Mark Fisher, Labour MP for Stoke-on-Trent Central since 1983, was born in 1944 and has been Shadow Minister for the Arts and Media since 1987. He read Englis' at Trinity College, C° cu-mentary film prod and scriptwrite cipal of Tattenhall Centre for Edu St dshire Cc mitt Service S of *City Centres*, itture and author of two plays, *Brave New Town* (1974) and *The Cutting Room* (1990). He is married, with two sons and two daughters, and lives in Stoke-on-Trent and London.

Richard Rogers was born in Florence in 1933 and came to Britain with his family six years later. Qualifying at the Architectural Association and Yale University, he set up Team 4 in 1963 with Su Rogers and Norman and Wendy Foster. In 1971 his partnership with Renzo Piano won the international competition for the Centre Pompidou. The Richard Rogers Partnership was established in 1977 with John Young, Marco Goldschmied and Mike Davies and in 1978 won the competition for the new Lloyd's of London headquarters. The practice has established a broad international base, with offices in London, Tokyo and Berlin and projects in Japan, Korea, Europe and the United States. The partnership recently won the first major competition in Berlin after the fall of the Wall and is currently building the Inter-national Court of Human Rights in Strasbourg.

Richard Rogers chaired the Tate Board of Trustees and is Chairman of the National Tenant Centre, the Building Education Trust and the Architectural Foundation. He was awarded the Royal Gold Medal for Architecture in 1985, was made Chevalier de l'Ordre National de la Légion d'Honneur in 1986 and in 1991 received a knighthood for his services to architecture. He is married with five sons and lives in London.

RICHARD ROGERS
MARK FISHER

A New London

Photographs by PETER BAISTOW

PENGUIN BOOKS

PENGUIN BOOKS

Published by the Penguin Group
Penguin Books Ltd, 27 Wrights Lane, London w8 5tz, England
Penguin Books USA Inc., 375 Hudson Street, New York, New York 10014, USA
Penguin Books Australia Ltd, Ringwood, Victoria, Australia
Penguin Books Canada Ltd, 10 Alcorn Avenue, Toronto, Ontario, Canada m4v 3b2
Penguin Books (NZ) Ltd, 182–190 Wairau Road, Auckland 10, New Zealand

Penguin Books Ltd, Registered Offices: Harmondsworth, Middlesex, England

First published 1992
10 9 8 7 6 5 4 3 2

Printed in England by Clays Ltd, St Ives plc
Set in 11.5/14.5 pt Monophoto Bembo

Contents

Foreword

This book has its origins in the Royal Academy's *London as it Could Be* exhibition of 1986. Since then we have been discussing, as architect and politician, what would be needed to extend that exhibition's spirit of confidence and innovation to the whole of London. We considered working together on a pamphlet or on articles, but it was only in late 1990, with the help of the Paul Hamlyn Fund in financing research and after the appointment of Ursula Owen as the Fund's Director, that we began to think of a book.

For the last year we have worked together on this project, meeting every week, visiting Barcelona, Paris and Rotterdam together, holding a series of discussions with architects, planners, politicians, specialists in urban design and community development. We also spent many days together looking at London at its best and worst.

This book is the result of that process. We intended originally to write the text together, but the pressure of work, with Richard's major new projects in Berlin, Korea and Tokyo and Mark in a pre-election year, made joint writing impossible. Instead this book combines our shared thoughts as the personal vision of an architect and a politician's report on what we have seen and learned over the past year. We hope that its perspectives and approach will fuel further the debate that is taking place on the future of this great city.

Richard Rogers and Mark Fisher, December 1991

Acknowledgements

There are many people we have to thank for their help and advice during the writing of this book, both here and abroad. In this country we are particularly grateful to Michael Manser, Colin Stansfield Smith, Ted Cullinan, Francis Duffy, Richard Burton, Richard McCormac, Gary Hart, Stuart Lipton and Anne Power. Brian Anson introduced us to the problems and people of Hoxton, and Father Patrick Towe showed us Broadwater Farm.

In Europe we were given generous advice and hospitality by David and Roser Mackay and Oriol Bohigas in Barcelona; Joseph Belmont, Emile Biasini, Pierre Hivernet, Roland Castro and Robert Lion in Paris; Maarten Hajer, Erik von Egeraat, Francine Houben Riek Bakker, Annemie Devolder, Audi Duyvestein and Peter van der Gugten in Rotterdam.

A host of people gave us help on aspects of the book – planning, architecture, urban design, transport, education, the Docklands development. These include Robin Thompson, past President of the Royal Town Planning Institute; Professor David Harvey of Oxford University; John Ellis, Dean Macris, George Williams and Alex Bash from San Francisco; Gordon Graham from the London Regeneration Consortium; Francho Bianchini from the University of Liverpool; Terry O'Rourke; Dr Ekhart Hahn; Michael Cassidy from the Corporation of London; John Montgomery; Robert Cowan; Bill Rodgers of the Royal Institute of British Architects; the architects

Sir Andrew Derbyshire and Bob Giles. Nigel Frost of the Building Experiences Trust helped us to appreciate the architectural projects that are taking place in schools. Leslie Gallery of the Philadelphia Foundation of Architecture, Simon Grieve from Melbourne, Stan Heuisler from Baltimore and Robert Oringdulph from Seattle gave us information on their respective planning laws and experiences.

MPs Bryan Gould and Clive Soley discussed the planning and environmental aspects of the book with us, as did Joan Ruddock, MP, on transport, George Nicholson of the London Rivers Association on the Thames and planning and Councillor Nicky Gavron, Vice-Chair of the London Planning Advisory Committee, on the work of LPAC. London MPs Brian Sedgemore, Nigel Spearing and Bernie Grant made helpful comments on the draft, as did Anne Page of the London Research Centre. Stuart Coombs of Olympia and York gave his time generously to show us around Canary Wharf.

Many people in the Richard Rogers Partnership contributed greatly to the book, including Philip Gumuchdjian, Laurie Abbot, Mike Davies, Marco Goldschmied, Jo Murtagh and Sue Sparks.

In Mark Fisher's office Ben Evans did invaluable and highly expert work in researching the book, collecting data and statistics and tracking down sources almost singlehandedly. We are also grateful for research undertaken in Paris and Barcelona by Bob Catterall. We would like to mention particularly the contribution made by Robert Clements, Richard Dewdney and the House of Commons Library Statistical Section.

Jo Pearce typed and retyped the text endlessly and always against impossible deadlines, and we are enormously grateful to her for her good humour, her patience and her ability to decipher illegible handwriting.

The book was made possible by the generosity of Paul Hamlyn, whose donation to the Labour Party, setting up the Paul Hamlyn Fund, funded the research for this book. The Director of the Fund, Ursula Owen, took the original idea of the book to Penguin Books and edited the text in its final weeks. Penguin has been supportive throughout, even when it looked as if we would never meet the deadline. We would like to thank Peter Carson for his belief in the book and Caz Hildebrand and Andrew Barker for their responsive design work. Mike MacCormack of BBC2 has been the model of patience in trying to film us together, an almost impossible task given our commitments this year.

Ben Rogers has been our most stringent critic, and we are both grateful for his editorial advice. I, Richard, especially want to thank him for his work on 'London: a Call for Action'. In the final week we retreated to an empty house in Cornwall, where we worked together intensively and enjoyably. He is, in effect, its co-author but would not let his name appear on the title page.

Last, but not least, we must thank our wives and families for their immense patience and support throughout the last year, when they must sometimes have doubted whether we would ever lead a normal life again.

To all these people, and to others with whom we have spoken too numerous to mention, our thanks and appreciation. Without their help and encouragement this book really would not have been possible. We are very grateful to them for their advice, which has guided and educated us. For any errors of fact or judgement we are entirely and solely responsible.

Photographic acknowledgements

Barcelona's Olympic Village, model of the Olympic Village, Olympic Port, general view, La Rambla, drawings of the scheme of the four Olympic areas, the sea promenade perspective, the Avinguda del Litoral perspective and the general view reproduced by kind permission of MBM Arquitectes, Barcelona.

Van Berkel bridge, Rotterdam, copyright © Jan Derwig; East London River Crossing reproduced by kind permission of Santiago Calatrava; Hillekop flats, Rotterdam, copyright © Piet Rook; L'Institut du Monde Arabe, Paris, copyright © Claude Bricage; La Défense, Paris, copyright © Deidi von Schaewen; La Défense, Paris, copyright © Georges Fessy; Paviljoen Boompjes restaurant, Rotterdam, copyright © Bastiaan Ingen Housz; La Pyramide at the Louvre, Paris, copyright © Patrice Astier/EPGL.

SECTION I

London: A Call for Action

BY RICHARD ROGERS

We are witnessing in Europe the emergence of a new generation of cities. No, more than that: we are seeing the emergence of a new urban culture. With the relative decline of the nation-state Europe is becoming increasingly defined by its cities. It is becoming, as it was until the seventeenth century, not a national but a city civilization. And the reappearance of the city-state has ushered in once again a very old and civilizing European phenomenon – inter-city rivalry and competition. The German state capitals – Frankfurt, Bonn, Munich, Hamburg, Stüttgart – are going from strength to strength, competing to outdo one another in the quality of their public transport, urban parks, galleries, opera, orchestras, schools and universities and commissioning some of Britain's most talented individuals to do so. With the decentralization in France the same thing is happening; what the mayor of Nîmes can do, the mayor of Montpellier will determine to do better. Germany and France provide the most striking illustrations, but you have only to look at the imaginative schemes that Rotterdam and Barcelona have unveiled to see that the race is on throughout Europe. Working as an architect in these cities, as I do a great deal, I get a sense of what it must have been like in *quattrocento* Italy, with Lucca emulating Siena, Siena striving to outdo Florence and Florence aspiring to upstage Rome. And if civic competition touches every part of these cities' policies, it is true to say that architecture has taken pride of place. Architecture, and especially urban design, has been the banner of cultural and political renewal in a Spain freed from Fascism, in a Germany overcoming division, in a France experiencing its first socialist presidency.

Make no mistake about it, at stake in Europe's new inter-city rivalry is more than status. The race in Europe is for pre-eminence not only as a cultural capital but as a financial one as well. Paris's and Frankfurt's city leaders make no secret of their ambition to lure business away from London.' Rising to their challenge and sustaining our position will not depend simply on offering a cheap deal on the rent, as was the strategy in London's Docklands. Rather they will involve providing the best of every aspect of city life: efficient transport, affordable homes, an attractive and clean built environment, as well as dynamic cultural facilities and a vibrant public life.

The fact that, in my experience, London is failing to keep up with the progress of its continental counterparts prompted me to work with Mark Fisher and the Hamlyn Fund on this book. Trafalgar Square was once the heart of an empire, Piccadilly Circus the centre of the universe. Today they are just two more jammed roundabouts in an shabby city playing a less and less culturally central role, at least where the vitality of city life is concerned, on the European and, indeed, world stage. When Europe was discovering the virtues of a loosely knit fabric of city-states, Britain saw the disappearance of its metropolitan authorities and the centralization of power in Whitehall. While Rotterdam learned from the mistakes of post-war housing schemes and embarked on a new generation of subsidized homes able to compete, in quality, with private developments, Britain simply stopped building low-cost homes. As Barcelona devised a great plan to revitalize entire deprived areas, London's housing estates festered, starved of the tiny investment that could transform most of them. As Paris opened its new opera house, the Royal Shakespeare Company at the Barbican went dark for a season. Above all, urban design and architecture were not given a chance. Europe is scattered, confetti-like, with prestigious cultural centres designed by internationally known architects; London gets only the odd extension here and there – the Sainsbury, the Clore and the Sakler – all of which are privately funded.

I know, of course, that these European cities are not Utopias – far from it: they still harbour areas of neglect, of poverty and unemployment. I know too that Britain is not without its successes. Glasgow and Birmingham, for instance, have put themselves back on the road to vitality, largely because they were among the first British cities to capitalize on the importance of culture in the economy of the post-industrial city. Nevertheless London still stands out; its citizens get a rotten deal.

I do not offer here a blueprint, the application of which would release London from its predicament in one fell swoop. But I do believe that an overview needs to be taken and policies developed that will see the city and its problems as a whole. Some of the actions advocated here are incontrovertible, like the institution of an elected metropolitan body or the establishment of a competition system to promote the quality of architecture. Other ideas are advanced as a challenge, inviting disagreement and discussion.

Why are cities so important? For one thing, they provide the public space without which, in this age of telecommunications, public life will wither. The paradigm of public space is the city square or piazza: without it the city scarcely exists. City squares are special because their public function almost eclipses any other use they might have – people come to them principally to talk, demonstrate, celebrate, all essentially public activities. (Note, if this is true, that London's great squares, all doubling as traffic intersections, don't constitute squares at all.) But other spaces are also forums for public life: the city campus, the railway terminus, the market, the municipal park, the pub (the *public* house) and, of course, the street, to name but a few. Unlike a public square, these may be used by citizens first and foremost for private purposes, but they are places that are nevertheless enhanced by the presence of other people. They are places where strangers interact not only for their own individual purposes but for the sake of interaction, because of the remarkable fact that strangers can simply give one another pleasure.

I admit that, to me, scarcely any pleasure compares with that offered by a city square. However, there are other, more practical, reasons for enjoying city life, reasons that may even appeal to the most hardened free-marketer, immune to the charms of the *agora* and the street.

A century ago the city was seen, almost universally and with good reason, as a vicious, degrading and dreadful place; in this country Dickens, Ruskin, Morris and Ebenezer Howard are only some among the best known of its nineteenth-century detractors. The city meant vermin, stench, darkness; it meant a large family and its pigs living in a small basement without light or fresh air: in essence it meant slums. As a result the ideal that dominated town planning in the first sixty-odd years of this century was of the thinner, greener, more spacious city. From Garden City enthusiasts to 'homes in the sky' disciples of Le Corbusier, almost everyone involved in the design of cities agreed that the dense nineteenth-century city, in which homes and factories were jammed together, was a very bad thing.

However, in the last generation there has been a major reassessment of city life and a recognition of its economic and ecological advantages. This forms the backdrop against which the resurgence of European cities has taken place. If once everybody agreed that the nineteenth-century model had to go, the multi-functional city is now being defended from the widest variety of perspectives; from Jane Jacobs's denigration of the Garden City tradition ('Ebenezer Howard's garden city was a place for Christopher Robin to go hoppety-hop') to the surprisingly impassioned tones of the recent European Commission Green Paper, with its call to 'recreate the diverse, multi-functional city of the citizen's Europe'.[2]

To begin with, there has been a renewed appreciation of the values of the intense public life that cities promote.[3] However, more material benefits of city life have also been highlighted. For one thing it has become increasingly clear that urban density provides the best setting for the easy, face-to-face interaction and communication that generates the scientific, technological, financial and cultural creativity that is the engine of economic prosperity in the post-industrial age. Economists and urban planners who once thought that telecommunications would render redundant the dense city, with its downtown financial district, now know otherwise.

Jane Jacobs extolled the city for rather different reasons, arguing that the rise in inner-city violence and poverty had its cause in the demolition of traditional neighbourhoods and their replacement by isolated housing estates placed in green, wide-open spaces.[4] Since then study after study has shown that city centres with a lively mix of activities, where daytime offices and shops and other places of work coexist with homes and places of nighttime entertainment, are safer than those that come alive for only eight hours a day. Furthermore, as city dwellers were encouraged to move to the new suburbs and satellite towns, it became ever more evident that such thinly spread peripheral development simply could not support good public transport, neighbourhood shopping or local industry nor generate lively communities. Finally, the thinner, dispersed city has proved to be ecologically unsound. It relies heavily on the car, creating unmanageable levels of congestion and pollution, and it eats up valuable green spaces.

So modernist and Garden City planning, arising from criticisms of the dense Victorian city, have themselves become the objects of criticism. In cities throughout Europe their rejection in favour of balanced, mixed development has formed the basis of the revival of urban culture. Nowhere is this clearer, perhaps, than in Barcelona, where Cerdà's grid of 1859 has provided the template for the enormous developments being undertaken in preparation for the Olympics. Barcelona's characteristic urban forms – the block, the avenue, the square – are being replicated, extended and newly energized by modern techniques, materials and forms.

But Barcelona is not alone. Paris, for instance, has embarked on an array of initiatives. Quite apart from the much publicized Grands Projets, strategic plans have been created for the eastern part of the inner city that aim to create entire and mixed-use residential areas on abandoned industrial ones. Meanwhile, on a smaller scale, numerous neglected local neighbourhoods are being revitalized and restored. There are two features of this imaginative programme that are especially worthy of note. The first is the way in which new cultural institutions are being established in run-down *quartiers* in order to act as catalysts for further regeneration. The second is that particular attention is being paid not only to buildings but also to the creation and rehabilitation of urban public spaces – streets, canals, squares and especially parks.

If on the Continent the lessons of the past are serving as a foundation for renewed, progressive urban initiatives, in Britain things have been very different. With the advent of the Thatcher Government the case against post-war planning did not become part of an endeavour to foster an urban community on new lines. Instead it became a pretext for leaving the evolution and implementation of London's re-development to the free market. The baby went out with the bath water.

Chief among the targets of the new free-market doctrine was metropolitan government, tainted as it was with a long tradition of, if not exactly socialist, at least interventionist policies. With the abolition of the Greater London Council (GLC) in 1986 the capital had lost the body responsible for developing a strategy for all of London. The GLC – or, more precisely, its forerunner, the London County Council (LCC) – had a more than reputable birth. The first modern, democratic metropolitan government in Europe, it was set up, a little more than 100 years ago, to tackle London's slums. But if London deserves an accolade as the first European capital with an elected government, it now has the dubious privilege of being the only European capital without one. Yet in continental Europe urban governments are the chief engineers of the new city vitality. Working as an architect on the Continent, I find that it is almost invariably the mayor or city council that is initiating new projects and developing new plans, always with an eye to the prestige and the prosperity of their city and, doubtless, always with an eye to the election returns. When Mark Fisher and I travelled to Barcelona, Rotterdam and elsewhere we were shown around by city politicians and officials excited by, and proud of, the improvements that they were making. Unlike these other cities, London lacks a voice to promote its interests and a body to decide issues that affect the city as a whole. Until one is created, initiatives to revitalize the city will fall at the first hurdle.

London is faced with a deterioration of its urban environment that is forcing people out of the city. Out of 3.5 million inner-city dwellers 1 million have moved out of inner London in the past three decades. If left unchecked, this trend could lead to a further spiral of decline. The number of its unemployed and poor is growing faster than that in any other European city. London is becoming more mono-functional, increasingly divided into ghettos of poverty and affluence segregated and disrupted by traffic noise and pollution. Nor are London's environmental problems of purely local concern. The global ecological crisis (to which cities are prime contributors) is forcing us to rethink current models of urban development along ecologically restructured lines. We must seek policies that will reduce urban traffic, energy consumption and pollutants and will produce a London with ecological balance and self-sustaining communities.

London needs a coordinated, interventionist policy. One issue that most of us hear about every day is the problem of the capital's transport system. The Department of Transport boasts that it is spending more, in real terms, on its roads programme than ever before, but, no matter how great the investment in roads, congestion in London will not be overcome. It has been demonstrated again and again that as fast as roads are built they are filled to capacity. One has only to look at cities such as Tokyo or Los Angeles to see this. In London the Westway is an object lesson. Once opened, it immediately clogged up the Marylebone Road, which had only just been widened in a futile attempt to anticipate the increase in traffic. Traffic is already increasing on London's latest urban motorways, the Ministry of Transport's new Red Routes, and it is hard to see how these too will avoid the fate of the Westway or, for that matter, of the M25.

Nor is the investment of public money in ever larger roads for London the only way in which Governments have subsidized cars in the capital. Subsidies for company cars are four times greater than those for British Rail; while today, more generally, taxes on drivers do not come close to reflecting the real cost of the car and the lorry in terms of the damage they do to the environment and to urban communities. Furthermore the congestion undermines the efficiency of a surface-based public transport system. If the emphasis of government subsidies and expenditure were shifted from encouraging private mobility to promoting public transport, London – and, indeed, other cities in Britain – could afford a radical reform of public transport policy, from free fares to new infrastructure.

Doubtless this promotion of the car looks worst – indeed, it is catastrophic – from a global perspective: road traffic is the fastest growing source of gases contributing to the 'greenhouse effect'. Its local consequences are also dire. Leaving aside the costs of lost productivity caused by congestion, leaving aside too the toll of deaths, injury and ill health, road traffic does perhaps more than anything else to undermine city neighbourhoods. Streets meant as places for shopping and meeting, green oases meant as a places of recreation and relaxation become respectively trunk roads and roundabouts. Brixton, whose town hall, church and public library make for an excellent composition, is just one example among hundreds in London of a place with real civic identity and importance all but destroyed by the car and lorry. Nor is it only local communities that suffer: witness Piccadilly Circus, where pedestrians, although more numerous than cars, have to be barricaded at its perimeter.

Up to a third of all households in London have no car, and it is not just a matter of time before everyone possesses one. Age, income, disability will always prevent a large number of people from driving. For these people the private car brings few benefits. It makes travelling by bicycle or on foot hellish, and it renders public transport less efficient and hence more expensive.

Any of these considerations alone should make us doubt the value of the car, at least as a primary means of getting around the city. Taken together, they represent an indictment of it. However, there is one facet of its tyranny that I have not mentioned but that, as an architect, I find particularly offensive, namely, the visual pollution that it spawns. How much longer must we put up with streets paved with scarred tarmac, avenues planted with lines of cars and public squares adorned with the paraphernalia of traffic control?

London suffocates while much of Europe is in the business of filtering out the car. The obvious goal, and the one being enforced

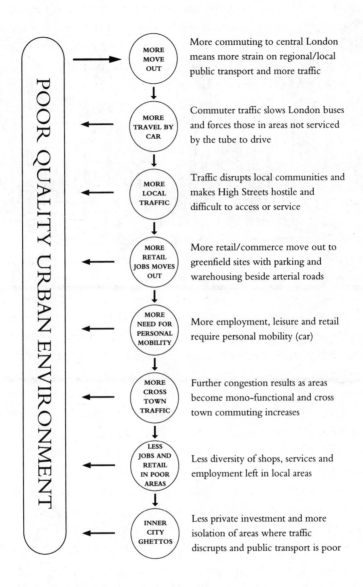

POOR QUALITY URBAN ENVIRONMENT

MORE MOVE OUT
More commuting to central London means more strain on regional/local public transport and more traffic

MORE TRAVEL BY CAR
Commuter traffic slows London buses and forces those in areas not serviced by the tube to drive

MORE LOCAL TRAFFIC
Traffic disrupts local communities and makes High Streets hostile and difficult to access or service

MORE RETAIL JOBS MOVES OUT
More retail/commerce move out to greenfield sites with parking and warehousing beside arterial roads

MORE NEED FOR PERSONAL MOBILITY
More employment, leisure and retail require personal mobility (car)

MORE CROSS TOWN TRAFFIC
Further congestion results as areas become mono-functional and cross town commuting increases

LESS JOBS AND RETAIL IN POOR AREAS
Less diversity of shops, services and employment left in local areas

INNER CITY GHETTOS
Less private investment and more isolation of areas where traffic discrupts and public transport is poor

The erosion of urban quality.

above: The chaotic streetscape.
below: Streets without cars.

everywhere else, is a lower ratio of cars to public transport the closer one gets to the inner city. The case has been made that the car actually enhances the liveliness of city spaces, but this romantic view flies in the face of the pollution, disruption and injury that the vehicle causes. Pedestrians, cyclists, buses, trams and taxis are not without vitality, nor are we proposing that all private vehicles should be excluded from the city. Of course, there are many badly designed pedestrian areas, but at least in those there is room for improvement, while in traffic-choked streets there is practically none.

Severely limiting cars in London could be effective only if investment were made in high-quality public alternatives. We need a much extended and thoroughly integrated urban transport network. The Thames, for example, offers an entirely unexploited means of transport that, in the long run, will prove cost-effective if linked up

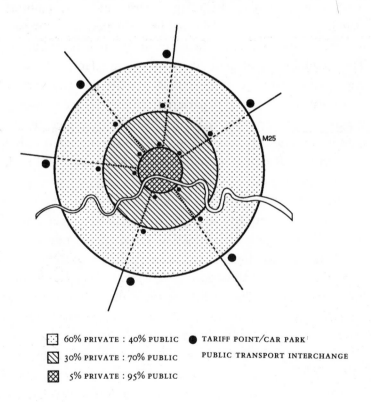

60% PRIVATE : 40% PUBLIC   ● TARIFF POINT/CAR PARK

30% PRIVATE : 70% PUBLIC   PUBLIC TRANSPORT INTERCHANGE

5% PRIVATE : 95% PUBLIC

Proposed public/private transport ratios.

to the main network by interchanges along its banks. (This would have the additional benefit of contributing to the revitalization of public life along the river.) New types of trams and buses are being developed and should be deployed, although here London is, in one sense, at a disadvantage. The lack of long, wide boulevards makes the use of trams and light railways less easy than in many of the more imperial European cities. Some distance can be gone in this direction, but proportionally more work must be done on improving the Underground, which needs to be supported by a rapid-transport system. Like the Réseau Express Régional (RER) in Paris, this would provide a new express service stopping at every fifth or sixth station and extending to the commuter belt.

The drastic reduction of private cars in London and the development of an alternative high-tech, integrated public transport network would involve designing a series of new transport interchanges, in the capital and around its perimeter, where those coming into the city could leave their cars and switch to public transport. The establishment of these would mean, in effect, the restoration of one of my favourite architectural types – the city gate. On the motorway arrival in and departure from the city are non-events. But the modern transport interchange, like its forerunner, the Victorian railway terminus, can evoke a sense of place. One has only to contrast Brunel's Paddington Station with the flyovers and underpasses at the beginning of the M1 in Hendon to get my point.

The extent of walking and cycling in Britain is already surprisingly high (37 per cent of passenger journeys and 32 per cent of travel time).[5] Encouraging the pedestrian and cyclist is rarely reflected in the design of London, where pedestrians are consigned to poorly maintained and badly designed pavements and constantly interrupted by streams of cars. The cyclist and the walker are second- and third-class citizens, at least in the eyes of the Department of Transport; its annual provision for bicyclists could build no more than 200 metres of motorway. Yet London could easily be woven together with green walks and cycle-ways (see page xl). Further, a substantial reduction in the volume of cars in London would permit wider pavements and avenues of trees.

Landscaped pedestrian and cycle routes.

If this new London is going to be realized, however, investment in public transport can be only a start. Government must also begin replanning the city so as to lessen the need for travel. We need a more defined city, made up of dense neighbourhoods with overlapping activities, so that people do not have to commute daily from a dormitory suburb to a financial centre or from a flat in the city to a business park. London, with its myriad villages, parks and towns, is especially well placed to develop polycentrally. The challenge is to consolidate this structure into a dynamic urban conglomeration.

The steady erosion of diversity of activity has been an unpleasant side-effect of *laissez-faire*, market-led development. London has seen the conversion into offices of ever larger areas that once contained markets, shops, light industry and even homes. Docklands is a glaring example. Unlike many of the flat, featureless locations of the new towns, the docks enjoy a beautiful situation on the Thames, facing the magnificent architecture of Greenwich and framed by the skylines of the City and Blackheath. The fact that the area was an integral part of historic east London, adjacent to the City and only a few minutes away from the West End, should have made it all the more possible to create from it a vibrant addition to the capital.

With no strategic planning guidelines, the concept of balanced development was all but ignored in favour of policies geared to facilitate fast, financially attractive exploitation of the area. Planning restrictions were lifted, and new commercial buildings were exempted from rates and land taxes. Lacking any brief to provide local housing or any duty to consider the social and cultural needs of neighbouring communities, the development did little to help its impoverished neighbours. The Government's quarrel with public participation extended even to the provision of proper transport. Instead of a rapid rail system, like Paris's RER or San Francisco's BART, the Docklands got a feeble overhead light railway, which, until halfway through 1991, was not even connected with the capital's Underground system. This amounted to nothing less than an invitation to drive to work through an already congested London. Contrast this with Rotterdam's new Kop van Zuid development, 'Manhattan on the Maas' (120 hectares of docklands), where the city council and its planner recognized that the integration of a variety of urban functions, including transport, was a priority. Hence, along with office and industrial spaces, provision has been made for 5,000 homes (half of them publicly subsidized), not to mention, shops, cinemas, theatres, schools and the like. The whole is linked to the city by means of a fully integrated public transport system.

However, it is not just the development of single-activity business zones that is threatening the vitality of London. Equally damaging have been developments in the high street. Historically shops have been the social heart of the city, generating a variety of overlapping activities quite apart from buying and selling. Different locations, on high street and side street, and varying leases offer sites for a wide range of shops and activities, from the twenty-four-hour café and corner shop to the street markets and supermarkets. Here there is time and place for people to meet, sit on benches, draw on pavements and while away the time as well as buy. As the high street is in the centre of a neighbourhood, it is possible for the majority of people to reach it on foot, for authorities to organize efficient public

opposite: Mono-functional activities.

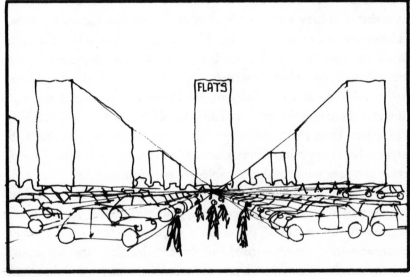

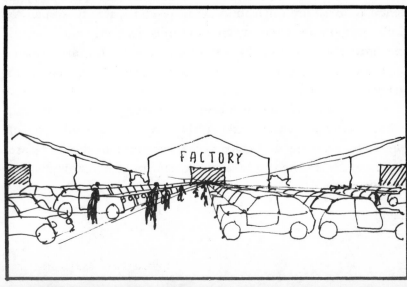

transport and for retailers to provide cost-effective private delivery services. It is not just that lively local shops confer 'character' on a neighbourhood; they also play a crucial role in policing the city and are the life-blood of the inner-city economy, especially for those who are effectively rendered immobile by not owning a car.

Yet London's high streets have become more standardized and more congested and have simply failed to compete with the secure, controlled environment of the shopping centres. Londoners wanting local shopping that is hospitable, intimate and diverse now have to travel to France! In the creation of this situation motor traffic has played no small part. The ceaseless flow of cars and lorries has turned London's community high streets into highways. Pedestrianizing many local neighbourhoods would boost their diversity and prosperity – that is, if they were not dominated by the national retail chains. (The ten largest retailers now control a third of all shop trade and, in many commodities, well over half.) Yet this development is not inevitable. Paris enjoys a dynamic retail economy chock-a-block with small shops because independent Parisian shop owners are nurtured by the city and pay very little in local rates and taxes. In Britain the system taxes the small shops and allows the owners of the high street – largely pension funds and insurance companies – to squeeze every last penny out of the rentable space they own.

Improving the quality of London's high streets is imperative, but action must also be taken to halt the spread of out-of-town shopping centres. As urban public places they are disastrous. Like the other institutions that have flourished in the last decade – the residential cul-de-sac, the business park and the financial centre – the shopping centre is an utterly singleminded and private space. It is open for only a proportion of the day and is guarded by men whose job it is to control entry and forbid any spontaneous activity. It may be sanitary, safe and prosperous, but it is not a forum of public life, just a machine for selling.

So why do people use such centres? Because the goods are cheap and there is abundant car parking. But at what cost is this apparent efficiency, economy and convenience achieved? In the first place, retail centres are sited to take full advantage of infrastructure (the

M25, for example) provided at no expense to the retailer but 100 per cent out of the public purse. Their proximity to arterial infrastructure permits accessibility for bulk deliveries by lorry and, crucially, creates a catchment zone for shoppers living, in some cases, many miles away (generally assumed to be the distance covered in under forty-five minutes at motorway speeds). The centres generate massive daily private traffic, which disrupts local communities, pollutes the environment and, when combined with the traffic generated by other centres that are taking advantage of the same infrastructure, eventually renders the roads incapable of fulfilling their original purpose – that of improving mobility between cities and, in the specific case of the M25, relieving town congestion. This process leads inevitably to further public road construction and so on.

It also undermines the financial viability of local shops, which pay high land costs and metropolitan rates. In addition, as more national retailers move to enjoy the economies of the periphery, so local, individually owned shops become less competitive by comparison: the consequence is less diversity, less local shopping, more congestion. And as for the communities of the non-car-owning poor to whom the new shopping centres are not accessible, they are denied cheap goods and potential employment and suffer instead the congestion, pollution and local retail monotony that are the legacy of the out-of-town malls. If these centres bore the true costs of their accessibility and of the environmental and social damage they cause, the relative commercial viability of local shopping would increase dramatically and would fuel the economic recovery and vitality of neighbourhood high streets.

Inner-city housing is the crucial component of a balanced city community. When we re-establish the tradition of planning and investing in British cities, the provision of new homes for sale or for rent (rent offers greater mobility) must be a priority, only this time not isolated on estates but mixed and integrated throughout the city. This is the way to cut down on congestion and preserve valuable green countryside. More than 5 per cent of London's built-up area is derelict, and many more houses stand empty, so there is no shortage of space for new homes.[6] The cost of housing, however, is

completely out of proportion to the earnings of most working people, forcing increasing numbers to move out of the city or live in
squalor. Families are losing their homes to mortgage companies for
failing to make regular payments, yet in 1991 fewer than 400 local-
authority dwellings were built in London. And with 80,000 people
homeless in the capital – a figure ten times what it was a decade
ago – the city must embark on the rehabilitation and reconstruction
of its housing stock without delay.[7]

We have been told so often that social housing is necessarily ugly
and unpopular, and that it violates the right to private property, that
we have almost come to believe it. It takes a journey across the
Channel to see this for the nonsense that it is. When Mark Fisher
and I visited the Netherlands, we discovered that in some cities as
much as half of new urban housing is publicly funded and that it is
generally of the highest standard. Designed by the Netherlands'
youngest, brightest architects, this new local-authority housing
avoids the mistakes of much early planning and tends to be highly
sensitive to urban context, yet incorporates the spirit of innovation.
There is one respect in particular in which the Dutch have learned
from the failures of the past: their housing associations ensure that
the future inhabitants of any scheme are identified at a very early
stage, so that they can be consulted, from the outset of the design
process, about the sorts of flats and houses they want. Each finished
building is the fruit of shared ideas and experience.

But there still remains the legacy of the failures of post-war housing estates or, more properly (because poverty is not confined to the
estates), of inner-city deprivation, where London's problems are
most critical and most brutal. In the case of an area like Hoxton its
poverty is horrible enough, but more disgusting still is the contrast
between it and the neighbouring City. One needs only to cross Old
Street to step from urban buoyancy to rank despair; you could see it
from the City of London. These places – and Hoxton is only one
among dozens – represent the worst underside of the developments I
have been discussing; they lie at the base of a downward spiral to
which post-war zoning and Thatcherite neglect have both contributed. It is perhaps easy enough to say what has gone wrong with

them: the question is, how can they be transformed? Investment, of course, is the key. Paris has identified its poorest neighbourhoods and placed them within a strategic framework; so must we. Architecture too can play a role; most of the housing blocks – like Sara Lane in Hoxton – can effectively be woven back into the city. In addition, the construction or rehabilitation of civic and cultural institutions can generate confidence and attract reinvestment.

Dr Anne Power, Director of Priority Estates Projects, who works with some of Britain's 15 million local-authority tenants, many of whom live in seriously run-down estates, has succeeded, with only a tiny government budget, in involving local tenants and training them to be responsible for their own estates. I shall never forget visiting Broadwater Farm and seeing how the morale of the community had been transformed by just such a process. A single message emerges from these estates: long-term improvement comes about by listening to the people and involving them in the 'plan'. Brian Anson, a pioneer of community planning, whose lifelong work with the disadvantaged has inspired me, has put it well: 'We must make it our premise that people have real knowledge. Out there is a fortune in environmental knowledge that lies dormant; it is the job of a community plan to tap it.' Perhaps this is still the most important lesson we have to learn.

The reassesment of current attitudes towards the city that I have been calling for – a move away from the traffic-dominated, segregated, non-place, unjust city that London is becoming – will not come about until there is a change in the way in which the built environment is administered, the public is involved and the quality of urban design is promoted. On these everything hangs.

The Department of the Environment should have overall co-ordinating responsibility for matters relating to the environment. Presently these are shared by several ministries – including, importantly, the Department of Transport. The latter, for example, does not have an ecological brief and consistently disregards the environmental impact of its policies because it takes as its goal not a reduction in the need for travel (the ecological approach) but the maximization of mobility. One day in December 1991 summed up the dilemma: as the Department of Transport continued to paint red stripes along its newly designated Red Routes, the Department of the Environment urged people not to drive into London because of the high levels of atmospheric pollution. Furthermore, the Department of the Environment should not be responsible for other matters, such as local government and taxes, as these are massive issues in themselves. There is a strong case for a Minister for Cities and, following the lead of many European states, junior ministers for transport, urban planning and architecture. Currently we have none.

Ministerial reform would be a good beginning, but experience since the abolition of the GLC has established one point: authority in matters of strategic planning (land use and transport) must rest with a body less centralized than the Government and greater than a local council. What is needed, if London is going to improve, is a strategic planning body with its own local tax base. It would then be in a position to experiment with land taxes, road pricing, tourism taxes and business rates. This type of restructuring would give the metropolitan body real power to tax the owner of the all-prevailing derelict London site and the unoccupied building, to encourage and facilitate the construction of affordable housing for rent and to share in the often huge increases in property values generated by new public investment in infrastructure, such as major road construction. These proposed land reforms are, in essence, the principles of Ebenezer Howard and the New Town programmes and, in some measure, of the Enterprise Zones, and they were succinctly summarized in a 1976 United Nations Resolution: 'the unearned increment resulting from the rise in land values from public investment ... must be subject to recapture by public bodies (the community).' The present situation, in which such incremental value is not shared by the community, represents little more than a somewhat haphazard transfer of public wealth to the fortunate landowner.

When the regional planning authorities and the GLC were abolished in 1986, the Council's responsibilities were divided between five government departments, thirty-three London boroughs, the City of London and about sixty committees and quangos. This proved to be the death knell of coordinated land-use planning in London, responsibility for which became the joint prerogative of all local boroughs, with strategic guidance handed down by government. Leaving aside the damaging fact that there is no voice to speak for London as a whole – consider the 1991 Olympic bid fiasco – this arrangement has had many shortcomings, chief among them the lack of an objective overview. There is, for example, little incentive for a borough to restrain a destructive commercial development if it can simply hop over to the next borough, taking business and jobs with it. On the other hand, initiatives that would benefit the whole city, perhaps at the inconvenience of the borough, are neglected. The whole system is inherently adversarial because local plans evolve primarily not through city-wide discussion but in the corridors of individual town halls. Thus no consensus about the shape of the city is built up before local guidelines are established. Instead every proposal, from a scheme for Coin Street, Paternoster Square or King's Cross to the domestic extension, becomes the occasion for a dispute about fundamentals, about the shape and character of the city.

Furthermore, the system is not open to public participation. The shabby town halls where designs are handed over a counter and then returned, having been accepted or rejected, are not forums of participatory government, and the process is ridiculously lengthy. The law requires local authorities to make a decision about a planning application within two months, but boroughs do not meet this requirement. And, of course, appealing to the Department is a still more costly and time-consuming measure, which few citizens can afford. No wonder most Londoners prefer not to involve themselves in their city's planning system. Nor does the quality of the judgement of the local borough, when it does make a judgement, offer much by way of consolation. There are honourable exceptions, but, generally speaking, councillors are ill-qualified to judge complex planning issues and rarely have the professional back-up they need.

All of this can be changed. How? In essence by establishing, democratically, a framework within which architects, developers, housing associations, community groups and everyone else with an interest in the planning of the city would cooperate. To this end I propose that the responsibility for planning and design that is currently exercised by local borough councillors should be transferred to a number of boards made up of elected councillors, independent specialists (architects, planners and transport engineers) and lay citizens (community activists, developers, architectural journalists). It is, I think, an open question whether these boards should also be metropolitan. The challenge is to create a system that can harness the needs of the citizen, the broad responsibility of government and the narrow efficiency of business.

It would be the remit of these boards to create, after the most thorough public involvement, local strategic plans. Their goal would be to take the holistic view of the city laid down in broad strokes by the metropolitan strategic body and to foster the balanced, ecologically sustainable and culturally vital communities that we so desperately need. The plans would cover, in quite a detailed manner, densities, land use, transport and conservation. As well issuing coarse-grained strategic plans, the boards would also be responsible for more detailed neighbourhood planning briefs that specified limitations of use, height, bulk and wind effect and ensured the proper provision of public space and amenities. The great advantage of this system would be that much argument could be avoided, and much time and money saved, because the major constraints within which the client and architect would have to work would be laid out as part of the planning framework at the outset of the design process. In most cases, as long as the architect met the requirements of the planning brief determined by the board, planning permission would be a formality. (In San Francisco, where a system like this operates, only a quarter of cases go before the planning commission.) A strict timetable would be established, and there would be automatic compensation for delays.

Although the number of reviews of applications could be expected to drop dramatically, there must still be a right of appeal. On the one hand, the owner of a site should have the right to argue for the suspension of certain planning codes if the projected design offered some extra benefit, perhaps design excellence, public amenities or civic space. On the other hand, community or architectural groups must have the opportunity to challenge a proposal that, while meeting all the planning requirements, would damage the city's balance. But, here again, discussion could be expected to be less adversarial precisely because the planning criteria would have been established.

Finally, an additional advantage of this system would be that issues of architectural style would take a back seat to more relevant questions, such as the size of a scheme, the type of activity it would enclose, its provision of public amenity. Currently planning decisions are frequently made on the basis of a scheme's style. As often as not, this represents illegitimate interference with the architect's creative freedom by a handful of councillors or their officials and is particularly irksome when the scheme concerns not a conservation area but a road of the utmost ugliness. Councils could generally deploy their resources better in improving the design of streets, parks and buildings than in playing architectural critic.

It can scarcely be emphasized enough, however, that the success of such boards would depend wholly upon the extent to which their plans were the product of a democratic process; like any planning procedure, this one would work only if the public were involved. How could this be achieved? First – and this is crucial – by holding all the boards' meetings in public forums that citizens were encouraged to attend. However, if London's inhabitants were to be prompted to take an interest in the development of their city, the designs under review would have to be exhibited and widely discussed in the media. London, and every city in Britain along with it, needs a Centre of the Civic Realm. Such institutions could play a crucial role in the democratization of urban planning and design. There would be two basic tasks for these centres: the meeting in public of the boards and the public exhibition of the plans before them. Beyond this they must be centres for the display of information about planning initiatives being taken in other cities at home and abroad; places where lectures, courses and debates about the city and its architecture, past and future, are held, so that new projects can be seen against the background of the past. At the very heart of these centres should be an adaptable working model of the city. Most important of all, we must interest children and their teachers, and the built environment must be integrated into the school curriculum. (The Building Experiences Trust is currently pursuing this objective.) The Centres for the Civic Realm that I am advocating could themselves become the focus of school programmes. Each must have its educational officer.

Nor should this institution, no matter how vibrant and popular it is, be permitted to monopolize discussion about the shape and nature of the city. There needs to be a much more widely publicized series of architectural prizes both for established architects, and, as in France, for younger ones. In France and in the Netherlands the Government has set up architectural funds that, among other things, are intended to support exhibitions, publications, television programmes, architectural competitions and research.

If the quality of Britain's architecture is to be improved and the public's attention engaged, the Government must take the lead by improving the standards of its own designs. A city is defined by its public buildings; if these are good, then it can well withstand a great deal of banal developers' architecture. At the moment the manner in which an architect is appointed is left entirely to the discretion of public officials. Just occasionally an imaginative and determined official will use his or her discretion to erect public architecture of the excellence; the remarkable series of buildings commissioned by Colin Stansfield Smith in Hampshire attests to this (as Mark Fisher shows in Chapter Nine). Like-minded government officials are rare, however. The greatest contribution to improving the design of public buildings in Britain would be the establishment of a nation-wide system of architectural competitions. We need a law that makes competition mandatory for all public commissions of any substance and a flexible system under which the type of competition – whether open to all or to a selected number and whether based on the architects' past work or on site-specific designs – may vary from case to case. Nor is it only public buildings that should be open to competition but also strategic plans and landscape design. And it is not only national and local government that should be obliged to institute competitions; the national corporations, such as British Telecom, British Rail and the London Underground, must be encouraged to take design seriously. Planning advantages should be extended to companies that run official competitions, create public spaces or offer other public amenities.

Over the past two decades France has put competitions to stunningly effective use. Mark Fisher describes in full the system that has evolved there. As an architect who has worked, competed and judged competitions in France, I will insist on just two points. First, the whole system would never have got off the ground if French politicians, civil servants and public figures, not least President Mitterrand himself, had not been singleminded in their determination to improve the quality of France's cities. A system of national architectural competitions may have the effect of arousing everyone's interest in architecure, but it arises itself from the commitment of public figures - Britain's politicians, take note! My second point is that, largely because of the architectural policies of the French Government − not just the promotion of competitions but also the establishment of high-profile architectural prizes and forums and a series of other initiatives − there has been a transformation in France's architectural climate. Mitterrand has set an example that everybody, especially city mayors, has followed, so that if it is true to say that twenty years ago France had arguably the lowest standard of public architecture in Europe, it now has probably the best. Everywhere you go in France you meet young architects excited by the opportunities facing them and rising to the challenges offered by what is nothing less than the emergence of a new architectural culture.

The newly unified Berlin provides a case study that draws together many threads of this discussion. With the demolition of the Wall and the environmental poverty of the eastern sector of the city, Berliners are presented with the opportunity of building a state-of-the-art, twenty-first-century city. Berlin enjoys a participatory and constructive urban-planning system. Two full-time senators, one in charge of planning and urban design and the other of the design and contruction of buildings, oversee the city's architectural development, and there are more architectural competitions held in the new capital than in any city in Europe.

With all important projects the public is involved from the

Proposals for Potsdamer Platz, Berlin.

beginning. Every Friday and Saturday, at fortnightly intervals, a public meeting is held in the Berlin Stadtforum, generally chaired by a
senator; here architects, and developers, planners and politicians,
present their schemes to a large public crowd. I recently experienced
this process at first hand. Our practice was appointed by five major
investors, including Daimler-Benz and Sony, to examine their needs
in relation to a site they had purchased in the very centre of the
newly unified Berlin. Two major squares, Potsdamer and Leipziger,
the ancient heart of the city, form the centre of this derelict 200-acre
development. At the same time, and in parallel to our work, the
Senate and the landowners agreed to run a series of competitions for

the site, based on our recommendations. By the time construction commences more than 100 international architectural teams will have submitted designs. The total area of building exceeds that of London's enormous Canary Wharf (where, incidentally, no public competition has been held to date), but Berlin's city leaders, prompted by their electorate, have ensured that nearly half will be devoted to shops, to places of entertainment and to homes, unlike Canary Wharf, which consists more or less entirely of offices. This is, hopefully, a vital new city quarter in the making.

It was our aim to create a great people's place in the historic Leipziger Platz; we therefore excluded from the square all vehicles apart from the tram, and we severely restricted traffic through Potsdamer Platz, which became the hub of the scheme, with tree-lined boulevards following the radial pattern of the historic streets. Below Potsdamer will be the largest public transport interchange in Berlin, if not in Europe, consisting of four existing and two new lines, including an express tube line *and* a trans-European express train connecting with Paris, Amsterdam, Zurich ... and (if we ever make the investment) London. It will be as quick to take the express from Potsdamer Platz to these other European capitals as it will be to fly. Electric monorails and trams are to run above ground. The efficiency and effectiveness of Berlin's public transport allowed us to suggested a public/private transport split of 90:10 for this, the heart of Berlin.

In the middle of the project lies a linear park, which links Berlin's great central park, the Tiergarten, with a canal to the South. This green ribbon, in which stand a number of cultural venues, forms a centre of sophisticated energy conservation. Among other things, this centre recyles the water and heat from the new buildings, so that their energy consumption can be cut by nearly half. Where the green ribbon crosses Potsdamer Platz stands an eco-centre – a bureau of information and a museum devoted to ecology. In our design we wanted a city centre that, while respecting the historical patterns of the past, looked to the future.

The London of the twenty-first century should not be a demolished and reconstructed city but one carefully woven into a consolidated union of richly diverse communities. Further expansion of the capital into the countryside is quite unnecessary. London abounds with every kind of opportunity for redevelopment, conservation and revitalization, from vast sites of derelict land in the East End to run-down Brixton or Hoxton and the unfulfilled potential of the South Kensington Museum site.[8] London cries out for a new generation of housing, schools and cultural centres like those being built by young architects all over Western Europe.

Yet a city is made up of more than object-buildings. It is the people's places – streets, squares and parks – that will always make up the greater part of the public domain. In the case of London the neglect of these is particularly galling because their regeneration would be relatively easy.

Of these public spaces the Thames provides the most striking opportunity. Today London turns its back on its river, yet it is, in embryo, the capital's greatest public amenity, a public space too of deep social symbolism, potentially linking the prosperous north and the depressed south. In the scheme that we exhibited at the Royal Academy in 1986, *London as it Could Be*, we demonstrated how the at least one part of the river could be transformed. We recommended the sinking of the noisy Embankment road from Westminster to Blackfriars and the linking up of the many pockets of existing green space to form a pedestrianized and continuous linear park. In the other direction we proposed the creation of a pedestrian route linking Leicester Square and Trafalgar Square with the South Bank and Waterloo Station. But this is only one among innumerable ways of exploiting the Thames's potential. In particular further pedestrian parks, paths and cycle routes could be threaded along great stretches of both banks.

If the Thames and its banks could be transformed into an east–west line of public parks and spaces, a number of landscaped public routes could be established that ran from south to north. Once again no demolition would be involved; rather, it would be a matter of linking existing parks, squares, commons and cemeteries by way of alleys, footpaths, canals, underused railway lines,

opposite: Pedestrianized linear park from Westminster to Blackfriars
(from *London as it Could Be*, 1986).

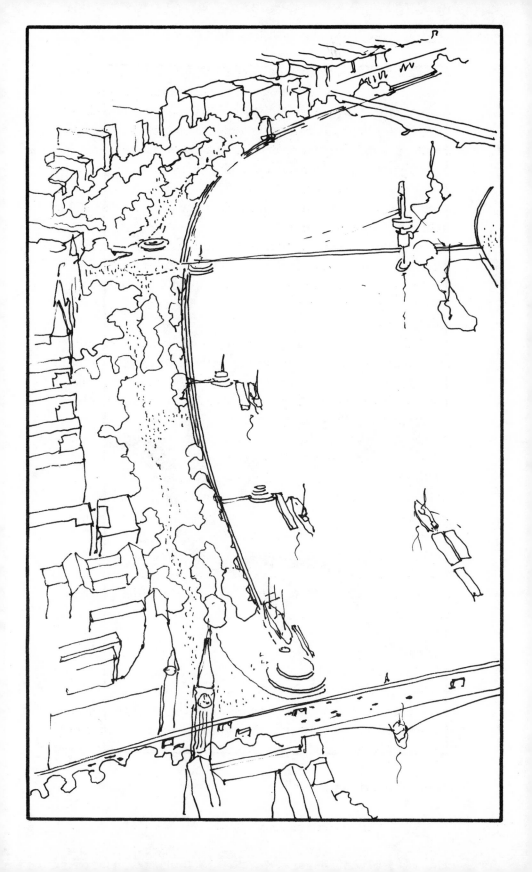

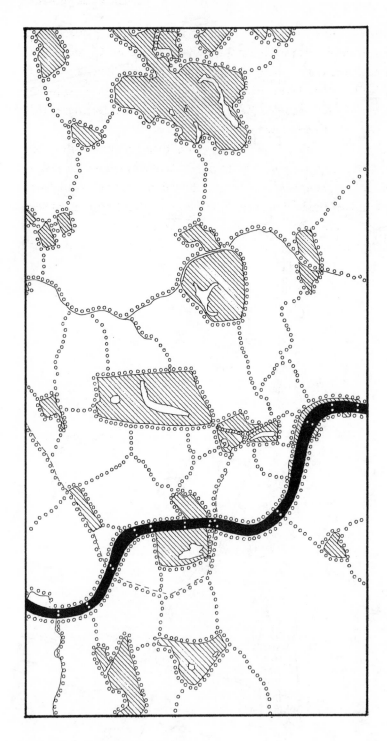

A network of landscaped routes.

pedestrian bridges and streets retrieved from the car. Routes could run, for example, from Richmond Park or Clapham Common, via Battersea Park, over a new pedestrian bridge to Chelsea Hospital, South Kensington, Hyde Park, through the Paddington Basin and along the Grand Union Canal to Regent's Park, Primose Hill, Hampstead Heath and beyond.

These projects are about weaving together and uniting existing spaces: to realize them will require the skills of an imaginative restorer and not necessarily those of a great painter. They are nothing beside some of the architectural interventions that London has seen in the past. They pale by comparison with, for example, Nash's creation of a sequence of spaces running from the Mall to Regent's

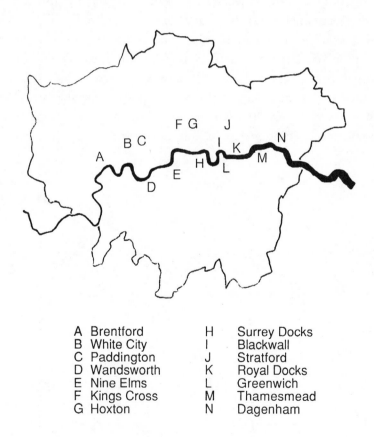

A	Brentford	H	Surrey Docks
B	White City	I	Blackwall
C	Paddington	J	Stratford
D	Wandsworth	K	Royal Docks
E	Nine Elms	L	Greenwich
F	Kings Cross	M	Thamesmead
G	Hoxton	N	Dagenham

Some of London's major development sites.

Park. However, London also abounds with great swathes of derelict land, the development of which needs larger, bolder strokes. Along the Thames alone there are vast neglected areas that, put together, would be the size of a small city: Wandsworth, Battersea, Surrey Docks, Blackwall, the Royal Docks and the Greenwich Peninsula all call out for development – development that is ecologically sound and respects the values of the public sphere.

London is still one of the great cities. It remains one of the three dominant financial centres; the long-standing quality of its performing arts and its galleries are world-renowned; the intimacy and the casualness of its historical spaces and buildings are universally appreciated; and the sheer quantity and variety of its parks are everywhere admired. But, as Michael Heseltine himself recently said of London's imperial past, it is 'what others have created'.

We have the imagination, talent and resources to revitalize this great humanist city, to create beautiful buildings, tree-lined avenues and new parks, where the commonest sounds are voices, footsteps and the buzz of the electric tram, a metropolis of social and ecological harmony. A new London, pre-eminent among Europe's new constellation of cities, is quite within our grasp.

London: A Plan for Development
BY MARK FISHER

PART ONE

The Problems

CHAPTER ONE

A Sense of Urgency

London has to change. For centuries it has been one of the world's great capitals. It is in danger of being so no longer. In its environment and its heritage, in its diversity and resilience, there is much to take pleasure and pride, but both pleasure and pride are beginning to sour as large areas of London life slip into decline.

London is a city famous for its grand monuments but loved for its domestic architecture. Wren's St Paul's, Nash's terraces, Hawksmoor's churches and the Royal Parks may all capture the eye, but it is the detail of its squares and terraces, alleys and passageways, its commons and its heaths that lodge in the heart. London is also the epitome of a cosmopolitan city, plural, ambiguous, changing. Its citizens speak numerous mother tongues, bringing the world's religions, customs and cultures into the city's streets.

But these streets are filthy with litter; its roads are choked with traffic; schools and hospitals are crumbling; major galleries and museums have holes in their roofs; shops, offices and factories stand empty. People sleep rough in doorways by night and beg by day. Women are frightened to go out alone. The extremities of wealth and poverty, display and despair, shame anyone who cares for this great city. Such inequalities are not only offensive; they are absurd in a city that contains such talents and skills, in the capital of a country that has enjoyed the windfall of North Sea oil for a decade.

Many of London's problems are shared by other Western

metropolises. Manufacturing industries have left. Traditional docks have closed as sea freight moved to new deep-water container ports. High-technology companies have relocated to greenfield sites. All this has left in the heart of London a legacy of unemployment and dereliction. It was the expansion of manufacturing industries that created cities in their present form; their departure demands that we rethink the future. Other European cities, such as Paris, Berlin, Barcelona and Rotterdam, are addressing these post-industrial problems by investing in ideas, energy and resources. Glasgow is investing in its culture. By contrast, London is drifting without direction.

All over Europe a new generation of cities is being born and, with it, a new urban culture. Europe is being defined by these cities, which are post-industrial in their economics, urban in their population density and planning and green in their environment. In all of them artistic and cultural life is a central element of regeneration. That urban regeneration, and especially urban design, is a banner of social and political renewal in a post-Franco Seville, Barcelona and Bilbão, in a Berlin no longer divided by the Wall, in cities like Lyon, Montpellier, St-Etienne and Dunkirk, which are challenging for the first time the central dominance of Paris.

If London does not respond to these developments with positive and progressive policies of its own, it will pay the price not simply in diminished status but in real economic decline.

It will also put at risk its position as a world city. At present there is a small group of such cities (New York, Tokyo, Paris, Berlin and London), with others like Frankfurt and Hong Kong attempting to attain that status. These cities are the international centres of finance and business; of transport, telecommunications and information; of learning and culture. The concept of a group of world cities is not simply a matter of prestige. Perceived membership generates both influence and wealth. London cannot afford to relinquish its leading position in any of these areas.

We have written this book to examine two questions: why, and how? Why is London not working? Why is the gulf between rich and poor districts widening? Why are people leaving? Why are other cities coping better with these urban problems? How can we build on the great strengths of London to ensure its recovery? How can we turn the city to face the river and so release the great potential of the Thames to benefit everybody and to enhance all aspects of London life? How can we enrich the city's environment and its urban design, strengthening those aspects that are already good (the parks, the squares, the villages) and improving the rest (the canals, the riverside, public buildings)? What policies will encourage innovation in architecture, in urban design and in planning? How can we reorientate London towards east and south? How can we ensure that such initiatives don't simply acknowledge those areas that are prosperous but also address the problems of inner-city dereliction in Hoxton, Dalston, Brixton, Newham, Peckham, Southwark and elsewhere?

We consider other questions – about participation and consultation. How can the people of London participate in their city's recovery? How can we increase public information about planning and architecture and so improve the quality of public debate? How can we reform the planning system, promoting approaches and initiatives that will mean that architecture and urbanism are taken seriously in Britain?

Implicit in all these questions is our passionate belief that London can do better; that people do not have to tolerate the problems that beset it; that London is selling itself short. Even in those areas that have benefited most from the consumer spree of the 1980s, where roofs are newly tiled, swagged blinds fringe the windows and estate cars line the pavements, even here there is a feeling that something is missing. People talk of a lack of vision for London. It is an overused, perhaps misused, phrase when what is lacking is, rather, a sense of sharing, of common purpose. But that common purpose needs to be inspired and articulated by a comprehensive view of the sort of city we want London to be – in short, by a vision.

To bring that to life there is a *prima facie* need for planning, intervention and investment in infrastructure, whether in transport, training, housing or telecommunications. A new partnership will have to be forged between public and private sector to implement those plans and coordinate that investment, but the experience of other

European cities is that strategic planning and public investment are major factors in creating urban regeneration.

There is no doubt that London has within it the talents to transform the city. The architects, designers, artists and planners are here, but they are not being asked to contribute. There is none of that excitement which flickered briefly in 1951, when, during the Festival of Britain, the South Bank displayed the work of artists like Henry Moore, Barbara Hepworth, Ben Nicholson and architects such as Leslie Martin, Philip Powell, Hidalgo Moya and Hugh Casson, and so turned away from the austerity of post-war Britain and imagined a new future, not just for London but for the country. Today there is no comparable feeling of a city that is bursting with ideas and confidence. But there can be little doubt that, given the slightest taste of such energy, the people of London would respond. The question is how to release those skills, begin that process and invent that future.

In this book our focus will be the physical environment of London, its rivers and canals, its parks and commons, its squares and streets. It is these that display the condition of a city; that affect our daily lives; that can be most readily changed, for good or for ill. That environment is of central importance to the efficiency of London and to the quality of life the city offers. If we neglect it, we transfer liabilities, rather than assets, to the next generation. It is the unbottled message we leave to the future. We are in danger of passing on a city lacking new ideas, imagination or collective pride. At present it would seem that office blocks, shopping malls, theme parks and car parks are likely to be the monuments of our generation. Where are the new parks and the new buildings? Where are we demonstrating how urban design and architecture can help to create balanced urban communities? At best we have marked time and are simply bequeathing a glorious past.

In London it is easy to be dazzled by the sweep of Nash's terraces around Regent's Park, or the grandeur and confidence of Cubitt's Belgravia, or the beauty of the Royal Parks, and so fail to see that many of London's landmarks, such as Trafalgar Square or Piccadilly Circus, are gradually being destroyed by the volume of traffic and are becoming little more than roundabouts. It is even easier to ignore those many areas of the city into which the tourist seldom ventures, those that are blighted by poverty and poor housing. In concentrating on the environment we will consider the ways in which new building, urban design and landscaping can contribute to turning these areas into more enjoyable, more accessible and safer places for people to use, for it is people who are at the heart of the environment, who make places live. Without them our environment is simply a collection of buildings and objects, little more than a stage set. Improving the built environment is not simply a matter of aesthetics. If designers and architects are to contribute successfully, their solutions must respond to people's needs.

What are those needs? What do people look for in a city? People want an opportunity to work and a home of their own. They want decent services: schools and hospitals, streets that are safe, public transport that is reliable. But they want more than that. Aristotle wrote, 'Men came together in cities in order to live. They remain together in order to live the good life.'[1] In pursuit of that good life they want choice and variety, of shops, cinemas, theatres, libraries and galleries, of pubs, restaurants and cafés. They want to feel a sense of identity and community, a sense of pride. They want to belong to a city. Above all they want each other, for it is the meeting of people that makes cities exciting, surprising and provocative places. But meeting people, in itself, is not enough. When Heinrich Heine wrote of Berlin that it 'is not a city at all, it is a place where people meet', he made a fine but crucial distinction. A city that is exciting to live in is one in which, once people come together, they create not just work and institutions but new ideas, events, a culture.

What these needs amount to is a desire for a various and balanced urban community, providing opportunities for work and for leisure, for efficient services and an attractive environment. It is the design of buildings and the space inside, outside and between them, in streets and squares, alleys, atria and arcades, that make up that environment. How we design those spaces, and particularly how we manage the balance between people and vehicles in our streets, will determine whether we can create that balanced community.

Almost all these needs and expectations have one common characteristic. They can only be achieved collectively, in public, with
others. Certainly the sheer size of cities offers privacy and anony-
mity, but, at root, cities are public places. They are communities in
which people are dependent to a great extent on each other.

In London the rich, living in Knightsbridge or Kensington, or the
visitor, in a West End hotel, may feel that they can insulate themselves from the city's problems and simply choose from among the
many delights still on offer. Private health care, private education,
bottled water may keep some of the realities of London life at
arm's length, but ultimately even those people have to walk along
broken pavements, further disfigured by unsightly litter, drive on
pot-holed roads, sit in the same traffic jams. Rich and poor are
yoked together. If London's economy, or its environment, declines,
we are all losers.

It has always been so. In the nineteenth century Parliament was
persuaded to introduce the great reforms that in effect created modern London – the formation of the Metropolitan Police in 1829, the
setting up of the Metropolitan Board of Works in 1855 to provide a
sewerage system and the establishment of the London County
Council in 1888 to tackle the 'pestilential human rookeries' that
were the slums[2] – by the fear that, if it did not act, crime, cholera and
disorder would spread to Westminster and Belgravia. The public
interest was a common interest.

In recent years the public interest has not been a concept much
prized by government. In this book we proclaim it. Without it cities
become jungles. This distrust of the public and preference for the
private has informed the present Government's attitudes to cities in
general and London in particular, to the detriment of all. In the early
1980s cities were viewed as problems. Instead of attempting to identify and tackle the root causes of the specific difficulties they faced
(rising crime rates, poor housing, low levels of skills) the Government found it convenient to lay all the blame on poor management
by local authorities. This hostility towards local authorities coincided
with the Government's desire, for macro-economic reasons, to
cut public expenditure generally. Accordingly central-government

financial support for local services in the form of Rate Support Grant has been severely cut. The cumulative loss to the thirty-two London boroughs now amounts to £7,936.9 million.[3] The councils' spending limits were cut back in the belief that spending in response to local needs was some wilful perversity for which councils should be blamed. Penalties were introduced, and finally central government took total control of councils' spending by capping their budgets. London suffered the additional penalty of losing its city-wide local authority, the Greater London Council (GLC), thus becoming the only capital in Europe without a democratic, strategic body to speak for it or plan for its future.

This Government's antipathy to the public sector and distaste for local government have been taken to ridiculous, and self-defeating, lengths. In 1991 only 302 council dwellings were started in London,[4] even though 38,000 households were accepted as homeless.[5] In the same period over 5,000 public-sector homes were built in Rotterdam, a city one tenth the size of London. Expenditure on infrastructure, in almost any form, was down while the Government held to its belief that generally the cheapest solution was the best. Both attitudes came together to undermine the development of Docklands with the Government's minimal investment in the area's infrastructure and its backing for the low-cost Docklands Light Railway (DLR), which is already proving inadequate for Docklands' needs and is incompatible, as a system, with any other form of transport in the capital. We will not improve London's environment, or tackle its fundamental problems, until these attitudes are changed, until we begin to invest in quality public services, not as a matter of ideology but on their merits.

It is just such a pragmatic approach that we have tried to bring to bear, in this book, on the challenges facing London. This is not simply a utopian vision of the city's future. There can be no easy, or cost-free, or quick-fix solutions for a city of this size. We don't start with a clean sheet. London's social, economic and political problems interact with each other. If they are to work, any interventions will have to synchronize and integrate with existing communities and services. That will make change complex, but, as Barcelona and other cities show, it does not mean that radical changes cannot be achieved.

Certainly we need to be ambitious in our dreams and expectations, to galvanize ourselves with a clear and exciting view of how London could be, but neither rhetoric nor brilliant initiatives can transform the whole mass of London, nor benefit all its people. For that reason we do not believe that large gestures, along the lines of Paris's Grands Projets, will by themselves provide an answer. There is both need and opportunity for some new buildings of this sort, but they will inevitably tend to enhance those central areas that are already well off.

Instead we need a wider diversity of detailed interventions all over the city under the umbrella of a process of strategic planning to co-ordinate and integrate such actions. But the emphasis must be on a strategic planning process, not one all-embracing masterplan attempting to lay out the city anew. For that there is neither demand nor time.

That process should be based on setting ourselves targets (for improvements in housing, public transport, pollution control, etc.) that can be monitored and updated as circumstances change. Frank Duffy and Alex Henney propose such a process in their book *The Changing City*.[6] They are describing what they see as necessary for the City of London, but the spirit of it could have wider application: 'We believe the way to improve the City lies in planning. We are not, however, advocating planning in the conventional and largely discredited sense of rigid, detailed and legalistic forms of development control based on how planners hope the future will unfold. We prefer the sense of planning commonly used in modern business – namely, setting regular targets which are used to monitor performance but which are readily modified as circumstances change. This form of planning provides a coherent and adaptable framework for determining what action is necessary to achieve common goals in an uncertain world.'

To favour such a process and to reject a masterplan is not to regard such an approach as un-English. A masterplan is suitable, even essential, when planning a town or city from scratch, as Bath,

Saltaire, Port Sunlight, Milton Keynes, Edinburgh's New Town and others show. But London has grown organically over 1,900 years, its expansion unplanned and spasmodic, determined by factors such as the shape of the river and movements in its economy. It is true that a considerable number of individual areas within the city (Bloomsbury, Belgravia, Hampstead Garden Suburb, Bedford Park and others) have themselves been planned, but the structure of London as a whole has not. Today there is neither opportunity nor need to interfere with the overall pattern of London's streets.

However, that does not mean that all that is necessary is a series of small interventions, with a few key sites such as King's Cross or Spitalfields, the Royal Docks or the Greenwich Peninsula being developed, or that all would be well if important buildings presently empty, like Battersea or Bankside power stations, were transformed and the river frontage tidied up. Such piecemeal improvements, desirable though they might be, would not begin to touch the city's real problems or provide a basis for its future. What is needed is something more radical.

If, for instance, the full potential of the Thames is to be realized, the river has got to be looked at in its entirety, not as a series of individual sites. If the south of the city is to play its full part in London's revival, there will have to be more bridges and better integration of transport systems.

For the east of London to develop, something more substantial will be required than a plan for the East Thames Corridor. If the development of waterfront areas, such as the Greenwich Peninsula and Thameside on the south bank and the Royal Docks, Bankside Docks and Rainham Marshes on the north, is to benefit the whole of east London, there will have to be an overview of the needs and potential of all east London boroughs and communities and a strategic plan through which to coordinate a range of initiatives. Central to that will be transport, with new investment in the Channel Tunnel rail terminus at Newham or Stratford, the extension of the Jubilee Line, the East London River Crossing bridge, the lengthening of the runway at the City Airport and improvements to the A13 all coming together to make a new transport mode that will link

London with Europe and both with the north of England. Only the combination of planning and public investment can achieve that.

It may appear that to advocate a strategic plan at the same time as dismissing any masterplan is contradictory. Not so. A masterplan implies a rigid prescription, imposed from above. By a strategic plan we mean a framework that brings together the key elements of a city (population changes, democratic structures, geographical limits, economic development, transport networks) and shapes them into a whole while at the same time allowing sufficient flexibility to respond to local needs and priorities.

Although we recognize the case for a strategic plan for London, this book is in no way an attempt to provide such a document. To be comprehensive, that would require the resources of government and the genius of a Patrick Abercrombie, whose *Greater London Plan: 1944*[7] set the context for post-war planning in London. In this book we can do no more than propose a general approach and consider, by way of illustration, some practical steps and policies by which it may be put into practice.

We believe the basic ingredient for that approach is to recognize the position of London within southern England and in a rapidly changing Europe. Both have considerable implications, particularly for transport and for economic expansion. At the same time we have to give greater consideration to the role of both technology and ecology in London's future. To preserve our pre-eminence in information technology and telecommunications, we need to invest in research and in distribution systems. With New York, London leads the world in services to commercial companies through optical fibre, with 400 office buildings served in this way compared with 110 in Tokyo.[8] However, our slowness in cabling the whole city and the absence of an overall policy will mean that Singapore and other cities will soon overtake us.

Just as we must anticipate those needs, we should be aiming to turn London into a city that can sustain itself more efficiently and more economically. To do so we must make better use of resources, particularly energy, in transport, in buildings, in manufacturing processes and in materials, and recognize the implications of the concept of 'sustainable development' outlined in the Brundtland Report[9] in 1987 and by the Pearce Report[10] in 1989 as the ability of humanity 'to ensure that it meets the needs of the present without compromising the ability of future generations to meet their own needs'. Failure to do so will mean that London and other cities will become urban black holes into which we will shovel ever-increasing amounts of resources without any significance as the quality of our lives inexorably deteriorates.

Within that context development should grow out of London's existing strengths and characteristics and, most crucially, in response to the needs of the people who live in and work in the city. The aim must be to create an environment that offers a productive and enjoyable life, not just for the richest 20 per cent but for all its people. To achieve that we will need to employ the skills and inventiveness of Britain's architects, designers and planners and to open ourselves to the contribution that Europe can make, thus beginning to turn the rhetoric of London as a world city and as a key European city into a reality.

In considering practical initiatives we will concentrate in particular on the Thames and on the potential of London's public spaces because we believe that improvements in these areas will have an immediate impact on the whole city. Flowing across London from west to east, the Thames is the key both to tilting the city again towards the east and to bringing together north and south. But its significance is not only strategic. The river is in itself a hugely underused resource that could contribute far more to the life of the capital. With a considerable proportion of the city's derelict or unused land along its banks, the Thames is waiting for London to reclaim it. If there is one Grand Projet we should adopt in the next few years, it is to turn the city to face its river and open up both banks so that they become places where people can work, live, shop, walk, eat, drink, sit, be entertained – in short, to make the Thames the heart of the city.

Behind all these proposals is a belief in the idea of the city. Current attitudes are far from positive. Too many people, in the media and in government, are at best ambivalent about, and at worst

13

dislike, cities *per se*. To such people inner cities are socially and politically unreliable, little more than breeding grounds for crime and
dissent. Riots, like those in the St Paul's district of Bristol, Brixton,
Toxteth or Meadowhall, do not happen in suburban or rural areas.
The condition of Liverpool in 1983 came as a shock to Michael
Heseltine even though he had been Secretary of State for the
Environment, responsible for inner cities, for four years. The experience of the previous seventeen years, as Member of Parliament for
first Tavistock and then Henley, had clearly not prepared him for
what he saw. To his credit he determined to try to tackle Liverpool's
problems. Others among his colleagues have continued to turn away
or to see in cities only disorder and electoral opposition.

It must be acknowledged that our generation is far from being the
first to view cities in such negative terms. Just as the idea of the city
as the home of civilization, culture, wealth and power has run
through our language and our thought since the Greeks, so too has
the image of the city as the place of corruption and crime, of danger
and decay. The city has been depicted as both heaven and hell. Since
nineteenth-century industrialization turned many of Britain's cities
into vast metropolises whose slums were an urban nightmare, attitudes towards the city have been increasingly hostile. The ideal has
been suburban, not urban. In this book we reject such a view and
are unashamedly pro-city. In our opinion, if cities are to be revived,
they will have to be made into places that are enjoyable and efficient,
places in which people want to live and work. It will not be enough
to assert that cities should offer opportunity and variety; we must
make sure they provide them. It is a circular problem. Once people
and businesses are attracted back, the income of inner-city areas
will increase and will be able to provide a quality of life that will
itself attract back more people and more work. To break into that
virtuous circle will require the right policies, political will and
investment by both private and public sectors. The experience of
other cities, in Britain and abroad, shows that such regeneration is
possible.

The choice is ours. We can either continue as we are, relying on
isolated projects undertaken by the private sector (such as King's

Cross and Broadgate), which are themselves dependent on the state of the national economy, or we can develop policies, at both national and local level, that take the initiative and promote the recovery that London needs. We can choose simply to be a city with a great past or one with a great future, a city of declining heritage or one of innovation, building on that heritage.

There are those who resist such action. Some say that what little is amiss with London is the consequence of its own success. Others insist that, even if all is not completely well, intervention of any sort is unnecessary and undesirable. Still more cling to the belief that once Britain pulls out of the present recession, all will be well.

We believe that such views are wrong-headed and perilously complacent and that they ignore the realities of London: the inadequacy of its infrastructure in transport, education, economic development and training; the appalling condition of much of its housing; the dangerous social divisions that are creating two cities, rich and poor, with little common interest to bind them. More immediately, that complacency underestimates the extent to which London is having to compete with other cities, both in Europe and beyond.

Because London is a world city, one of the three leading financial centres, and enjoys the advantage of speaking the key international language, it is tempting to suppose that its pre-eminence is impregnable. In their time the people of Constantinople, Alexandria and Venice must have thought the same. Fifteenth-century Lisbon, which had been turned by Miguel I into the trading (and slave trading) centre of Europe, went from pre-eminence to obscurity in the space of thirty years after 1421.

Today competition between cities is growing more intense every year, for inward investment, for tourism, as centres for finance markets or as locations for international headquarters. When other cities are investing in airports, convention centres, new universities, cultural and sporting facilities, London cannot afford to be left behind. Its inability in 1991 to agree on a committee that could present a bid for the Olympics in 2000 was in itself not of great moment, even if it made London look faintly ridiculous to the outside world. But it was symptomatic of a lack of clear leadership and common purpose that, unless it is rectified, will threaten more important prizes than the opportunity to host the Olympics.

London remains a great city but one with great problems. All of them can be tackled. We have the skills and the talents. We have the technology. Our architects and artists have the imagination. The question is, do we have the courage to be ambitious and audacious and the political will to drive such plans through? Above all, can London be galvanized into action with a sense of urgency that has not been a feature of British life in recent years? The response to these questions must be 'yes'. The solutions themselves will be easier to identify once we have assessed the strengths and weaknesses of London today.

CHAPTER TWO

The Rights and Wrongs of London

London has substantial strengths and major weaknesses in its culture, its economy and its environment. It would be foolish either to talk the city down or to ignore the scale of the problems it faces. But over everything looms the appalling condition of its transport system, wrapping the city in a grisly embrace and threatening to strangle the life out of it.

Travelling into London or across it, whether on public or private transport, above or below ground, is a dire experience. Descend into the Tube and take the Northern Line into central London during the rush hour: 406,000 people do so every weekday and suffer the overcrowding and squalor of a system that is as exhausted as its thirty-five-year-old rolling stock.[1]

If you are deterred by the prospect of that start to the working day, try staying at street level and taking a bus. In spite of the introduction of special priority bus lanes and other improvements in traffic management, it is likely that you will sit for long periods in streets that have been brought to a standstill by the volume of private cars. Consequently 50 per cent fewer people take buses into the centre of London than did so thirty years ago,[2] and the average speed at which traffic moves has fallen to 11 mph, the same as it was before the introduction of the motor car a hundred years ago.

The congestion is intensified by the 458,000 men and women who commute into central London each day by British Rail,[3] many of them on trains that, like the Northern Line's engines and carriages, are over thirty years old. In terms of mobility and transport, London isn't working. Not only does this make the city an increasingly unattractive place in which to live or work; it is also a considerable drag on the economy. The Confederation of British Industry (CBI) estimates that deficiencies in London Transport cost up to £1,000 a year in lost productivity from each employee and increase distribution costs by 30 per cent.[4] Overall it has calculated that infrastructure deficiencies add at least £15 billion a year to business costs in Britain, two thirds of that falling on London and the South-East.[5] It is the sheer scale of these transport problems and their impact on the city's economy that demands that any assessment of London's strengths and weaknesses must begin with transport. As Colin Clark wrote in 1957, transport is the 'maker and breaker of cities',[6] touching and influencing every person and every aspect of city life. We will make little progress until the city's transportation systems are improved.

Certainly there are some indications that things could be beginning to change. London Underground's investment programme has been increased from £370 million in 1991 to £590 million in 1992 and £780 million the following year. This will allow it to accelerate work on the core projects of resignalling, replacing redundant stock and station renovation. But London Underground has estimated that it will need £750 million in each of the next ten years to 'establish an acceptably modern network'.[7] Work on a new cross-town link between Paddington and Liverpool Street, which is funded separately, is scheduled to begin in 1994. The Jubilee Line is being extended. British Rail has spent £160 million on an excellent modernization of Liverpool Street Station[8] and has commissioned architect Nicholas Grimshaw to restructure Waterloo. But these initiatives, welcome though they are, are no more than piecemeal improvements to a system that cannot meet the demands made of it. What transport in London needs is a new coherence, integrating networks and policies.

Experts have been calling for that comprehensive planning for more than fifty years. Abercrombie detailed massive plans[9] for new road and rail systems that were updated and amended by the Greater

London Development Plan of 1966–9. A joint GLC and Department of the Environment committee chaired by Sir David Barran in 1974 produced a major report on the city's rail needs. Nationally the 1963 Buchanan Report, *Traffic in Towns,*[10] and the 1977 Leitch Report on trunk roads[11] made proposals that could have led to significant improvements in London, but although some specific recommendations were implemented, the complexity of the problems and the vast cost of the solutions meant that what was done was partial and cripplingly slow. What we need is an integrated mass-transit system as a key part of wider transport policies to reduce pollution and increase energy efficiency.

We will never develop an effective transport system, secure the scale of investment needed or, above all, spend that money efficiently until London is able to plan its transport needs coherently. One glance at the existing networks makes the case for integration. Rail, Underground, buses, taxis and roads are all administered and financed separately. The gauge of the new Docklands Light Railway synchronizes with neither rail nor Underground systems. It is a far cry from an integrated mass–transit system that would provide feeder links and common fares between all forms of public transport.

We could plug the more obvious gaps. We could probably link the rail systems with a Thames Riverbus service. But to introduce a proper regional transportation network would require, even as a first move, the active cooperation of British Rail and London Regional Transport, not the rivalry and competition for passengers that exists at present. What people want is to be able to buy one ticket and to travel into and around the city on one linked network. London has taken tentative steps in this direction, as rail passengers travelling into the capital can now combine their rail and Underground journeys on a single ticket, but there are no signs of coordination in the network itself.

In *London 2001*[12] Peter Hall discusses how we could adapt what we have to form a system not unlike the French Réseau Express Régional (RER). He claims, 'it could be built quite parsimoniously, without large-scale new construction, because most of the network is already there'.[13] It would connect many of the suburban routes south of the Thames, making them in effect part of the Underground, and it would link some of the far-flung suburbs, giving commuters direct access to central London for the first time. There would be two rings, an inner orbital rail route, connecting existing British Rail lines to London Underground's east London services and then, in the future a wider orbital rail route, a rail M25. These are proposed by the Labour Party and supported by private developers. A London RER of this type would transform transport for both Londoners and commuters.

But as important would be the wide-ranging policy decisions that are necessary: the shift away from roads to rail, from private to public. Lyon is aiming for an 80:20 public/private mix of transport, as is Berlin. Only targets like these would get to the heart of London's transport problems and tackle the damage done to its environment, where traffic accounts for most of the air pollution. The city is increasingly dominated by the most voracious god that man has ever worshipped, the motor car, which daily spreads noise, smell, dirt, vibration, injury and death throughout the city when moving and takes up valuable space when stationary.

To correct that imbalance requires coordination, not just of physical systems but of government departments and their policies. It is not hard to identify the range of options available. We need to employ a combination of deterrents and incentives, of fiscal and regulatory measures. We could manage the movement of traffic more rigorously, or we could penalize the unused, stationary vehicle more heavily. We could have fewer, or more expensive, parking spaces. We could enforce the existing parking regulations more efficiently, though that would require more than doubling the 1,671 traffic wardens currently employed. The Metropolitan Police aims for 2,350 by 1995, and, combined with local-authority wardens, this figure could reach nearly 4,000.[14] We could end the positive encouragement that we now give to company cars through tax relief and by granting planning permission for huge car parks in new office blocks.

Around the world there are examples of good practice for us to consider. The Dutch *woonerven* slow vehicles to walking speed in residential areas with 'sleeping policemen' humps, chicanes and tree planting.[15] In Singapore people are charged for driving into central areas at peak times, using a system devised by the GLC in the 1970s. Hong Kong has also experimented with electrification pricing. Stockholm County in Sweden and Bergen in Norway have piloted schemes for road pricing aimed at reducing traffic volumes and exhaust emissions.[16] Nationally Sweden, Norway and the Netherlands have set themselves a series of targets for reducing damage to the environment, traffic casualties and parking spaces by the year 2000. In Athens, where transport accounts for 86.4 per cent of air pollution, a five-year plan, in operation since 1988, is coordinating measures to reduce traffic volumes (restricting access to inner-city areas and the gradual relocation of ministries and public corporations away from the central business area), to improve public transport (two new metro lines and the extension of the trolley-bus service) and to tackle pollution directly (the reduction of lead in all petrol by 62 per cent and incentives for taxis to convert to unleaded fuel). Although the implementation of this programme is behind schedule, it shows, in the words of an Organization for Economic Cooperation and Development (OECD) report, that 'such comprehensive packages are an effective way of integrating the various aspects that contribute to air pollution caused by traffic in urban areas'.[17]

London could benefit from adopting any or all of these initiatives. What it cannot do is nothing. Nor can London hide behind the excuse that such radical plans are unachievable and utopian. Certainly the intervention and investment involved would require a degree of political courage that would be unlikely without a clear demonstration of public support. But change on this scale is possible, as London's history shows. Frank Pick and Albert Stanley (later Lord Ashfield) achieved it when in the 1920s and 1930s they took the Underground empire of the American Charles Tyson Yerkes and turned it into what was then the finest metropolitan transport system in the world.

Yerkes had arrived in Britain in 1900, fresh from building the EL, Chicago's elevated railway, and from a spell in prison for financial impropriety. He brought together the District, Bakerloo,

Piccadilly and Hampstead lines but couldn't make them pay. Central government investment was needed and regulation in the form of a Passenger Transport Board, which created London Transport in 1933. But it took the vision and drive of Pick and Stanley, as managing director and chairman respectively, to forge it into a coherent system, and one key technique they employed was design.

Yerkes had already seen the potential of good design in giving his lines an identity, and he finished his early stations in deep-red glazed tiles, which in many places survive to this day. But it was Frank Pick who employed design to establish a corporate identity for London Underground, with its bull's-eye logo and the typeface he commissioned from Edward Johnson. Pick was determined that the quality and appearance of every aspect of the system – its stations, carriages, signage, posters – should celebrate the freedom and mobility that London Transport was providing for people in London. Some of the stations, such as Southgate and Arnos Grove, designed by his principal architect Charles Holden, rank with the finest twentieth-century architecture in London, elegant, functional and efficient.

In particular Holden's redesign of Piccadilly Circus, with its Art Deco concourse, beige marble fittings, subdued lighting and shopping arcade, set new standards for the quality of public spaces. In the booking hall was a painting placing Piccadilly at the centre of the Empire – indeed, of the world. This was something more than just a transport system. No wonder the architectural historian Sir Nikolaus Pevsner lauded London Underground as a 'civilizing agent'.

Comparable energy and determination had been demonstrated across Britain by our forefathers in the nineteenth century, when they built 10,700 miles of railways in only twenty years, an achievement made possible by Parliament's passing 229 Railway Bills at the rate of one Bill every two working days throughout the entire period. We should compare that with the five years it took to pass the single Act of Parliament giving approval for 1.5 miles of tunnel to link the Docklands Light Railway terminal to Bank Underground station.If we have the will, everything is possible.

Although transport overshadows everything, London also faces other major problems. Fortunately all of them have within them major strengths on which to build.

At one level London's economy has weathered remarkably well the initial impact of post-industrialization, which saw the city lose 427,000 jobs between 1973 and 1983,[18] almost all of them in manufacturing or the handling of goods. In the same period services, and particularly financial services, boomed, and the City of London remains one of the world's three most important financial centres, with jobs growing in the Square Mile by eight times the national average in the 1980s.[19] Although this growth has been reversed by the present recession, the City has proved itself overall to be resilient and successful. Net annual overseas earnings from banking rose, in the ten years prior to deregulation in 1986, from £290 million to £2,295 million[20] and financial earnings generally from £3,745 million to £9,375 million.

London remains a major force in international financial markets, although Tokyo is closing the gap fast, increasing its share of international banking loans from 10 per cent to 18 per cent between 1985 and 1987, while London's business dropped slightly from 24 per cent to 22 per cent.[21] At a corporate level London is responding to this challenge, and to the requirements of new technologies that involve three quarters of all banking employees working on video screens, by adapting both the volume and the quality of office space. The architect Frank Duffy, who specializes in corporate development, is convinced that 'the financial services companies in the City are changing more rapidly than anywhere else in Europe, if not the world. The growth of the City as a world financial centre requires building resources of the highest quality, making the City, along with – if not ahead of – New York and Tokyo, one of the most exciting places for the development of both the "hardware" of office design and the "software" of managing buildings.'[22] However, any optimism gleaned from the City's success must be qualified by analysis of London's wider economy, as is made clear by the Henley Centre's survey *London 2000*.[23]

Britain's top companies are beginning to move out. In 1985, 48 per cent of the top 500 companies had their headquarters in

London. By 1990 this figure had fallen to 42 per cent. With city-centre office rents twice as high as in Paris and two and a half times those in Frankfurt, it is not surprising that London's share of world banking had fallen from 25 per cent in 1985 to 19 per cent by the end of the decade, while Europe increased its share overall from 28 per cent to 31 per cent.

The Henley Centre, an independent research organization, is in no doubt about the inability of the market to cope with these trends. 'The economy functions more efficiently when the future plans of various elements of the infrastructure are known. They should encourage growth to gravitate to where capacity is cheapest and less congested and to where existing services save time. Unfortunately, with increasing privatization, competition tends to drive plans into secrecy.'[24]

For London as a whole the effect of de-industrialization has been traumatic, with the capital suffering more severely than any other British city, including Liverpool.[25] Some boroughs face high, and seemingly permanent, levels of unemployment: 20 per cent of Hackney's population is out of work and 18.2 per cent of Haringey's.[26] Not only is the city's employment economy becoming geographically unbalanced, but some groups of people are being particularly disadvantaged.

Among ethnic minority groups unemployment is running at 13 per cent, compared with 7 per cent for white people.[27] It is inevitable that such people will feel despair and disillusion. They will certainly take little comfort from the prosperity of those in financial services, nor believe that growth in the Square Mile will trickle down and assist people in Southwark or Dalston. Their scepticism is confirmed by all available research.[28] No one supposes that there is any easy solution to such employment inequalities. Policies that increase resources for training and education will have a general impact but will be, at best, long-term and even then may not succeed in helping people who are presently unemployed to become potential employees of companies that are demanding increasingly sophisticated skills. At present 'participation rates in education and training for those aged between 16 and 18 years old are lower in the UK than in any other country hosting a world city', according to estimates published by the Department of Education and Science.[29]

Because this problem is so intractable some experts[30] are beginning to advocate that people living in inner-city areas who have below-average chances of unemployment should be encouraged to move out – the employment equivalent of Ebenezer Howard's determination in 1898[31] that relocating communities was the best way to cope with poverty, slums and high population density in cities. In our view any such policy is abhorrent and dangerously wrong-headed. Economic migration of this sort, whether forced or 'encouraged', offends against all democratic principles, effectively penalizing the unskilled and semi-skilled with exile. If carried through to any extent, it would turn inner cities into professional ghettos, as undesirable and unbalanced as ghettos of poverty. The problems of inequality, low skills and deprivation cannot be exported in this way. Transferring them to new locations does nothing to address either the causes of unemployment or its effects.

In the medium term there is no alternative to investing heavily in education and training, but we should be under no illusion about the extent of catching up that London, and Britain, needs to do. Tokyo, Paris and New York are already tackling the challenge of what the Tokyo metropolitan government's report describes as 'the rise of soft economics', those services based on information, communications and high-technology engineering and electronics.[32] All are intent on turning their cities into major academic and research centres. London is making no such investment, either to enhance academic education or to boost the potential of the unskilled and semi-skilled, who account for 21 per cent of the working population.[33] The census shows that managers, professionals, scientists and technicians account for 28 per cent of the working population.

Once London commits itself to such an investment strategy, we could augment it by attempting to disperse what growth there is. Left to the market, future development in London will tend, in imitation of Docklands, to be in exclusive locations, separated from, not part of, surrounding communities.

To ensure greater balance in development, we will have to use strategic planning in a positive way. Before people cry 'centralist' or criticize such an approach as meddling with the market, they should consider that Docklands was just such a central government intervention in the natural or free market, offering an artificial financial context with incentives on rates and other taxes.

We should give special emphasis to development in the south and east of London, in the Royal Docks, the Greenwich Peninsula, Woolwich, Thamesmead and the East Thames Corridor generally. In many of these areas, particularly the Greenwich Peninsula and Thamesmead, development will have important implications for London's ecology and its green environment, either enhancing them with new parks and wildlife habitats or inflicting greater volumes of traffic on them. To find this balance between the city's economic needs and its environmental future is one of the major challenges facing London and every other comparable city.

Both the Brundtland Commission and the EC Green Paper on the environment identify this problem, but neither is clear how to resolve the conflicts that inevitably ensue, the EC Green Paper noting cautiously that the implications of 'sustainability' for urban environmental management 'need to be explored in detail'.[34] London approaches this difficult issue from a comparatively strong position, at least from the point of view of existing provision, having a better ratio of parks to office space than any other world city apart from Berlin.[35] The Royal Parks, Hampstead Heath, Blackheath, Epping Forest and the city's many commons are justly famous and greatly cherished. But their beauty can distract us from recognizing that the majority of the parks and open spaces are concentrated in the centre and the west of the city. Some boroughs, particularly in the east, have little or no open space. Tower Hamlets has 65 hectares, Islington only 54, compared with Camden's 352 hectares and Richmond's 1,889.[36]

We have done little in the past fifty years to improve this situation. Haggerston Park was made in 1951; Holland Park was opened to the public the same year; and Southwark, with help from the Greater London Council, created Burgess Park, off the Old Kent Road. But our record of renewal compares unfavourably with that of other European cities. Similarly there is little evidence of any reconsideration of the role, or design, of existing parks. The Government, in 1991, initiated a review of the Royal Parks, asking a working party to report on 'whether the parks meet the needs of today, and how they can meet the needs of tomorrow',[37] but as the working party deliberates, the gardening of the Royal Parks, along with the catering and the provision of deckchairs and rowing boats, are all being privatized. Doubtless the working party will point out the Royal Parks' potential as locations for concerts, art exhibitions and other events, but the Government's brief, with its emphasis on maximizing the income from the Parks, will mean that such cultural events will be viewed primarily from a commercial viewpoint. This will risk ignoring the contribution the Parks can make to the educational life of the capital, providing an opportunity for London schoolchildren to study wildlife and flora. A wider strategy is needed if London's parks are to be enhanced to the benefit of all, just as it is needed for the development of the city's cultural life.

London's cultural life is unquestionably one of its greatest assets. This is due partly to the dominance of English as a world language, partly to the excellence of British artists, musicians and performers and partly to the extraordinary collection of arts companies and cultural institutions in London. To have the Royal National Theatre and the Royal Shakespeare Company (RSC), the Royal Opera House and the English National Opera, the four major orchestras and the London Sinfonietta, the National Gallery and the Tate Gallery, the British Museum and the Victoria and Albert, the South Bank and the Barbican all located in one city is remarkable. Add the West End theatre, the fine-art auction houses, the fringe theatres, the BBC and London's design and fashion industries, and it can quite clearly be seen how strong is the city's cultural life, making it a magnet for tourists and an exciting place to live. It also continues to contribute to the economy of the city, providing employment for 214,500 people and generating a turnover of an estimated £7.5 billion annually.[38] At the same time it promotes the city internationally, being one of a very small number of activities in which London leads the world.

London ought to be building on this enviable reputation and position. Instead, while other cities such as Glasgow, Birmingham, Frankfurt and Seville are investing in arts festivals, new museums and new concert halls, London is marking time, even slipping backwards.

The Tate Gallery has holes in its roof and needs £27 million worth of basic repairs. The National Gallery needs £20 million, the Victoria and Albert £100 million. All have had their purchasing grants frozen by the Government for seven years, with the result that they cannot develop their collections. The Tate's grant allows it to buy one major British painting a year. The RSC was so underfunded that it had to close its London base at the Barbican for four months in the winter of 1990–91. Question marks hang over the future of the Royal Opera House, which receives a government subsidy of 38 per cent of its costs, compared with a subsidy of over 70 per cent for every other major opera house in Europe.

This catalogue of woes owes something to the lack of priority given to the arts by both Mrs Thatcher's and Mr Major's Governments, but one further reason why it remains unaddressed is because there is no one to assume full responsibility for the arts in London. That responsibility is shared between the Minister, the Arts Council, the London Boroughs Grants Committee (LBGC), the London Arts Board (LAB) and the thirty-two boroughs, plus the City of London. There is no common strategy.

The priority given by the Government to cutting public expenditure meant that in 1991 the LAB received a grant increase of 2 per cent while inflation was 8 per cent; the LBGC was unable for many weeks to set a budget within the Government's guidelines; and the boroughs, faced by the poll tax and the capping of their budgets, cut £8 million from their arts and libraries budgets.[39] The result was that, although the finances of most of the major arts organizations remained relatively intact, small arts companies and venues in the boroughs were closed down. This harmed the communities they served and the audiences they were building up, but it did greater damage to the young artists and performers who relied on these small companies for work.

What should be one of London's greatest strengths is being put at risk. The Government has got to bring these bodies together to form a city-wide strategy, has got to support the boroughs rather than penalizing them and has got to begin to celebrate the city's cultural life instead of neglecting it.

In no area is this neglect more apparent than in architecture. Where are the major new buildings of the past ten years? It is not a long list. Norman Foster's ITN headquarters, Nicholas Grimshaw's *Financial Times* printing works, Michael Hopkins's Lord's cricket ground pavilion, John Miller's Royal College of Art extension, James Stirling's Clore Gallery. After you add Ralph Erskine's Ark at Hammersmith and Ted Cullinan's Petershill House there is a temptation to start looking back ten, twenty, even fifty years to the Smithsons' *Economist* Building, Denys Lasdun's Royal College of Physicians, Daban and Darke's flats at Liddington Gardens, Leslie Martin and Peter Moro's Royal Festival Hall, Crabtree and Reilly's Peter Jones department store and Lubetkin's High Point flats. What is notable is that, the Royal Festival Hall apart, all those buildings are in the private sector. It is a thin record for a city with such a glorious architectural past.

Overall, in spite of the fact that each contains a worm of weakness, London's strengths (its economy, environment and cultural life) all offer foundations on which to build the capital's future. However, any easy optimism begins to wither when you consider the city's local services, particularly education, health and housing. These are the bedrock of any city and have the greatest impact on people's lives. For London all are barometers of its decline. London's school buildings need £1 billion spent on them,[40] and 148 schools have closed since 1980.[41] Staff turnover runs at the rate of 22 per cent each year.[42] Homelessness has risen from 16,579 households to 37,740 households and 65,000 single homeless in the last decade.[43] Local authorities have a statutory duty to the homeless, but London's are unable adequately to respond, since their building programme has fallen from 9,131 new starts in 1979 to 302 in 1990.[44] The criminalizing of squatting will inevitably add to the homeless problem. Crime figures rose from 584,000 to 834,000.[45] It's a cocktail of social deprivation that would daunt any city. In tackling this crisis London has been constrained by the very factor that has exacerbated many of these problems, namely, the Government's implacable hostility to any local-authority expenditure. Boroughs have had to cope with a policy of penalties and controls implemented by nine pieces of legislation since 1983.[46] Fourteen London councils, and the Inner London Education Authority (ILEA) and the GLC, have been rate- or poll tax-capped in that period, with the result that £7.9 billion have been lost to London boroughs since 1979.[47]

Poorer boroughs, such as Hackney, face a cycle of decline. As unemployment rises and the income levels shrink in real terms, so the local economy is squeezed, as are the council's finances. Social problems increase, demanding initiatives that require expenditure. Instead financial realities, reinforced by government policy, make cuts necessary. As the quality of services such as education declines, many of those people who are able to do so move out, further weakening the local economy. It is a vicious circle, undermining communities and threatening to create a dangerous void in the middle of the city. In it different elements like housing or crime, which by themselves can be coped with, interact to dire effect. Once again, it is in the field of transport that this process can be seen most clearly.

As the quality of life declines, people continue to move to the suburbs and beyond, but many are still commuting in to work, so putting greater strain on regional transport, on roads and on the environment. The scale of this population shift is enormous: inner London lost 0.5 million people between 1961 and 1986.[48] This exodus has been not only to the Outer Metropolitan areas (Reading, Southend, the M25 towns), whose populations have increased by 1.2 million, but beyond, to a belt of counties (Wiltshire, Oxfordshire, Northamptonshire, Cambridgeshire and Suffolk) to the west, north and east of London. As Peter Hall says, 'the movement has been and will be outward, from core to ring, from ring to fringe.'[49] The Office of Population Censuses and Surveys predicts that this trend will continue until the end of the century and that an additional 1.3 million people will move to these areas. Inevitably this shift is both stimulating, and being fuelled by, parallel shifts in industry and employment.

The case for a regional perspective and some planning of the relationship between London and this wider region becomes overwhelming, not least to prevent urban sprawl beyond the M25 and to give some coherence to what is becoming a series of interrelated towns and cities ringing London. That in turn requires us to define London, which has always tended to defy definition.

London consists of a series of geographical Russian dolls. At the centre is the City of London, around which is the 10 square miles of central London, including the West End, Westminster, Kensington and Chelsea. Beyond that are the boundaries of the old London County Council/ILEA, with a population of 2.5 million,[50] themselves surrounded by the 620 square miles, 32 boroughs and 7 million-strong population that were the responsibilities of the GLC. Further away still is Outer Metropolitan London (12.5 million population), the South-East (20 million)[51] and the western and northern belt referred to above, which takes in Bournemouth, Swindon, Northampton, Milton Keynes, Peterborough and Ipswich. When considering transport, population movements, industry and jobs, the map must include these outer areas. For the built environment, particularly for discussion of the Thames and London's public spaces, a narrow definition is used in this book, coinciding with the boundaries of the old GLC.

Whatever the definition, the trends are clear. People are moving out, and employment in London is declining, in spite of a short-term increase of 126,000 new jobs between 1984 and 1988 following deregulation in the City.[52] To some extent that move away from the inner city is nothing more than a marked acceleration of a process that has been going on for most of this century. Ebenezer Howard, in *Garden Cities of Tomorrow*,[53] made the first coherent case for decentralization, taken up enthusiastically by disciples like Patrick Geddes and Lewis Mumford. Howard's ideas were a response to appalling inner-city housing and health conditions and to a population density three times higher than London's today. But Howard intended that migration to garden cities should relieve the metropolitan blood pressure, not destroy it. The migration has taken place, but it has not satisfactorily been accompanied by the other aspect of his strategy, which was to use the breathing space to rebuild and reinvigorate central London. Abercrombie understood this in his plans, but, as with Howard's garden city strategy, the implementation of the Abercrombie Greater London Plan was only partial. The tower blocks that replaced slum housing or bomb sites were often cheaply built, poorly designed and without any communal provisions. There is nothing inherently wrong with high-rise apartments. Rich city dwellers all over the world pay huge rents for penthouses. The towers of Roehampton continue to be praised and remain popular. They may fail to be the 'villages in the sky' that Le Corbusier intended, but the absence of a neighbourhood street life can be seen as a positive attraction by rich people in search of privacy. By contrast, the poor, lacking the cushion of disposable income, have greater need of the support of neighbours and a community. For them tower blocks – where the lifts don't work, which have no caretakers or security system and whose walkways therefore become no-go areas – are a nightmare. High-rises such as these have only speeded the exodus from inner London. We are faced today with ominous signs of the breakdown of city life, as crime figures reach record levels. A car is stolen every minute in London, and over the last ten years violent crimes have increased by 120 per cent and burglaries by 39 per cent.[54]

We have to make a choice. We can continue with the present Government's policies, doing as little as possible and tightening control over the inner-city boroughs, both physically, with the aid of stronger policing, and politically by means of financial restraints. Behind this approach is the hope that the awfulness of living in London will either drive people away (to where?) or goad them to effect a recovery (how?). It is a punitive strategy, whose essence is captured by a favourite phrase of Conservative politicians, 'No pain, no gain,' and it shows little respect or concern for the reality of people's circumstances. Moreover, implicit within it is the danger that the breakdown will become a collapse and the decline plummet into free fall.

The alternative is to take a wider view, to attempt to restrict the suburbanization of the outer metropolitan area and beyond while putting together a package of policies designed to begin to turn the inner city around. As people cannot be compelled to return, those policies will have to make inner-city life so attractive – with better services, better facilities, improved transport – that they want to do so. To achieve that will require investment on a large scale, both public and private; it will need to harness the talents of the people of London and the inherent strengths of the city, and it will have to involve the strategic planning that London has lacked in recent years.

A guiding principle of that planning should be the concept of 'decentralized concentration' that runs through the London Planning Advisory Committee's (LPAC) strategy for London.[55] Decentralized concentration has been a characteristic of Danish planning in recent years, but it has much in common with the network of village communities identified by Patrick Abercrombie in his *Greater London Plan*.[56] In both, urban development is concentrated in local centres spread throughout a metropolitan area, so that these centres act as foci for a wide range of activities, commercial, retail and cultural. The advantages of decentralized concentration are that it reduces the demands for transport in and out of the centre of cities, encourages higher densities of population and makes the best use of available land, all of which help to maintain varied and balanced communities. In its strategy LPAC envisages thirty-three such centres, or nodes of activity, around London, but a city-wide authority would be needed to implement a plan of this sort.

Alone among the capitals of Europe, London has no city-wide authority that could formulate such a strategy, no democratic forum in which to debate it, nor even a voice to speak specifically for the city. Central government has not assumed these duties. Instead responsibility is fragmented between the thirty-two boroughs and the Corporation of the City of London, which too often have been competing with each other rather than cooperating, point scoring rather than problem solving. The issues have become political footballs, with the Government and Conservative-controlled boroughs, like Wandsworth, positively relishing the difficulties of Labour boroughs, such as Lambeth and Camden, as they grapple with huge social problems. It is an attitude that may yield short-term party-political gains in local elections, but it ignores the fact that a city is one community and the existence of such pockets of deprivation diminishes the whole of London.

At last the Government seems to be acknowledging, albeit with reluctance, that some form of strategic body for London is essential. But what form? Those who, for political reasons, will not coun-tenance a democratically elected council cannot agree on the type of non-elected body. Should it be a quango of the great and the good or an executive composed of unelected bodies or advisory bodies such as the London Planning Commission, which was proposed in the 1983 White Paper *Streamlining the Cities*?[57] Some favour an American-style mayor as an elected figurehead.

The problem with all these proposals is that, unlike a democratic-ally elected council, they would have no constituency, no money, no power and so no teeth. The existing advisory bodies, LPAC and the Standing Committee on South-East Regional Planning (SER-PLAN), have in many respects done well, having given intelligent consideration to the problems of London and the region, but they are without power to effect anything.

The cautious, the sceptical and the hostile believe that macro-planning of this sort is un-English. In fact London has been the sub-ject of strategic plans ever since the war, with Abercrombie's great documents of 1943 and 1944 being updated by the Greater London Development Plan of 1970, itself amended in 1976. However, only in the period 1965–86, between the Local Government Act of 1963 and the GLC's abolition, did London truly have a strategic metropolitan planning body, and even then it was only after 1969 that the GLC was both a highways and a public transport authority. Others, like the Secretary of State for the Environment, Michael Heseltine, feel that such planning is unnecessary. In 1983 he foresaw the end of 'the heyday of a certain fashion for strategic planning, the confidence in which now appears exaggerated' and discounted any strategic role 'which may have little basis in real needs'.[58] The in-coherence of London since then indicates that he was wrong.

However, neither the existence of a strategic authority nor that of a strategy is any guarantee of success. Most plans are overtaken by unforeseen events. The time is surely past for all-embracing and detailed schemes like Abercrombie's, not least because the boroughs will not return the powers that they have enjoyed since 1986. What is needed now is a slimline, strategic body with limited responsibility for the macro-elements of London's life – its transport, its economic development, the Thames. Its role will be to provide a general framework within which Urban Development Plans (UDPs) and detailed area plans can fit, to speak to government on behalf of London and to liaise with the region and with Europe. This last is important. As the map of Europe changes and its centre of gravity shifts rapidly eastwards, so London's position will alter in relation to the rest of the Continent. Unless we upgrade its air and rail facilities, London will be in danger of being sidelined both physically and politically.

What is certain is that only London can save itself. The problems of unemployment and industrial decline elsewhere in the UK mean that there will be limits to the amount of government investment that London can hope to secure, even though the future of the capital is as significant and as essential to the success of Britain nationally as it is to the people of London.

Time is not on our side, as London is already several years behind other European cities in addressing the challenges of post-industrialization that face them all. This gives us the opportunity to learn from their mistakes and profit from their successes. To do so, we must first study what other European cities have done in the 1980s and assess their performance.

Much of the grandeur
of central London was
created in the early nineteenth century by John
Nash. He redesigned
St James's Park in 1828

(*above*), converting
Charles II's canal into a
lake and marking what
should have been the
southern end of his tri-
umphal route between

Regent's and St James's
parks with the Duke of
York's Steps, flanked by
his majestic Carlton
House Terrace (1827–32)
(*below*).

London is loved as much for its village communities and its domestic architecture – Hampstead Village (*above, right*) and Flask Walk (*below, right*) – as for its famous landmarks. Little Venice (*above*) is the best-known area of a canal network that runs for 54 miles through the north of the city. Much of it needs renovation, but, when completed, it will add greatly to the life of the capital.

The Law Courts in Fleet Street (*left*), and Greenwich (*below*), with buildings by Inigo Jones, Christopher Wren, John Vanbrugh and Nicholas Hawksmoor, show different faces of the splendours of London's architecture. These are the images that visitors to the city cherish. Today the pleasures of these sights are soured by the condition of many of the capital's streets (*right*).

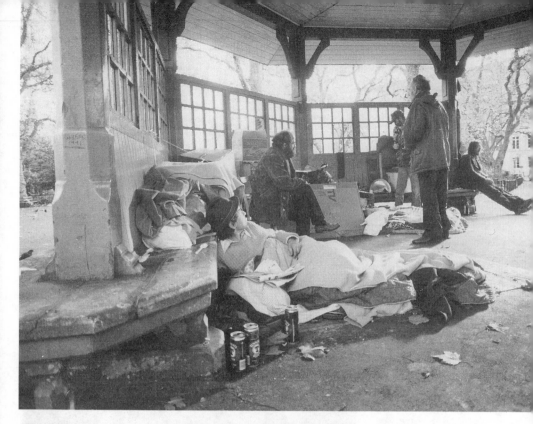

Men and women sleeping on the streets and begging in the Underground have become features of London life in the past five years. Here a group of homeless men has made a base in Lincoln's Inn Fields. The Government's solution is to remove them from the streets by offering them hostel accommodation. What they need is homes, but London boroughs were allowed to build only 302 homes in 1990.

In the 1930s London's Underground was admired all over the world for the quality of its management, its engineering and its design. Years of under-investment and neglect have reduced much of it to the present impoverished state of the Northern Line (*above*). If we are to reduce the volume of traffic in central London (*below*), we must develop a coherent, integrated policy for all London's transport networks that will get people out of private vehicles and on to public transport.

The Sara Lane flats (*right*) in Hoxton have been described as being 'as bad as the Divis flats in Belfast'. But blocks as depressing and squalid as Sara Lane can be found all over London. The corridor (*below, left*) resembles a prison, with barred and padlocked gates, rather than a home. The lift (*below, right*) doubles as a part–time urinal.

CHAPTER THREE

The European Example

Wherever you look in Europe a new generation of cities is emerging, competitive and confident: Seville, Barcelona and Madrid; Berlin, Frankfurt and Düsseldorf; Rotterdam and Amsterdam; Paris, Lyon, Montpellier and Dieppe – all are transforming themselves.

Such changes are not easy either to achieve or understand. 'Does not this vastness of world cities present a less or more foggy labyrinth?' asked Patrick Geddes.[1] When a million, when several million, people come together in one place to work and to live the complexity of the ensuing problems, and their scale, is daunting. Nor do they vary significantly between cities in different European countries.

Almost all have been important manufacturing cities. Almost all are experiencing the problems of post-industrialization as new technologies replace old and service industries replace manufacturing. Cities with an industrial past need to create new work and a new role for themselves.

Work is like ballast for a city. Shift it, and the balance between areas, between uses and between needs changes. Since in most of Europe the prevailing winds are from the west, industrial development has tended to be concentrated in the east of cities. It is certainly true of London and Berlin, as of Paris and Barcelona. A vicious cycle ensues. In the east pollution is higher, land values are lower, housing is poorer, community income is less, services like education and health are worse. Remove manufacturing, the economic linch-pin of such districts, and these problems intensify.

In addition to the need for a new urban balance, some European cities share one particular problem: the decline of their docks. Most freight is now carried in containers, in larger vessels that demand deeper docks and in fewer of them. The nineteenth-century quays, which boomed with traffic until fifteen years ago, are redundant. Hamburg and Glasgow, Rotterdam and Dunkirk, Barcelona and Liverpool, all join London in the search for a constructive use of these sites.

Industrial cities on rivers, like Paris on the Seine and Berlin on the Spree, are experiencing comparable problems. Their manufacturers polluted their rivers with effluent, forcing the cities to locate their housing, theatre, restaurants and parks well away from the river banks, leaving freight transport as the main activity. Now these rivers are cleaner, and less used, but are overlooked only by largely empty warehouses and derelict land.

Political and economic circumstances are determining how each of these cities is groping its way through this labyrinth of difficulties, but among them London stands out. It alone faces all these problems without any strategic plan of action to address them. London can profit by learning from any of them, from Paris and Rotterdam, from Berlin and San Francisco, but most particularly, perhaps, from Barcelona.

For five days in June 1991 Barcelona stopped and gaped as, high on the hills of Collcerola overlooking the city, Norman Foster's vast telecommunications tower rose 30 metres a day into the sky towards its final height of 288 metres. In the streets beneath, the temple of the Sagrada Familia, begun by Barcelona's native architect Gaudí in 1879, is still not complete. The people of Barcelona have learned to be patient. 'They'll still be finishing the Sacred Family in another 112 years' time,' they say with amused resignation. But Foster's tower will be in operation in early 1992 and will broadcast to the world the changes that are taking place in Barcelona.

The city is transforming itself. In addition to this investment in telecommunications, it is reclaiming 4.5 kilometres of coastline. The rail network has been moved, much of it underground. There is a new ring road and a renovated sewerage system; new bridges; over 2.5 kilometres of road tunnels; a total of 350 major public building projects. Few cities can ever have attempted a planning revolution on this scale. The occasion for this frenzy of construction is the 1992 Olympics, for which Barcelona is the host. But the city is using its success with the Olympics as a means to look beyond the Games and to tackle problems whose roots go deep into its industrial past.

For over 500 years Barcelona has been one of the major ports of the western Mediterranean, in competition with Marseille, Genoa and Naples. In the nineteenth century Spain's first railway line was laid from the docks. The route chosen was along the seafront. Manufacturing industries followed in its wake, polluting the beaches, which became unusable. Beside the docks a statue of Christopher Columbus continued to look eastward, but the city looked west.

Confronted by the industrial wasteland of its waterfront, it turned its back to the sea to face the surrounding mountains and, beyond them, the hinterland of Catalonia, of which Barcelona is the capital. It was not surprising that, when Ildefons Cerdà devised his masterplan for Barcelona's development in the 1850s, his *ensanche* grid pattern of avenues and street blocks stopped 200 metres short of the sea. But the transfer of freight to the new container port south of Barcelona presents an opportunity for the city to restore its seafront. The railway lines serving the old port have been moved, providing land both for housing development and for a new park.

Barcelona's history is punctuated by attempts to replan a city whose limits are defined by rivers to north and south, by the sea to the east and by the mountains inland to the west. The French planner Léon Jaussely was invited to adapt Cerdà's plan in 1905 and proposed a ring road. Le Corbusier collaborated on the Macià Plan in 1932. Neither was fully implemented. Under the Franco regime strategic planning was considered dangerously political. People confined their demands to the small and the specific – paved squares, traffic lights, zebra crossings, better street lighting.

With the return of democracy people recognized the need for large-scale planning and investment, but there was no money to implement such aspirations. The new city council, the Ajuntament, was limited to a programme of 'small actions'. In 1980 the mayor, Narcís Serra, appointed Oriol Bohigas as director of a new Urban Design Office. Bohigas had a radical past. When Dean of Architecture at the University Polytechnic, he had been imprisoned by Franco for supporting his students in a dispute. In his new post he worked on the premise that large-scale planning had failed the city because no one understood it, because it did not communicate with people. His solution was simple: to respond to specific demands. His Urban Design Office brought cohesion to the work of surveyors and lighting engineers from the roads department and landscape gardeners from parks.

Dozens of neighbourhood projects were completed, and a sense of confidence was engendered in people, but Bohigas was unable to tackle the more strategic problems. For those major investment was needed, and this became available only with the success of the Olympics bid.

From the start the city's approach to the Olympics was daring and innovative. The council had been purchasing land and commissioning plans from architects for more than a year in anticipation of the success of its bid. The plan it offered was unlike any other in recent years.

It rejected the safe and conventional option of placing the Olympic Village and arenas in a suburb, thus centralizing and simplifying construction, transport and security. Instead it proposed to integrate the Olympics with the whole community by locating the facilities on four sites throughout the city, linked by a new ring road. Such an approach inevitably creates considerable disruption, but it has allowed Barcelona to tackle several of its long-term problems and so ensure that the impact of the Olympics will not be confined to the Games themselves but will leave a lasting benefit. As the placards around all the roadworks and construction sites declare, '*Aquí estem construint la Barcelona del '93*' ('Here we are building the Barcelona of 1993').

In the past cities that have hosted the Olympics have found it more than sufficiently challenging to prepare facilities for the Games. To undertake a twin-track policy of Olympic preparations and a reconstruction of a city requires brazen audacity.

In Barcelona's strategy the most striking element was the plan to link the city with the sea by siting the Olympic Village, where athletes and officials will live, on the coast near the site of the 1888 Universal Exhibition. Here at last was the opportunity to reconnect city and coastline. The commission for this was awarded to architect Oriol Bohigas, now back practising in the private sector, and his colleagues David Mackay, Josep Martorell and Albert Puigdomènech.

Their Village has a central concept of brilliance and simplicity. They have extended the central, historic axis of the city along the Passeig de Carles I, so that it now leads triumphantly from Gaudí's Sagrada Familia down to the water's edge, where it is flanked by two forty-four-storey towers. Beside them the old district of run-down industrial buildings between the old city of Barcelona and the nineteenth-century settlement of Poble Nou has been demolished and the railway rerouted.

In its place is a new linear park, the Parc de Mar, extending along the seafront, sited in front of a new residential area with shops, banks, offices and 2,012 apartments that lead back, through arches, to Cerdà's grid pattern of city blocks. To build this the city has commissioned the architects who have won Barcelona's annual prize for best building of the year in each of the past thirty years.

Their work encompasses a range of styles and perhaps even of quality, but Martorell, Bohigas, Mackay, Puigdomènech (MBM Arquitectes) have ensured a unity to the scheme in part by specifying the use of brick throughout and in part by adapting Cerdà's grid plan so that the coherence of each block is determined by the placing and the shape of the block's corners. In doing so they have designed an area containing a great variety of architectural styles but one that is held together by the traditional structure of Cerdà's *ensanche*. It is a piece of planning intervention that is both daring in its imagination and respectful of the city's past.

At the foot of the two towers is the new Olympic port. Like the

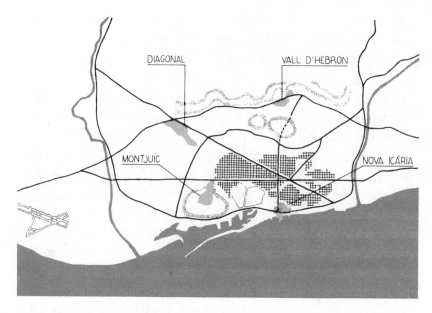

(*Above*) Scheme of the four Olympic areas.
(*Below*) The Olympic Village, general view.

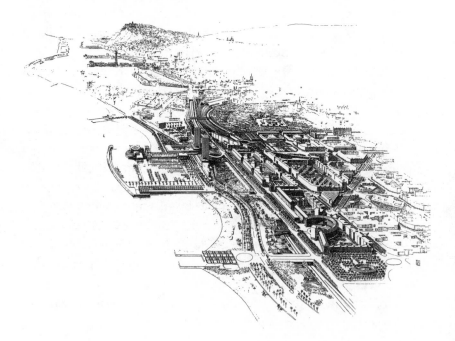

(*Above*) The Olympic Village, Avinguda del Litoral.
(*Below*) The Olympic Village, the Sea Promenade.

linear parks, this marina has been designed by the MBM architects to be a public space with shops, restaurants, bars, a sailing school and a conference centre. Even the breakwater has been built in such a way that, instead of being formed by a mass of boulders, it consists of steps from which people can fish or swim, the weight of the waves being sucked under a series of submerged off-shore breakwaters set at 45 degrees. Marinas such as this are so expensive, and the rents for yacht moorings so high, that invariably they are developed by private companies and operated as exclusive private clubs. The MBM architects were determined that Barcelona's new port and marina should be a public place that everyone could enjoy.

The creation of new public space is a feature of all four areas of the city that are being developed for the Olympics. Up on Montjuïc two new parks are being created beside the 1929 Olympic Stadium, adapted by the Italian architect Gregotti and the Spaniards Correa and Milá. Beside it a new sports hall, the Palau Sant Jordi, designed by the Japanese Arata Isozaki, gives on to a plaza and terraced gardens that themselves lead down to a new Sports University built by Ricardo Bofill's Taller de Arquitectura.

Over at Vall d'Hebrón, a suburb previously without any major public amenities, the American sculptor Claes Oldenburg is designing a park beside the courts and stadia for tennis and *pelota* that are being built by young architects such as Toni Sunyer as part of Eduard Bru's masterplan for the area. Oldenburg's will be a park with a difference. Around it will be scattered giant matchsticks, yellow and red, leading to a restaurant disguised as a monster book of matches.

All this is part of a conscious policy to link up the green spaces through the city, and Barcelona is implementing that policy with flair and imagination, commissioning major international sculptors to create work for specific sites in these parks or, as in the case of Oldenburg, to design the park itself.

In the Parc de la Cruetta del Coll, hewn out of a disused quarry on the hillside, Eduardo Chillida has suspended a huge concrete claw of a sculpture, poised to grasp some unseen boulder from the lake below. The Parc de l'Espanya Industrial features a large work by

Anthony Caro, while the American artist Barbara Pepper has designed a new park in the heart of the city at the Plaça de les Glòries. For these spaces the word 'park' fails to convey either their appearance or their atmosphere. Forget the green sward of English parks, lacking only sheep to transport you back to the eighteenth century. Forget the neatness of English municipal gardens, where regiments of marigolds and geraniums line up in serried beds. These are parks for a city of sun. Their elements are trees to provide shade, fountains to soothe, hard surfaces to replace scorched grass. These are parks for pleasure, for games of *petanque*, for jazz concerts at dusk, for food and for drink and for sleeping. In recognition of the quality of these parks and squares the city was awarded the Prince of Wales Prize for Urban Design at Harvard in 1991.

These parks will contribute to the life of the city long after the Olympic winners are forgotten, but they also capture something of the spirit of the city and the way in which people live in it. Barcelona is a city of enjoyment. In summer the streets and pavement cafés are full. There is bustle but little aggression. Shops are individual and distinct, not units of retail trade. As you pass them, you move through waves of sweet smells – coffee, fresh bread, flowers, soap. This is the spirit of the Rambles, whose broad, tree-lined centre is packed with pedestrians and whose flower stalls are banked with blooms: lilies, irises, roses and brilliant primaveras. Fifty metres along from the Palau de la Virreina museum is a covered market, the Boqueria, with its fruit and fish displays of stunning opulence. It is as far removed from the average British municipal market as Fundador is from syrup of figs.

This is a cosmopolitan city whose people will tolerate the inconveniences of reconstruction, the noise and dust, the drills and the scaffolding, but only on the condition that the result is quality. This is a comfortable city, whose people are proud of their history, of their Catalan language, of the wonders and idiosyncrasies of Gaudí, but who are pragmatic, not pretentious. So it is appropriate that this transformation of the city has been driven by a sense of social purpose, by the needs of the future rather than by the short-term imperatives of the Games.

Only the Olympics, however, could have released the £3.5 billion that is being invested and could have held together the disparate group of political partners necessary for an enterprise of this size. Capital has come from the central government in Madrid, where Maragall's predecessor as mayor, Narcís Serra, is now Vice-President. But even such a sympathetic friend at the heart of government cannot dissolve the tensions that invariably exist between Madrid and Catalonia. Both the central government and the city council may be run by socialists, but the socialist parties of Spain are a federation in which neither interests nor ideologies necessarily coincide.

In Barcelona itself the mayor, Pasqual Maragall, also faces problems. In the Plaça de Sant Jaume the headquarters both of the city council, the Ajuntament, and of the regional government, the Conservative-dominated Generalitat, glare impassively at each other across the square. Ever since the Generalitat abolished the metropolitan area of Barcelona in 1988, separating the city from the surrounding twenty-seven communes, relations have been poor. The president of the Generalitat, Jordi Pujol, has little enthusiasm for the Olympics and none for Maragall's vision of his city's future. Cooperation has been minimal.

For the Olympics there has been an uneasy truce, but an incomplete one, with political in-fighting and delays by Pujol ensuring that the metro extension to the Olympic Arena on Montjuïc will not be ready until months after the Games are finished. In this game of political chess Pujol has been outmanoeuvred and has had to watch Maragall's personal popularity rise as inexorably as the Olympic buildings. But Pujol is determined not to be left behind in the post-Olympic phase, when Barcelona is set to become a major European cultural capital.

The Ajuntament has refurbished and extended the Palau de la Música Catalana, the city's concert hall. The Generalitat is laying the foundations of a new National Theatre of Catalonia, designed by Pujol's favourite architect, Ricardo Bofill. Beside it in the Plaça de les Glòries the socialist central government has commissioned Moneo to build a new concert hall. Plans are well advanced for a new Museum of Contemporary Art, designed by Richard Meier and subsidized by the Generalitat, the Ajuntament and a private foundation. Pujol has also responded by entrusting the design of an art centre to two architects, Piñón and Viaplana, whose previous work has been for the socialist Ajuntament. The winners of this cultural Olympiad of investment will surely be the artists and audiences of Barcelona.

The scale of the reconstruction, and the speed with which the parts relating to the Olympics must be completed, has brought other problems. The Nova Icària area had to be demolished entirely to make way for the Olympic Village when at least some of the existing industrial buildings might have been retained if time had allowed. The need for private-sector finance has meant that the apartments in the Olympic Village will all have to be sold at high market prices, ending Maragall's hopes of maintaining a balance between social and private housing in the new area (the dangers of yuppification are not confined to London's Docklands), but the decision to situate Barcelona's fourth university here will mitigate this to some extent.

To complete the work on schedule skilled construction workers have had to be imported from all over Spain and even, semi-legally, from Poland. A deal has had to be struck between the city council and the construction trades unions guaranteeing, for a price, a no-strike moratorium until after the Games. Of greater significance, perhaps, has been the inability of the city council to participate fully in the rise in land values that has resulted from the Olympic boom. The council had managed to purchase some land, but the bulk of the gains from the development of the triangle behind the Olympic Village will go to estate agents and speculators.

The impact of these problems may not be felt for some time. The physical disruption to the lives of people living in the city is more immediate, being an everyday irritant and pressure. With the relocation of the railway, much of it underground, and the renovation of the sewers, there is scarcely a major street that is not affected by building works. Journeys take longer. Noise levels are higher. Dust in the summer, mud in the winter are facts of life. It would not be surprising if the tolerance and patience of people cracked, but

47

opinion polls show high levels of acceptance, even approval. In part this may result from the attempts of the city council to inform people about what would be involved with the aid of a four-month exhibition in 1988, before construction began, and a further exhibition staged between November 1990 and March 1991.

Allied to this is Barcelona 93, an outreach service that goes into neighbourhoods to explain the scheme and last year contacted 1.2 million people. The success of such initiatives depends on whether people can recognize the benefits that will come to them, as well as to the city, in future years. With the Olympic Village, the sports and cultural facilities and the parks that is not an impossible task. The gains from the ring road, from the relocation of the railway or from the new sewerage system are less tangible. To try to rectify this the council has produced an excellent exhibition on the reconstruction of the sewers, siting it 20 metres below ground. (Perhaps the location has accounted for the modest size of the audience.)

Such exercises in public relations are the simple part of maintaining the support of the community. Consultation with people whose homes and neighbourhoods are directly affected is less easy. Every development has been subject to the normal rights of public consultation and appeal. One community in the north-east of the city, Tibidabo, complained vociferously when it became clear that an intersection of the ring road was going to part split, part encircle their neighbourhood. Heated public meetings with council officials and politicians, one lasting until 3 a.m., failed to resolve their grievances, and only the creation of a new public park in the area covering the ring road gained the withdrawal of the objections to the road.

Despite all these problems morale is high. There is excitement and confidence in the city. At last things are changing. The elderly remember the Universal Exhibition of 1929, whose developments up on Montjuïc were never completed, and the failed bid to hold the 1936 Olympics, which were awarded to Berlin. In protest at Hitler's Games, the republican government of Catalonia convened an alternative Olympics in Barcelona. On its opening day the Spanish Civil War broke out.

The preparations for the 1992 Games are burying these memories, along with the years of frustration and restriction under Franco. Here is an opportunity to celebrate the powers of self-determination that democracy has brought. Here is a chance to assert the future. It is not surprising that people enthuse about new ideas and new architects and can pass over temporary inconveniences without breaking step. For the people of Barcelona this reconstruction has been hard-won.

It is also hard-headed. Pasqual Maragall understands clearly that Barcelona needs to establish a role and an identity if it is to hold its own as competition between European cities, for economic development and for tourism, intensifies. The Olympics will help, but the city must attract longer-term investment. For some years in the 1980s Barcelona maintained links with Japanese banks and industry. Sony and Yamaha and others have already established a European base in Barcelona, and the city is full of Japanese tourists who have discovered a passion for Gaudí's architecture.

Maragall recognizes that the industry and commerce of the twenty-first century will place far higher premiums on telecommunications; hence the enthusiasm for Norman Foster's tower, which is augmented by a further mast, designed by Santiago Calatrava and situated on Montjuïc. He knows too that to sustain the city's momentum after 1992 will require something more than additional amenities and improved infrastructure. Art galleries and museums will help to establish Barcelona as a cultural force in Europe, but Maragall will also want to return to some of the major plans that have been deferred in the pre-Olympics period, particularly the commercial development of the old docks by the Port Authority. These large developments will be important, but it is the small-scale interventions that have laid the foundations of Barcelona's transformation, and it is from studying these that other European cities will most benefit.

The projects have been of three kinds – parks, plazas and streets – and in total 140 have been completed.[2] Some have been renovations (the Plaça Reial, off the Rambla Sant Josep); some have been new developments (the Plaça dels Països Catalans); some have been large (the Parc de l'Espanya Industrial), some small (the Plaça de la Mercé in Ciutat Vella, the old town); some have been solely for the local community (the Plaça de la Palmera, with sculpture by Richard Serra), some for the benefit of the whole city (the Parc de Joan Miró), but, whatever their scale, all have been designed to respond to the particular needs and potential of each site. As the American architect Henry N. Cobb says, this programme 'cannot be ascribed to any sort of aesthetic or ideological consensus among its [Barcelona's] citizens, nor even among its leading architects and politicians. Both the new urban spaces themselves and the public's response to them are far too varied to support such a claim.'[3] This variety is a positive source of strength in a body of work that has not only given Barcelona a sense of pride and identity but has also been extremely useful in regenerating the city.

There are considerable similarities to the public art projects direct-ed by Bob McGilvray in the Blackness district of Dundee, where the work of sculptors and designers has also been the force behind urban renewal, but in Barcelona the relationship between these 'small actions' and the wider work of David Mackay and Oriol Bohigas has effectively taken forward thinking about urban design in a dramatic way.

To achieve so much so fast has demanded political will on the part of Maragall and his council, not least to carry the people of Barcelona with him and to sustain their confidence. In part that sup-port may have arisen out of frustrated energies, pent up for so long under the Franco regime. But cultural momentum of this kind can no more explain the way that the city is tackling its future than can Maragall's undoubted political determination. Both have had to be channelled and translated into action by specific policies from which London has much to learn. Of course, direct comparisons can mislead. The importance of the opportunity occasioned by the Olympics cannot be overestimated, but, in contrast to Barcelona's successful bid in 1986, London was incapable even of agreeing on a proposal to host the 1996 Olympics.

Certain lessons, however, are clear. Barcelona has had one body representing it, one voice speaking on its behalf. It has had a coherent strategy and a good sense of what it wanted to achieve. The city has been viewed as a whole, its history and future, its people and their environments, its economy and its culture. Successive mayors have been skilful in appointing key people, such as Bohigas. Above all they and the council have had the courage to see their strategy through. What is surprising, perhaps, is that in Paris, in different circumstances, facing different problems, in a different scale of city, the strategic approach adopted has had many similarities.

Suggest that a Chinese American architect be commissioned to build something for a site next to the National Gallery, or that a young design team be asked to rethink the layout of St James's Park, and you would have an uproar. The conservation lobby would have a corporate coronary. Letters would speed to *The Times*. Questions would be asked in the House. Yet that is what has happened in Paris. With I. M. Pei's Pyramide in the Cour Napoléon in front of the Louvre and Pascal Cribier's, François Rouband's and Louis Benech's redesign of Le Nôtre's Jardin des Tuileries, Paris is embracing the future, and the results are exhilarating.

London and Paris have much in common. Both are the historic, as well as the political, centres of their countries. Both share a rich architectural heritage that has tended to constrain new thinking. Notre Dame, the Ile de la Cité, La Sainte Chapelle, Les Invalides, the Louvre and Haussmann's boulevards match anything in London. Both cities have endured some undistinguished post-war architecture. Both suffer from major social problems and imbalances.

Yet while London drifts, Paris has tackled its problems with enterprise, even daring. In the last fifteen years the French have begun to transform their capital, most noticeably by a series of Grands Projets. The first, the Centre Pompidou, was completed in 1977 by President Giscard d'Estaing, who also approved a park and a Cité des Sciences et de l'Industrie at La Villette and the conversion of the Gare d'Orsay into an art museum of the nineteenth century. He also gave preliminary approval to the Grande Arche de la Défense in his final weeks in office.

His successor, François Mitterrand, picked up these initiatives with even greater enthusiasm. At his first presidential press conference in 1981 he announced a major transformation of the Louvre. Within months he had plans for a new opera house at the Bastille, the conversion of the Arche de la Défense into a tele-communications centre, an Institut du Monde Arabe and a new Finance Ministry, which was to be moved from the Louvre to Bercy in the east of the city. This last would make sufficient space within the Louvre for the contents of seven separate museums, or departments, to be exhibited coherently.

There was a brief hiccup when, in 1986, Mitterrand had to 'cohabit' with a right-wing government. The new Prime Minister, Jacques Chirac, was not enthusiastic about these Grands Projets, which, he felt, were adding too much lustre to the President's popularity. Work slowed on the Pyramide, while the communications role of La Défense was abandoned, but both projects survived, and in his second presidency Mitterrand added three further schemes, a vast Bibliothèque Nationale to rival the new British Library in size and cost, an international convention centre and the renovation of the Museum of Natural History. Small wonder that satirists dubbed him Mitterrameses II.

The French have always had a taste for monuments on a grand scale – witness the Tour Eiffel and the Arc de Triomphe – but this programme outstripped any since Haussmann's for the number of projects, the speed of construction and the scale of investment, over £11,550 million[4] having been spent in the last ten years. It proclaimed a new confidence in France, but Mitterrand made sure that it was firmly rooted in the city's former glories and traditions. The Pyramide at the Louvre and the Grande Arche are both on Paris's historic axis, which connects the Louvre to Bernini's statue of Louis XIV, to the Place de la Concorde, to the Arc de Triomphe and on to La Défense, in a line through France's history. The symbolism is clearly stated, as can be seen by considering the genesis of the Pyramide itself.

I. M. Pei said, when presenting the project to the Commission Supérieure des Monuments Historiques, 'The pyramid can only be justified and explained as the emerging part of an underground architecture ... It constitutes the ultimate visible gesture of a buried architecture' – in this case the archaeological treasures buried beneath the Cour Napoléon, the remains of the walls of Philippe Auguste's thirteenth-century fortified castle.

The original brief was to avoid building anything above ground level in order not to obscure the façade of the Louvre. However, Pei became convinced that the buried architecture had to communicate directly with the outside world. To permit this the underground concourse needed to be large, spacious and lit by natural light, and visitors below ground should always be able to see the Palace itself. Pei experimented with domes and cubes before choosing the pyramid, which took up the least space and provided the best upward view. Moreover its geometric shape echoed the layout of the gardens designed by Le Nôtre. In short, the Pyramide, far from being a work of outrageous impertinence, was born of Pei's great respect for – indeed, homage to – the Palace and its history.

Nevertheless it provoked outrage. *France-Soir*'s headline of 24 January 1984 declared, '*Le nouveau Louvre fait déjà scandale*,' while other newspapers weighed in with 'a megalomaniac and disastrous scheme', 'a bomb crater' and 'fit only for Disneyland'. In the face of such protests most governments would have beaten a retreat. It required nerve on the part of the Secretary of State in charge of the Grands Projets, Emile Biasini, and of Mitterrand to withstand this critical battering. Their confidence in Pei's plans has been more than justified by the breathtaking beauty of the Pyramide.

A criticism that is harder for Mitterrand to refute is that he has a compulsively sweet tooth for the grandiose presidential gesture, that he is a junket junkie. Undoubtedly these projects exhibit a strong strain of Gaullism, which revels in *la gloire de la France* and evokes a national pride in the French people. But the Grands Projets are rooted equally in an economic reality. Mitterrand has understood that, however much the European Commission may talk of partnership and cooperation, the future of Europe is going to be highly competitive and that it is between cities that competition will be most acute. In the promotion of Paris as the financial centre of twenty-first-century Europe the Grands Projets have been Mitterrand's flagships. Judged by column inches in the world's press, it has been a successful marketing strategy, which has enhanced and updated Paris's claim to be the Cultural Capital of Europe.

The strategy has included investment in, and modernization of, France's rail network, not least the rail link between Paris's Charles de Gaulle airport and the city centre that aims to enable Paris to compete with Heathrow as the most heavily used airport in Europe. If it is effective in capturing an increasing share of the European financial market, then investment on such a major scale in rail and in Charles de Gaulle and the £2,920 million spent on the Grands Projets will have been vindicated.

Mitterrand's daring in backing Pei's design, and in risking public investment on this scale, was compounded by his choice of architects for the first six Grands Projets, all of whom were foreign.[5] Xenophobia is not unknown in French public opinion, but Mitterrand's decision, taken on the advice of Emile Biasini and Joseph Belmont, was to put all of these designs, with the exception of the Louvre, out to 'blind' international competition.

By the 1970s French architecture was at a low ebb. Belmont was appointed first as Directeur de l'Architecture in 1978 and subsequently as Président de la Mission Interministérielle pour la Qualité des Constructions Publiques in 1985, with a brief to initiate a system of competitions for all new public buildings, at both local and national level. The international competitions for the Grands Projets demonstrated the Government's commitment to this process. Two of the projects were won by unknowns. Otto von Spreckelson, whose proposal for the Arche was successful, had never before built anything bigger than a church. Carlos Ott, the architect of the Opéra de la Bastille, was also little known.

The competitions were genuinely open. Young French architects knew that they could, and eventually would, begin to win them. In the meantime the opportunities offered by other central and local government competitions for smaller public buildings, such as junior schools, libraries and factories, have provided a career structure that has been even more effective in raising standards than the presence of great international figures and the public interest that this stimulated. Jean Nouvel, the first Frenchman to win a competition for one of the Grands Projets, the Institut du Monde Arabe, had previously built the Clinique de Bezons and the Centre Culturel at L'Aube-la-Ville.

In Dominique Perrault's ten-year career between qualifying and winning the competition for the £720 million Bibliothèque de France at the age of 36, he had completed eight buildings, all in the public sector, all won by competition. His Hôtel Industriel at Bercy, in which he has his own practice's offices overlooking the vast Bibliothèque de France site and the shunting yards of the Gare d'Austerlitz, is a remarkably assured and accomplished building for so young an architect. Were Perrault British, he would probably consider himself fortunate if he had succeeded in designing a shop interior, a private art gallery or a house, always presuming he had the right contacts, entrepreneurial flair and good luck. Perrault came to the Hôtel Industriel having already built a factory at Châteaudun (1983), an Ecole Supérieure d'Ingénieurs en Electronique et Electrotechnique at Marne-la-Vallée (1984), forty apartments at Rezé (1986), offices at Bar-le-Duc (1989) and a waterworks at Ivry (1989).

In his earlier work he incorporated a jumble of ideas, often in conflict with one another. The experience seems to have cleared his mind, for the Hôtel Industriel is crisp and simple, a rectangular box distinguished by Perrault's use of light, both reflected and glimpsed. Interest in light is becoming his signature. In his plans for the Bibliothèque Nationale the bookstacks are in four L- or open-book-shaped towers at the corners of a piazza the size of the Place de la Concorde. As the towers fill up with books internal wooden shutters will vary the amount of light shining into, or through, each floor.

What this building has in common with the best of the other Grands Projets (the Centre Pompidou, La Défense, the Pyramide) is that it is exciting, it provokes. To see the Pyramide at night, its reflection dancing in the water around it, to walk down its stairway, suspended free and moving with your step, to stand in the concourse with the sky and the Louvre above and, all around you, subterranean secret entries to the treasures – these are moments that catch your breath and put you in awe of man's ability to turn steel and stone and space into wonder.

That wonder should not suspend criticism. These buildings are not perfect, even in their own terms. To refinance La Défense, after Chirac withdrew public finance, two extras floors of offices were squeezed in, with the result that the office ceilings are set lower than normal. To feel cramped inside a building of such majestic size is ironic and oppressive. Having only one entrance to the Pyramide necessitates a mess of crowd barriers outside to marshal the queues, frustrating the eye as well as inhibiting one of the building's key purposes, to improve access. The commanding position of La Défense, on a hill, turns it into a wind tunnel that the suspended 'cloud' canopies and an arrangement of small glass panels do little to deflect. The vast elevated piazza between the four towers of Perrault's proposed Bibliothèque Nationale threatens a comparable wind blast for visitors. But such criticisms are dwarfed by the ambition and the achievement of these buildings. Following a long-established tradition of symbolism in French architecture, each gives form to an idea. Each reasserts the belief that buildings are more than mere constructions. Each makes you grateful for having seen it.

Although these Grands Projets are the standard-bearers of Mitterrand's plans to transform his capital, they have around them a company of other projects: buildings restored and new, factories and apartments, public spaces and parks. In addition to Les Tuileries and the new urban park at La Villette, two major parks are being created at either end of the city, the Parc Bercy in the east and the Parc André Citroën in the west, both overlooking the Seine. For a city to create new parks calls for considerable vision, determination and money.

The pressure on land use drives up the price, making it hard for even the most ecologically minded city council to justify putting inner-city land out to grass (though other European cities, such as Amsterdam, have made progress). Few new parks have been made in London since the war. One exception is Burgess Park on the Old Kent Road, only a small proportion of whose acres have been landscaped. The borough council, Southwark, wants to finish it but cannot find the £20 million that is necessary. Contrast that with the £32.5 million and the £32 million spent on Bercy and Citroën

Cévennes respectively. Such diversity of size, scale and use should defuse some of the criticism that Paris is giving priority to the glamorous and the glitzy and that care and attention is being lavished only on the centre of the city visited by tourists and journalists. But defuse it doesn't, and for solid reasons. In spite of its image and its Haussmann elegance, Paris is a deeply divided city with areas of considerable poverty, particularly in the north and the east. The Arche and the Pyramide are irrelevant to the problems of such areas. Even La Villette, in the industrial north-east of the city, can do little to help upgrade the surrounding area, which includes a substantial Arab quarter with high unemployment and low incomes.

As in London and so many other European cities, the prime strategic challenge is to tilt the social axis of the city again towards the east. Both the region's structure plan, the *Livre Blanc*,[6] and the urban policies of Mayor Jacques Chirac are attempting to do this. Chirac's Plan Est includes major Zones d'Aménagement Concerté (ZACs), within which the housing, schools, factories and leisure facilities are being upgraded and rebuilt. However, the boundaries of Chirac's city extend only to the Boulevard Périphérique, which encircles the centre of Paris. Beyond that lies the *banlieues*, the suburbs, with problems no less acute.

Like London, Paris is a Russian doll of a city. Outside the centre and the Boulevard Périphérique is the 'first crown' of the *banlieues*, and outside that is the 'second crown' of the new towns. These areas have a rigidity whose origins are rooted in Paris's history as a walled city. In the 1780s the architect Claude-Nicolas Ledoux was commissioned to design a new wall encircling the city, the wall of the Fermiers-Généraux, which, to restrict trade, allowed entrance to be made only through its fifty-four toll gates. Little of its structure survived the Revolution, but its line has been retained ever since, resisting even the interventions of Haussmann. Today it is the route of Paris's ring road, the Boulevard Périphérique, and the 400 metres outside it remains a no-man's-land beyond which the suburbs grew both in population size and as breeding ground for social problems. In 1981 this social unrest erupted in riots.

The causes of these riots were easy enough to identify. The

National Commission for Districts' Social Development, set up in October 1981 in response to the riots, reported 'a population accumulating various handicaps, and victims of the crisis: families, often of foreign origin, who are not given a chance to become socially integrated; cohorts of unemployed youths who have never known what having a job is and considered as foreigners in estates where they were nevertheless born and brought up; the dreary decor of sad-looking façades and abandoned gardens; the marks of exclusion and rejection far from the city; finally, an environment with a pervading feeling of insecurity'. It proved less easy to agree on solutions.

The Conservative mayor of Paris, Jacques Chirac, put his trust in achieving renovation and prosperity through rising land values. Mitterrand's Government placed the problem within a wider social context, setting up the National Commission for Districts' Social Development, which initiated a rapidly increasing number of community projects (twenty-three in 1982, 130 by 1984)[7] that attempted to tackle social problems such as crime and low skills levels, as well as housing. As Prime Minister Michel Rocard said, 'How can we talk about liberty, equality and fraternity in towns where exclusion is the order of the day?'

In practice neither Chirac's nor the Government's approach was conspicuously successful. In frustration Roland Castro, an architect whose student days had been influenced by the student upheavals and radicalism of 1968, formed Banlieues 89. This pressure group operated on two levels. It promoted a visionary masterplan, 'Le Grand Paris' (June 1990), on the basis that '*le territoire du Grand Paris n'est pas à défricher: il est à déchiffrer*' ('for Grand Paris it is not just a question of reclaiming the land but of making sense of it'). This plan identified four new areas in addition to central Paris – Paris-Presqu'île (north-west), Paris-la-Plaine (north-east), Les Hauts-de-Paris (south-west) and Paris-Amont (south-east). These areas would act as new magnets for development.

At the same time Banlieues 89 was working on 107 community projects, mainly in smaller towns. The Government responded by appointing a minister with special responsibility for

urban development, Michel Delebarre, and setting up a Délé-
gation Interministérielle à la Ville, within which Banlieues 89 was
included as a unit. However, the ministerial appointment was at a
junior level. Delebarre was given few staff and too small a budget to
make any real impact. His approach has been essentially technocratic
and certainly has been incapable of fulfilling the wider ambitions
outlined by Banlieues 89 – to rebuild the suburbs, not just for the
workers but with them.

The physical rebuilding of run-down areas is taking place all over
Paris. In the ZACs private developers cooperate with the local
authority, which provides at least 51 per cent of the finance. The
developers get to build homes for sale; the local authority gets a
school for the children in those homes; and in the process the whole
area is upgraded. The principle behind ZACs, that of a positive
relationship between public and private sectors, is a long-standing
feature of French political life. 'Going back to the Monnet Plan after
World War II,' writes M. V. Savitch in *Post-Industrial Cities*, 'the
French have planned and directed private enterprise to achieve
national ends. The link between what is the public and private
spheres is not so sharply demarcated in France as it is in Anglo-
American culture.' In continuing that tradition ZACs have been
successful, but they cannot address the wider metropolitan problems
of Paris. For that a planning strategy is needed.

The Ile-de-France region, comprising central Paris and the surrounding eight *départements*, has attempted such a strategic view in its
planning document, the *Livre Blanc*. It asks the right questions, even
though, like any regional planning document, its scope can be criticized. By restricting consideration to the Ile-de-France region, it
cannot tackle the transport or demographic shifts that have resulted
in large sections of Paris's economy migrating to Orléans, Nantes
and other cities well outside the region. It is a document of aspirations rather than prescriptions. Its blandness stems from its determination to cling to a consensus between left and right, between
local and national government. That consensus is genuine enough
with regard to the long-term objectives of the *Livre Blanc*, but it con-
ceals substantial party political differences over how to achieve those

ends and, in particular, over the powers of the city in relation to the state.

On the left the Government favours an element of central government control to ensure that the interests of business are balanced by those of people who live in poorer communities. On the right Chirac and his adviser, Pierre-Charles Kreig, insist that subsidizing poorer districts will only drag down the successful commercial areas that Paris needs if it is to prosper.

In practice it is not ideologically so simple as Chirac favouring the prosperous west and the Government inclining to the run-down east. Chirac has authorized ZACs in the east of the city and has approved the new Euro-Disneyland only 32 kilometres to the east of Paris on a site one fifth the size of the city. This theme park, described as the 'future juvenile capital of Europe',[8] is set to bring 13 million people a year from Britain, Germany, Spain, Belgium and the Netherlands, on super-fast trains, making the Paris region the focal rail point in western Europe.

Being only a consultative paper, the *Livre Blanc* cannot reconcile these different approaches and priorities, but it remains a useful and worthy strategic view of Paris in a regional context. London could benefit from such a document, as it could by studying what is happening in Paris. However, London should not make the mistake of uncritical imitation, since Paris's regeneration is far from being an unqualified success. Much criticism, both within France and from abroad, is directed at the emphasis placed by the French Government on its programme of Grands Projets.

The French have always had an appetite for grand architectural gestures. Louis XIV built Versailles. Napoléon Bonaparte made Paris fit to be the centre of his empire. His nephew, Napoléon III, commissioned Haussmann's masterplan. The Great Exhibition of 1889 was marked by Alexandre Gustave Eiffel's tower. The present-day programme of Grands Projets, initiated by President Pompidou and President Giscard d'Estaing but associated principally with President Mitterrand, will undoubtedly rank with the projects of those former eras.

François Mitterrand is neither unaware of, nor averse to, comparisons with Pericles' building programme, which culminated in the Parthenon and transformed fifth-century Athens. Both leaders shared an ambition to turn their respective cities into the intellectual and cultural capitals of the world, not simply for vainglory but for solid political and economic reasons. The very arguments deployed by Thucydides, son of Melesias, against Pericles have been directed at Mitterrand: the cost is too high, and the buildings are irrelevant to the real needs of the city and its citizens. For Mitterrand both criticisms have considerable force. An unemployed worker in Bobigny is going to derive little direct benefit from grand buildings. Nevertheless the Grands Projets have undoubtedly helped focus the attention of the world on Paris and have created a sense of adventure and excitement in France.

The debate can be illustrated too by considering La Défense. Its critics maintain that this huge new business district in the already prosperous west of the city further unbalances Paris. La Défense is also vulnerable, as is London's Docklands, to the charge that it is a self-contained commercial area which has no relationship with surrounding neighbourhoods. But there the comparisons with Docklands end. Unlike the London scheme, La Défense is also a major retail area with 200 shops, three supermarkets, twenty restaurants and nine cinemas visited by over 50,000 people a day. Its urban park, containing fountains and sculptures, is also remarkable and makes an attractive and popular place for that urban pastime, promenading.

The most telling criticism of the Grands Projets is that they are imposed from on high and are parachuted in to sites. The same cannot be said of Barcelona, where the Ajuntament has gone to great lengths to involve the whole city and to respond to the needs of neighbourhoods. In spite of that, Barcelona does not provide an ideal model either. Although the benefits of Olympic investment have been spread around the city, there remain areas that still have very poor environments.

Whatever the imperfections in the ways that Barcelona and Paris have approached their city plans, both have displayed ambition, both have taken interesting risks and both are progressing with extraordinary speed. This urgency may result from the fact that both cities have entrusted key parts of their development to individuals (in Paris to Biasini for the Grands Projets and Belmont for architectural policy generally, in Barcelona to Bohigas and Mackay, together with Martorell and Puigdomènech, for the Olympic Village and seafront) and then backing their judgement.

The same is true of Rotterdam, where the director of the city council's Urban Development Unit, Riek Bakker, has the status and authority to push through the city's strategic plan. The problems confronting her are acute, but by comparison with London or Paris, the scale is smaller, Rotterdam's population being 700,000, with a further 500,000 people living in the surrounding suburbs.

The city council was faced by a number of problems. The city's economy had always been narrow, being based on the docks, both for shipbuilding and for trans-shipment. But in the late 1970s and early 1980s the success of South Korea, Japan and others in capturing a large share of the international shipbuilding market forced Rotterdam to take positive steps to widen its economic base. To do so it needed to attract back the professional middle-class residents who had been encouraged to leave the city centre in the 1960s and move to satellite towns under the Government's overspill policy.

In addressing these two problems the river was the key. 'The river is the capital of the city,' said Riek Bakker, but although it is central to the city's life, it splits Rotterdam both geographically, being crossed by only one bridge and two tunnels, and socially, with the population on the south bank being almost entirely working-class.

The council's 1985 strategic policy, the Binnenstadsplan, and its subsequent White Paper, *Vernieuwing van Rotterdam* (1987), gave a framework to a policy for urban regeneration, out of which arose its major development, the Kop van Zuid plan. This will span the river with a new bridge in the centre of the city, open up the left bank for building and investment, attract new companies to the city and so provide an economic boost to the three low-income districts that adjoin the proposed development area, Feyenoord, Katendrecht and Afrikaanderbuurt. The plan will provide additional retail space (60,000 square metres), offices for rent and sale (60,000 square metres), 5,500 housing units divided equally between public and private sectors as well as a major convention centre, a court house and much needed hotels.

A comprehensive plan of this size, which has been in the planning pipeline for five years and will take a further fifteen years to realize fully, has inevitably been hard-won and has involved compromises, notably over the line of the bridge and the balance of the development. What Riek Bakker has refused to dilute is her insistence on quality in the architecture, building and urban design, as is illustrated by the long-running controversy over the choice of design for the bridge. The developers proposed a suspension bridge, elegant but conventional. She and her committee favoured a design of great beauty by the Dutch architect Ben van Berkel. It too is a suspension bridge, but the suspension will be from a single pylon, which will achieve balance by leaning away from the vertical at an angle of 20 per cent. The concept is similar to Santiago Calatrava's new bridge over the Guadalquivir river in Seville, and it is no surprise that van Berkel has worked with the Spanish engineer. Ben van Berkel's bridge will cost about 12 per cent more than the developers' but will provide a central feature that will enhance Rotterdam for years to come. Finance for the Kop van Zuid will come from both public and private sources, with the majority of infrastructure funding being met by central government, which will pay for 85 per cent of the cost of the bridge and 50 per cent of the cost of the roads. In practice public/private deals are made easier by the council's ownership of 60 per cent of the land in the city and all of the land in the harbour area. 'In Rotterdam we never sell land, ever,' says Riek Bakker. Instead the council will sell long leases for shops, offices, hotels and houses.

Because most of the centre of Rotterdam was razed by bombing in May 1940, the city has had a long tradition of rebuilding, with the result that redevelopment is not seen as a threat to a loved and cherished heritage, as it is so often in Britain, but is welcomed. In the 1946 Basisplan, which was much influenced by the thinking of Le Corbusier, Rotterdam was redesigned as a functionalist, radial city with the business and shopping district (the Lijnbaan) in the centre and with housing concentrated in suburban areas. The resulting city centre was well planned and well executed – indeed, Lewis

Mumford in *The City in History*[9] holds it up as a model of urban planning – but its public spaces were essentially formal, intended to impress rather than delight.[10] As the limitations of the Basisplan's rigid or rational prescription became apparent in the 1960s and 1970s, a new generation of architects and politicians pursued ideas that would reclaim the city centre as a real public domain that could belong to the people of Rotterdam and would encourage them to use and enjoy it. Much could be, and was, achieved with flowers, trees, pavement cafés, market stalls, even narrowing the width of the central boulevard, the Coolsingel, but finally structural changes had to be made, laid out in the 1985 Binnenstadtplan.

Running parallel to these changing attitudes to the public domain has been a great emphasis on, and interest in, social housing. The city council's responsibility for housing has been devolved to non-profit-making companies, comparable with British housing associations, and both the quantity and the quality of public housing that have resulted have left British cities far behind. In 1991 over 5,500 homes were built in Rotterdam, compared with just over 300 in the London boroughs, whose population is more than six times the size of Rotterdam's.

The districts that result have some interesting characteristics. Rotterdam's education system does not have a tradition of schools surrounded by playing fields, with the result that they can be sited, literally, in the middle of communities, next to shops or in the bottom floors of apartment blocks. The effect is to integrate schools with their surrounding communities. This concern for local communities and for redevelopment led by social housing distinguishes Rotterdam and at the same time has provided a solid foundation for local architects to build careers based on social housing. A practice such as Erik van Egeraat's and Francine Houben's Mecanoo, which formed part of the Netherlands' contribution to the 1991 Venice Biennale, has built 120 housing schemes in the ten years of their partnership.

Activity like this fuels a real interest in architecture in the city, fostered by the Rotterdam Arts Council, which promotes architectural exhibitions, festivals and competitions, such as the one it initiated in 1988 for the redesign of three squares, the Bospolderplein (a vast space to the west of the city centre), the Zuidplein (a shapeless area dominated by traffic) and the Eendrachtsplein (a junction where various districts met). The competitions were won, respectively, by the Spanish architects Bach and Mora, Piñón and Viaplana and by the Dutchman Jo Kormeling.

The Rotterdam Arts Council is right to identify the design of urban space as a present weakness. Many of the excellent housing schemes' surrounding spaces are underdesigned, being in appearance at best functional and at worst bleak. But overall the architectural quality of these schemes and the coherence of the Kop van Zuid plans provide lessons not just for London but for the many British cities that will be redeveloping their port areas in the 1990s.

The differences between Paris, Barcelona and Rotterdam, as cities, are obvious, but all three are notable for their attempts to remake themselves. What can London learn? Any lessons have to be general rather than specific, since good urban development, by its nature, should respond to, and arise out of, particular circumstances and needs.

In these general terms, all three cities are trying to take a comprehensive view of their futures and are formulating strategic plans that include infrastructure investment in road, rail and telecommunications, as well as cultural and urban objectives. It is only when you explore behind the generalities of those aims and means that differences begin to emerge, and it is from considering these that London could profit most.

No city can have only one purpose behind its plans for regeneration. It is inevitable that the pragmatic and economic aims of improving the marketing of the image of the city as lures for inward investment and tourism are major considerations that all three cities share. It is, after all, the motive that is most likely to trigger, and to justify, the scale of public investment that is necessary. But beside that it is crucial that a balance is struck between the view of a city as a 'work of art' and as a 'living space' in which priority is given to the use of public places by people.

Both Paris and Barcelona exhibit strong elements of 'the city as work of art' and would make no apology for doing so. Gaudí's

Sagrada Familia, Isozaki's Palau Sant Jordi, Calatrava's Felipe II–Bac de Roda bridge and Foster's telecommunications tower are intended to impress, as are Pei's Pyramide, von Spreckelson's La Défense, Perrault's Bibliothèque de France and the van Berkel bridge in the Kop van Zuid plan. However, in Barcelona and in Rotterdam more thought has been given to the use of the spaces around the monuments and greater priority to the needs of the city's own people.

In seeking this balance Paris and Barcelona, more than Rotterdam, have the added problem of relating redevelopment to the demands of conservation. In Barcelona there is concern for the shape of the medieval city, for the work of Gaudí and his contemporaries and for more recent landmarks like Mies van der Rohe's German Pavilion (1929) on Montjuïc, recently restored. In Paris the respect for the city's structure and historic landmarks is obvious, but, as Pei's Pyramide shows, this need not prevent or inhibit new buildings. Even in Rotterdam, what remains of the pre-war city is being restored – whether in the Kiefhoek district or in particular buildings such as J. J. P. Oud's Café de Unie.

With regard to financing, there are inevitable compromises for which a price has to be paid. Both Barcelona and Rotterdam are having to rely on the principle of leverage, using public investment in infrastructure to stimulate private capital. In the Olympic Village the gains that come from the new marina, the recovery of the seashore and the linear park alongside it are being paid for by the almost total elimination of social housing at affordable rents in the new Olympic Village apartments. In Rotterdam there is already criticism that the Kop van Zuid scheme will concede too much to the commercial demands of the development on the south bank of the Maas and so fail to relate effectively to districts like Feyenoord.

If these are salutary warnings of the real problems and difficult choices involved in development, which London should heed, we can without reservation profit from the excellent example all these cities set in their openness to ideas from abroad and to the work of foreign architects and artists. Barcelona is employing Foster, Isozaki and Richard Meier, as well as artists like Ellsworth Kelly, Anthony Caro, Barbara Pepper and Claes Oldenburg. The choice of non-

French architects on all the early Grands Projets has already been noted, and only last year Ken Armstrong won the major competition for the Centre Japon. In Rotterdam Aldo Rossi, Derek Walker, Bernard Tschumi and O. M. Ungers have all designed major buildings. By contrast almost no non-British architects, apart from the Americans Cesar Pelli, Harry Cobb, Skidmore Owings and Merrill, and Kohn Pedersen Fox in Canary Wharf, have been invited to build in London, and none at all by central or local government.

More crucially, London can benefit from the experience of three cities with some vision of the city as humane, as a place in which people can mix, move, meet and, as Richard Sennett writes in his book *The Conscience of the Eye*,[11] 'step out of themselves' into an environment that is stimulating and complex, one in which people can be participants rather than observers. Sennett traces this attitude back to the work of Robert Park and the Chicago sociologists and urbanists of the early twentieth century who saw urban living as providing an opportunity for us to confront and embrace the 'differences of class, age, race and taste outside the familiar territory of oneself'.[12] Such an attitude is particularly relevant in these three cities, and in London, all of which have populations that incorporate a wide range of ethnic cultures.

This approach challenges the idea of the city as monument and as work of art, and it may appear to be in conflict with the Grands Projets of Paris, which are nothing if not monuments, but it should not be forgotten that the first of them, the Centre Pompidou by Renzo Piano and Richard Rogers, is as notable for its open invitation to the public, in the building and in its piazza, as it is for the innovation of its architectural design. That open approach towards the public is similarly a feature of Bernard Tschumi's Parc de la Villette and of La Défense, visited by thousands every day.

Barcelona, Paris and Rotterdam are all trying to see the city as a whole. Barcelona is perhaps taking the most comprehensive view, spreading its four centres of development and tackling them at the same time as renewing the city's infrastructure at all levels, telecommunications, sewers, road and rail. Paris, in spite of the *Livre Blanc*, has a less complete strategy, but it is attempting to retilt the city towards the east and is also investing hugely in transport. Rotterdam's city-wide plans are rather overshadowed by the Kop van Zuid, but the programme of social housing is something that benefits the entire city.

None of them has plans that show real signs of getting to the root of the social problems of the city, but all are at least addressing the issue, and all are doing so by means of investment in social housing.

All are putting a premium on commissioning the best architects they can find, regardless of nationality, to design their new buildings, bridges and parks. Foster, Isozaki and SOM in Barcelona; I. M. Pei, Aulenti, Bernard Tschumi and Armstrong in Paris; Aldo Rossi, Tschumi and O. M. Ungers in Rotterdam.

All are making special plans for their waterfronts and using the opportunity offered to address wider problems: Barcelona, to link the city to the sea; Rotterdam, to bring together the rich north bank and the poorer south bank; Paris, to help rebalance its economy to the east.

All enjoy strong political leadership. Even when, as in Paris and Barcelona, there are party political conflicts between different tiers of government, there is general agreement on the need for action.

All are investing hugely in the future and using the leverage of public-sector funding for infrastructure to stimulate private finance.

None of these approaches is peculiar to Paris, Barcelona or Rotterdam. Cities all over Europe are developing comparable strategies. Birmingham is reshaping its city centre. Berlin's first move after the Wall came down was to invite the world's best architects to rebuild the new city. Frankfurt, like Glasgow, has invested in new museums. Smaller cities are commissioning strategic plans: Nîmes from Norman Foster; Nantes from Ahrends, Burton, Koralek; Montpellier from Ricardo Bofill; Dunkirk from Richard Rogers.

What these cities demonstrate is that it is possible to draw up strategic plans and to realize them. The one question they cannot answer is: does London have the will to act? If the answer is yes, then the place to start must be the Thames.

Grasping the opportunity offered by the 1992 Olympics, Barcelona has reclaimed its seafront while making a superb new marina, designed by David Mackay and Oriol Bohigas. This will be open to the public, with cafés, shops, restaurants, a breakwater and a sailing school.

The masterplan for the
Olympic Village, by
David Mackay and Oriol
Bohigas, and for the
extension of the Passeig
de Carles I, which
reconnects the centre of
the city with the sea, are
shown both in a model
and in reality.

Barcelona's transforma-
tion since the end of the
Franco regime has been
marked by the city
council's commitment to
creating new parks, such
as the Cruetta del Coll
(*above*), and to commis-
sioning artists like
Eduardo Chillida,
Barbara Pepper, Anthony
Caro and Ellsworth
Kelly. The Rambla St
Josep in the centre of
the city (*below*) shows
the benefits of giving
the pedestrian priority
over traffic.

I. M. Pei's Pyramide in
the Cour Napoléon at
the Louvre is a symbol of
how France's investment
in the Grands Projets has
married adventurous
contemporary architec-
ture to a respect for the
city's heritage.

La Défense is a new business area in the west of Paris that demonstrates superficial similarities to London's Docklands. But unlike Docklands it has, in addition to offices, a wide range of other facilities and amenities and is distinguished by some fine architecture, notably von Spreckelson's Grande Arche. This is set on an elevated site at the west end of Paris's historic axis, which runs through the Arc de Triomphe, the Champs Elysées and the Jardins des Tuileries to the Louvre. An extension to the Métro can take you from the centre of Paris to La Défense within twenty minutes, again in contrast to the Docklands Light Railway, whose gauge prevents its integration with the London Underground system.

Two of Paris's Grands Projets, the Grande Arche de La Défense (*above*) and Jean Nouvel's Institut du Monde Arabe (*above, right*), demonstrate the French Government's commitment to contemporary architecture. Rotterdam is also investing in the future, with the Kop van Zuid dock-development scheme having as its central feature a new bridge by Ben van Berkel (*below, right*).

Mecanoo is a young architectural practice whose work formed part of the Netherlands' entry for the 1991 Venice Biennale. Although they have been in partnership for only ten years since leaving college, Erik van Egeraat and Francine Houben of Mecanoo have completed over 120 social housing projects, such as Hillekop in Rotterdam (*below*), as well as the striking Paviljoen Boompjes restaurant overlooking Rotterdam's docks (*above*). In Britain architects of their age would be fortunate to have designed one or two small buildings or interiors.

PART TWO

Strategies for Change

CHAPTER FOUR

Turning to the Thames

'Two cities divided by a river' is how Angela Carter describes London in her novel *Wise Children*.[1] The question is, can the river help to bridge that divide and bring London together again? Can reviving the Thames revive London?

Stand on any central London bridge at 9 a.m. on a weekday morning and look down at the brown water. While the rush hour seethes around it and traffic grinds at less than walking pace along its banks and across its bridges, the river itself is often undisturbed by a single boat. It is emptier now than it has been at any other time, probably since Roman engineers first bridged it in AD 43 and certainly since Peter of Stonechurch laid the foundations of the old London Bridge in 1179.

It is because of the river that London exists. It is the river that has witnessed, and participated in, so much of London's history, and it still has great power and beauty. But at the moment the potential of the Thames is being wasted. Once it pulled into the city money and tributes, materials and manufactures, from all the corners of the earth. Today few people even make a living from it. There is little trade or transport on it and scant life beside it, apart from the jammed traffic. If you want to walk along its banks, or sit with a drink beside it, or enjoy a meal overlooking it, your options are limited. In places it is hard even to get near it.

But if London is to be revitalized, then the Thames is the place to start. There can be no new London without a reawakened river. It is the Thames that can help remarry the south and the north and retilt the city west to east, creating new housing, new jobs and new hope.

To achieve any of this we must build on the river's great strengths: its size, as it twists the 96 miles from Teddington to the sea; its variety, from rural Richmond to industrial Dagenham and from domestic Barnes to the pomp of Parliament; the beauty of its views – the Tower from St Mary Overie; the Queen's House, Greenwich, from the Isle of Dogs; Chelsea Bridge illuminated at night; the ecology of the Barking Creek reedbeds; the technology of the Thames Barrier. The river both connects us to London's history and touches the lives of almost everyone living in the city today.

It is the consciousness of that great history and variety that should make anyone who loves London angry to see the present waste of the Thames: the 300 acres of industrial desert on the Greenwich Peninsula; the silence in the Royal Docks; those monuments to energy by Gilbert Scott, Bankside and Battersea power stations, standing idle, giving neither power nor pleasure; the views of St Paul's obscured; County Hall empty for six years, lit outside each night, dark within. The length of the Thames through London is littered, literally, with land and buildings that are misused, underused or derelict.

Judy Hillman wrote in her book for the Royal Fine Art Commission, *A New Look for London*, 'The greatest opportunity for creating a chain of open space and transforming an underused thoroughfare into a place for people lies, of course, in the Thames. This broad waterway provides the city with its largest open area, not firm beneath the feet, as in a traditional park, but offering a tremendous sense of freedom from the congestion and tension of urban life, and a backcloth for industrial buildings, bridges, spaces and human activity of grey living water, constantly changing according to tide, wind and weather.'[2] The rest of the world finds it incredible that we can allow this great river to be so neglected.

We must look at the history of the Thames if we are to understand how it has reached this parlous state. Before the population of London became too large for its primitive sewerage system, the river was free of pollution, and the rich and the powerful chose to live beside it. Monarchs built royal palaces at Westminster, Greenwich and Hampton Court. The aristocracy followed suit. In the sixteenth century, on the river bank between London Bridge and Rother-hithe, were clustered the mansions of the Earls of Warren and of Surrey, the Prior of Lewes, the Abbot of St Augustine's, Canterbury, and the Monastery of Bermondsey. By the eighteenth century the Thames resembled Venice, with the palaces of Lambeth and West-minster and the houses of the Earls of Somerset and Arundel, Salis-bury, Worcester and Essex leading down through their gardens and terraces to the river bank. Small wonder that when Canaletto paint-ed his view of London's river (*circa* 1746) with 'ships, towers, domes, theatre ... all bright and glittering in the smokeless air', and with St Paul's against the skyline, he did so from Richmond House and, in the foreground, depicted fourteen ladies and gentlemen enjoy-ing themselves on a terrace overlooking a distinctly blue river. Reminders of these times can still be found along the river west of central London, in the Bishop of London's former palace at Fulham and Syon House (1547) dating from the sixteenth century, Ham House from the seventeenth, the Palladian villas of Marble Hill House (1724–9, built by George II for his mistress Henrietta Howard) and Chiswick House (1729).

As the population grew to 1 million in 1800 and 4 million in 1900, the river ceased to be desirable and became an open sewer, but it was the industrial waste of the nineteenth century that really fouled the Thames. The commerce that had given names to the guilds and companies, Haberdashers, Salters and Vintners, in 1700 still consisted of only about 1,000 ships a year, and most produce was traded, rather than processed. By 1800, 3,500 ships were berthing, and these were bigger vessels, requiring specialist docks. The Port of London became one of the largest in the world. Much of the fish and flax, corn and coal, sugar, salt and skins, ostrich feathers and iodine, tea and tobacco, rice and rubber, talcum powder, timber and treacle, pitch and tar, had to be transformed by boiling, tanning, bleaching, dyeing or other processes. The East End became a great manufacturing slum whose effluent was discharged into the Thames.

William Wordsworth was able to stand on Westminster Bridge on 3 September 1802 and observe that 'Earth has not anything to show more fair ...'[3] Some fifty years later, in 1858, the 'Year of the Great Stink', Parliament was so disgusted by the stench of the river that it draped sheets soaked in disinfectant over its windows before finally admitting defeat and suspending the session. By then the rest of London had already turned away from the river, moving west to Cubitt's Belgravia or north to the hills of Highgate, Highbury, Notting Hill and Hampstead. Let the river become the centre for the city's industrial life: London society could enjoy itself elsewhere.

For the next hundred years river trade grew inexorably. Five million tonnes had been handled in 1850; the tonnage had risen to 15.5 million by 1900, and new docks were built to cope with the volume. In 1961, 60 million tonnes were handled.[4] But the introduction of the container, and the consequent need for larger vessels, transferred activity to the deeper wharves at Tilbury. London's docks began to decline. In 1967 the East India and the Regent's Canal docks shut. They were followed by St Katherine's, London and Surrey docks. By 1981, with the closure of the Royal Docks, London's dockland had gone from its zenith to its death in the space of twenty years.

London is left with a challenge – to find a new use for its river. In this it is not alone. The rise of the container ship, together with the exodus of manufacturing industry from the inner cities, has presented other European cities located on rivers, or with docks, or both, with precisely the same problem. The difference is that they are treating this as an opportunity and are engaged in tackling it. Only London is failing to do so.

Apart from the initiatives being taken in Paris, Barcelona and Rotterdam, Dunkirk, mentioned in the previous chapter, Antwerp, Hamburg and Berlin are all working on this problem. Here in Britain, Liverpool, Salford, Bristol, Cardiff, Swansea and Hull have completed schemes, while others, like Glasgow and Ipswich, are drawing up plans. As a result there is no shortage of examples or ideas to inspire us. What is absent in London at present is political will and direction. More crucially, what we do not have is any vision about what sort of river we want the Thames to be. Growth is inevitable. The profusion of derelict sites ready for development will ensure that. What is at issue is whether we shape the future of our river with a coherent strategy or whether the future of the Thames will be determined for us by property companies and financiers. Michael Heseltine recognized this during his first period as Secretary of State for the Environment when, in February 1981, he called for 'an initiative to be taken in the preparation of a coherent plan for development along the river',[5] but no action was taken. The GLC conducted a comprehensive survey and audit of the river in the form of an environmental design handbook, but it was published in March 1986 within weeks of the Council's abolition. Since then, in the absence of any city-wide authority, nothing of substance has happened.

Not everyone agrees about the need for such a strategy. Some people support the Conservative Government's reliance on the private sector. It is ridiculous that the future of the Thames should be left to the whims of developers who will inevitably want the maximum financial return for riverside development and will therefore concentrate on luxury apartments, hotels and office blocks. This is already happening. The development at Chelsea Harbour consists of precisely such high-cost, high-rise apartments, alongside other facilities that are not open to the general public.

The London Planning Advisory Committee (LPAC) maintains that the Urban Development Plans (UDPs) that every borough has to draw up, will, when stitched together, provide a Thames strategy. We believe that its confidence is misplaced. The degree of concern and policy thinking on the part of boroughs with river frontages varies considerably. Some are excellent. Greenwich has produced a substantial waterfront policy.[6] Others feel that the river is not one of their priorities. Even when brought together, UDPs will not be able to provide a coherent overview. What is needed is a vision, a strategy, for the Thames that trumpets the importance and potential of this great river. We must make the Thames London's Grand Projet for the 1990s.

Paris's Grands Projets are exciting, but, as we have seen, they are vulnerable to the criticism that, as monuments in the centre of the city, they are primarily of interest to tourists. By contrast, the revival of the Thames, running through the city, could touch the lives of almost everybody. Such a diverse project would involve bridges for pedestrians; the development of derelict sites; the creation of new walks and gardens; a uniform approach to lighting the banks, bridges and key buildings beside the river; a renewal of interest in river transport. There would be space for new housing, offices, shops, jobs. The project would enhance and excite the whole city.

The first principle behind such a strategy must be that the Thames is primarily a public space, not a private opportunity. This is the basis of everything that other European cities are doing. In Barcelona they have made the Avinguda del Litoral (the linear park running along the seashore), the three other public parks and the new marina the focal points of the waterfront development around the Olympic Village as a means of achieving their aim of a 'strategic urbanism ... which in particular is directed towards redefining the public sphere'.[7] In Paris the fact that the city was originally established on the Ile de la Cité and grew out from there on both banks means that the river frontage has always been a central feature of the city's life. The Louvre, Les Invalides, the Eiffel Tower, the Tuileries are all beside the Seine, and this tradition is being continued with the new parks at Bercy and at the former Citroën works.

Secondly, London should be turned to face the river once again, an ambition that is easy to have but hard to achieve. Since medieval times, when the City of London made the banks of the river its southern limit, the river has been an administrative boundary line, Richmond being the only borough to span both banks.[8] The responsibilities of the boroughs included the maintenance of the river bank, but the river itself was held by the City of London Corporation on a freehold that had been purchased from Richard the Lionheart when he needed additional money for the Crusades. In 1857 the Thames Conservancy was established and took over the City's functions until these, and the ownership of the riverbed and foreshore to the high-water mark, were transferred to the new Port of London Authority (PLA) in 1908.

At no time were the boroughs involved in the river, so it is not surprising that they tended to see it not as an opportunity but as marking the limit of their powers. In most of the riparian boroughs this lack of interest was made inevitable by riverside industrial development that often spread back hundreds of yards from the waterfront – one of the reasons why many London bridges, such as Waterloo, do not span the river from bank to bank but begin as much as half a mile back. It will need a major effort to reverse this and to turn the river into the focus, and natural centre, of the city. Development of sites will be necessary but will not by itself be enough. Transport links will have to be established. At present few buses serve the existing riverside roads. On the north bank the stretch from Blackfriars Bridge to Battersea Bridge is virtually a bus-free zone. The new Design Museum, and indeed the whole of Butler's Wharf, is hard to reach by public transport. The new homes, workplaces and amenities to be built along the Thames will require better access than this.

This type of balanced development of the river is precisely the opposite of what has taken place in Docklands. Although praised by the Government, it is generally regarded abroad as a disaster. 'What we must not do,' said H. B. Cools, the Burgomaster of Antwerp, when planning his own city's docks development, 'is to do to our redundant docklands what you have done to your docklands in London.'[9] Indeed, when Antwerp displayed its own plans at an exhibition, Baltimore and Barcelona were used as examples of what could be achieved and London of what should be avoided.

With its emphasis almost exclusively on commercial development, London Docklands has been concerned only with offering short-term profits to developers and bankers who are ready to take a gamble, especially if that gamble is handsomely subsidized by the taxpayer in the form of tax relief and fiscal incentives. The second stage of development, Canary Wharf, shows welcome signs of learning from the early, blinkered, approach. There the developers, Olympia and York, are providing landscaped public spaces, shops and restaurants at street level, some housing and an extensive cultural programme. It will make for a much more balanced and attractive working environment, but this will not constitute a community. For most people that means a district with houses, schools, libraries, a health centre and a life of its own, twenty-four hours a day.

The Government has learned some of these lessons. Apparently rejecting more single-site developments like Docklands, Michael Heseltine, the Secretary of State for the Environment, has now set up a working party to consider a coherent plan for the East Thames Corridor. That is a major step forward in thinking and is welcome. In announcing it he recognized, correctly, the significance of transport infrastructure, in that it is only the coming together of the extended Jubilee Line, improvements to the A13 (the main road into the City from the east), the Channel Tunnel rail terminus at Stratford, the East London River Crossing and the lengthening of the City Airport's runway that will open up the potential of the whole area.

However, it is likely that, in the short time scale of three months within which it must report, the working party will not be able to consider more than the immediate implications of any strategy. To have the maximum effect, both economically and socially, developments in the East Thames Corridor should relate to the whole of the east of London in general, and to the hinterlands on either side of the river: Plumstead and Shooters Hill, south of Woolwich and Greenwich; Newham and Bow, north of the Royal Docks and the City Airport. Viewing the East Thames Corridor in isolation could create almost as many problems as it solved.

A further weakness of the plan is likely to be that the Government will offer no substantial infrastructure investment to open up these opportunities. When announcing the Channel Tunnel route into the east of London, Malcolm Rifkind, the Secretary of State for Transport, insisted that British Rail would have to look for private-sector funding, with the result that the link will not be completed before 2005, more than fifteen years after the French finished work on their line between Paris and the Channel. A comparable ideological refusal to invest public money in the East Thames Corridor will similarly delay, or even prevent, the balanced and coherent development of this area, which is so vital to London's future.

To consider what might be involved in a balanced development of the whole river, let us start with its wider economy. Cultural amenities, such as the redesigning of the South Bank or a new public park at Barn Elms, rightly generate excitement, but in our enthusiasm for them we must not forget that the Thames is a living river whose economy has been founded on work, on freight and on transport.

Although the docks have closed and their traffic has moved to Tilbury, there is still much industry beside the river, and central London remains a major cargo port, handling 10.7 million tonnes in 1990. That trade is up on 1986's 8.5 million tonnes – scarcely a renaissance but still a substantial industry, which is steadily reorganizing itself. The number of working wharves has fallen from sixty-four in 1986 to forty-nine in 1990, but those remaining are busier, and five new wharves have opened, while the six largest account for two thirds of those 10.7 million tonnes.[10]

London is certain to continue to need the aggregates, newsprint, cement, wood, oil, grain and steel that comprise this trade and to want to go on disposing of one third of its household refuse each year (650,000 tonnes) downriver by barge. Some of this work, particularly the delivery of aggregates, is unsightly and creates noise and dust, but it is likely to increase as demand for aggregates grows in the future, and there is no doubt that river transport is the cheapest and most efficient way of handling it, reducing traffic in London's streets by millions of lorry-road miles a year.

Industry will continue to be a central feature of the Thames, which must remain a working river. But industrial activity need not inhibit cultural and commercial developments. There are no wharves above Wandsworth and only three above Tower Bridge, which between them account for only 5 per cent of all trade. The forty-six wharves below Tower Bridge are split equally between north and south banks; twenty-six are above the Thames Barrier and twenty below. This area is precisely the one that offers the greatest opportunities for development, and Greenwich's waterfront strategy shows that a balanced approach is possible.

Greenwich is made up of several distinct village communities, spread over 7 miles of waterfront from Deptford to Thamesmead. The borough's policy is to help regeneration, in an area in which unemployment is high, by striking a balance between ensuring an adequate supply of industrial land, improving the environment for local residents and attracting new inward investment, particularly for housing and cultural purposes. The Greenwich Peninsula offers an ideal opportunity to realize many of these objectives. The site is no longer needed for gas production, power generation or metal manufacturing, and plans have been drawn up for a mixture of housing, retail, leisure and open space.

The borough's policy envisages that the same mix of uses would be appropriate in Thamesmead, the historic centre of Greenwich, and in Woolwich, with special emphasis on the cultural tourism potential of the Woolwich Arsenal to add to the attractions of the Naval College, the National Maritime Museum, the Royal Observatory, the Queen's House and the Royal Park. This would leave Angerstein's Wharf, the North Charlton Waterfront and the west bank of the Peninsula for container and industrial development.

This area is of crucial importance to the development of the Thames and of London. On its south bank are 350 acres on the Greenwich Peninsula, 90 acres in Woolwich town centre and a further 450 acres in Thamesmead, whose potential can be more fully appreciated when its 7 miles of water frontage is compared with Barcelona's reclaimed seafront of 4.5 kilometres.[11] On the north bank Brunswick Wharf (28 acres) and the Royal Docks (400 acres) invite development on an equivalent scale.[12] This area is the key to the London of the twenty-first century. If these sites can be brought back into use with balanced developments that are not driven by short-term considerations, then London will benefit enormously. If commercial companies are allowed to pick individual sites piecemeal, for a hypermarket here, a hotel there, then the capital will have squandered an opportunity that will not be repeated in our lifetime.

The overriding consideration must be quality – in planning, in infrastructure, in urban design and in architecture. It is encouraging that the Secretary of State for the Environment has refused to accept the first masterplan for the Greenwich Peninsula. Nothing but the best can be good enough for this area.

We can learn also about the practicalities of balanced development, and of retaining a strong industrial sector on the river, from the Port of Paris. In the last three years the Port Authority has increased the river transport of bulk materials by more than 70 per cent, to 3.5 million tonnes a year and has embarked on a programme of modernizing quays, improving road and rail connections, purchasing land and building 1.3 million square feet of new warehousing. However, in the regional planning document, the *Livre Blanc*, industrial use of the river is totally forbidden in the centre of the city, which is reserved exclusively for leisure and cultural use. Denied access to central Paris, the Port Authority has built a new port with tipping facilities, a ready-mix concrete plant and a building-materials supply depot. This has been architect-designed, so that, in the words of Rémi Loth, the Head of Research and Maritime Operations, 'The result is what looks externally like a series of very classical pavilions and shows that an industrial port can be implemented with the aid of architectural quality.'[13]

If industry is to mix with non-industrial users, one thing is essential, regulation, and that can come only from a master planning strategy. If a free and unregulated market exists, the cost of riverside land will be driven up by office and hotel developments or whatever uses offer the highest profits. A working river needs land-use planning controls as acutely as do public cultural places such as parks.

Turning from developments on the banks to the river itself, it is transport above all else that will bring life back to the Thames. For hundreds of years the river was one of the city's prime thoroughfares. On land the streets were narrow, dangerous and often dirty. In winter the dirt turned into mud, so it was not surprising that those who could went by water. When Wolsey visited Henry VIII at Greenwich he always travelled by barge, disembarking at Old London Bridge while his boatmen shot the rapids between the narrow arches to wait at Billingsgate for their master, who had proceeded along Thames Street on a mule, covered with crimson velvet, his Great Seal and cardinal's hat carried before him by attendants.

Others, less elevated, used the ferries that plied for hire to row people across or along the river. John Stow, in his sixteenth-century *Survey of London*,[14] claimed that the river provided work for 40,000 watermen and lightermen. An overestimate, perhaps, but certainly it teemed with rowing boats, as a print such as Vissher's view of London's river (1616) bears evidence, showing a river bustling with boats and skiffs. If all well-to-do people used the river as frequently as Pepys, whose diaries are peppered with references to it – 'by water to Whitehall', 'so by water Home', 'down by water to Deptford' – perhaps Stow's figures are accurate.[15]

Those who wistfully compare the empty highway of the river today with the weight of traffic on London's streets point to the nineteenth century, when for over fifty years a regular steamboat service operated. Starting in 1826 with a Richmond to London Bridge service, the company expanded until it was operating fifty-seven steamers and, between 1866 and 1876, claimed to carry 20 million passengers a year. But in 1878 the *Princess Alice* collided and sank one Sunday evening near Woolwich. Seven hundred people were drowned, and within a few years the company had ceased to trade. In 1904 the LCC reopened the service with thirty 'Penny Steamers' running from twenty-eight piers between Hammersmith and Greenwich every fifteen minutes between 7 a.m. and 6.30 p.m. throughout the year. In the first full year 4.7 million passengers were carried, but accidents, a hard winter and poor administration led to a working loss of £79,159, requiring a subsidy equivalent to a 1 farthing rate. In the council elections of 1907 the Municipal Reformers turned it into the main issue of what was dubbed the 'Steamboat Election' and, having gained a majority, axed the service.[16]

The attractions and good sense of travelling by boat in London could not be dismissed so easily, and between the wars several attempts were made to revive the service, particularly by Sir Samuel Instone, who in 1924 tried to persuade the LCC to let him use the piers still in place if he put up the finance for all the capital and running costs. The LCC refused, and by the mid-1930s, when more schemes were aired, responsibility had passed from the LCC to London Transport and its General Manager, Frank Pick.

These new schemes owed much to the enthusiasm and promotion of A. P. Herbert and J. H. O. Bunge, an oddly assorted pair of eccentrics. Herbert was the Independent Member of Parliament for the University of Oxford, a barrister and a writer of novels and plays, one of which, *The Water Gypsies*,[17] both novel and play, was set upstream on the Thames. He probably knew more about the river, and loved it better, than any living person, as his book, *The Thames*, bears witness.[18] He lived by the Thames at Chiswick, frequently travelled to the Commons by boat and spent much of his life championing the knowledge, care and use of the river he loved, ending up, proudly, as the Chairman of the Thames Conservancy Board.

Bunge was an enthusiast of a different kind, a man of detail, turning out plans and calculations that reinforced Herbert's larger-than-life advocacy. Unfortunately, neither was a man of great financial or business experience, nor were the direct promoters of the scheme that was presented in June and July 1934 to a Ministry of Transport inquiry formed to look into the 'desirability and practicability' of running a regular service.[19] The local authorities, including the LCC, were in favour, and London Transport was interested, Frank Pick himself attending the inquiry. But when London Transport discovered that the viability of the service depended on taking passengers from London Transport trains and buses, its support was withdrawn and the inquiry rejected the proposal.

In spite of these set-backs regular river transport is an idea that will not lie down. Having emerged again briefly during the Festival of Britain in 1951, it is once again a live issue today. The developers of Canary Wharf, Olympia and York, promised a Riverbus service between Westminster and Docklands as part of their original proposal for the site. They have kept their word but in the process have discovered that the capital cost of seating a passenger on a road bus is £1,000 compared with £10,000 on a Riverbus. Not surprisingly, they are having to subsidize their service with £3 million a year.

The financial implications of this are severe. It is possible that they may be insurmountable, but without more detailed economic studies it would be foolish to dismiss the river as a potential contributor to London's transport needs. What has to be established is the distinction between the running costs and the scale of infrastructure investment that would be needed for a regular and comprehensive service. All schemes to date have operated from only a handful of piers and so have inevitably not been viable.

Together with the PLA, the Riverbus Partnership has set up a working party to look into the future of river transport and has presented its findings to the Department of Transport through the Docklands Joint Consultative Committee. The report argues that the river can contribute seriously to London's transport needs only if it is integrated with London Regional Transport. This would involve a regular, timetabled service not just for tourists but for people living and working in London, with many more piers, proper stations linked with bus and Underground routes on both banks and car parking at stations outside central London. River-traffic control would also have to be improved, with traffic lights being erected on bridges to separate large vessels from small. Above all, the infrastructure costs would have to be publicly funded, at least in part. Only in these circumstances could fares be reduced sufficiently to make a regular Riverbus a reasonable alternative to other services for Londoners. The Government shows no sign of accepting the case for public investment. However, it does understand the advantages of such a service. In *Strategic Guidance for London* the Department of the Environment writes, 'Rivers and canals in London offer uncongested routes for both freight and passenger transport, and have the potential to relieve road traffic and provide services which customers want.'[20] The Department goes on to make it quite clear that it is the boroughs, not central government, that should find the money: 'Boroughs should recognize the potential contribution of London's rivers and canals to the capital's transport systems, reducing pressure particularly on east–west, west–east travel at peak times. UDPs should provide for piers and wharves where appropriate. Boroughs should consider when new or enhanced facilities, with suitable access arrangements, should be encouraged.' At the same time the DoE was rate-capping several boroughs and preparing the introduction of the poll tax the following year.

In spite of central government's negative attitude, the Thames is being developed with more housing, workplaces and amenities, and the developers will stimulate demand from potential passengers, which in turn will alter the cost equations. Research shows that the running costs of a river vessel are considerably lower than those of a vehicle on land: a small 350-tonne barge has an equivalent of oil consumed per tonne/kilometre of between 10 and 20 compared with a road bus's 50–10.[21] Whether the benefits will sufficiently outweigh the high costs to make river transport viable will probably depend on how intense the pressure becomes on all other forms of transport in London, both public and private. A further factor will be the speed at which the Thames-side population grows. It is a safe prediction that both the number of people living or working beside the Thames and the pressure on transport will increase. If so, A. P. Herbert's dream of a river-transport service may at last become a reality.

The economics of these operations would be somewhat different if the Thames was non-tidal. For at least sixty years people have been considering the possibility of eliminating the tides in central London, and in the 1930s the partnership of Herbert and Bunge nearly achieved it. Herbert wrote a book, *No Boats on the River*,[22] in which he raised the issue, and Bunge outlined two plans for a dam or barrage, either at Woolwich or just above the Royal Docks. In either case the water level above the dam would have been 18 inches below the mean high-water springs or at just about the level of the water in the Surrey, West India, St Katherine's and other docks. Bunge later described these plans in greater detail in a book, *Tideless Thames in a Future London*.[23]

The PLA was unenthusiastic, and so too was the Government, leading the Earl of Dudley to remark in a speech in the House of Lords in 1937, 'In these matters the Government are merely in the pocket of the Port of London Authority.' Under pressure the PLA agreed to a formal inquiry, but on the day before it was to start taking evidence, 28 March, it was cancelled by the Government 'on defence grounds'. A. P. Herbert introduced a Parliamentary Bill a year later,[24] but, with the Government opposed, it stood no chance of success.

Herbert and Bunge made their case not only for reasons of transport and amenity but also on safety grounds. London has always been vulnerable to freak tides that bring with them danger and destruction. In 1928 fourteen people died when the river rose and overflowed into the city. A tidal surge on 31 January 1953 flooded Canvey Island, drowning 300 people and causing devastation to farmland, stock, twelve gas works, two power stations and 200 miles of railway. The tides are getting higher: the high-water level at London Bridge is 27 feet today compared with 18 feet in 1953, 16 feet in 1881 and 14 feet in 1791.[25] The geological reason is that Britain is on a plate that is still rebalancing after the instability caused by the end of the Ice Age; north-west Scotland is rising and south-east England is sinking. The Thames Barrier will provide protection at least until the expected end of its life in 2030, but the case for a dam or barrage persists on transport and amenity grounds.

The PLA bases a substantial case against a non-tidal Thames on practicality. In a speech in 1991 David Jeffery, chief executive of the Authority, claimed that, as the Thames is an alluvial river, a barrage would cause the river to silt up and need dredging, at a current cost of £7.50 a tonne. The balance of salt and fresh water would change, altering the ecology of the river and perhaps damaging it. The impact on the city's water table could be considerable, with consequential problems for sewerage and water quality, as well as the likelihood that basements and foundations would be flooded.[26]

Supporters of a barrage point out that similar considerations were faced by the city of Boston, Massachusetts, when it decided to turn the Charles River into a non-tidal estuary with a freshwater lake 2 miles long. The technical problems can be overcome; as engineer Sir Jack Zunz writes in his contribution to the Royal Fine Art Commission's Thames study, *Capital Assets*,[27] 'The engineering skills are there ready and waiting to be harnessed.'

A. P. Herbert always believed that London would opt to eliminate the tide eventually. 'One thread runs through this rough record of the river,' he wrote in his book *The Thames*. 'First it was the fight for locks, which are dams with plentiful and quiet water behind them; then it was the demand for docks, which are dams with plentiful and quiet water behind them; now it is the big Dam in the river, with plentiful and quiet water behind it. One day this will come too.'[28]

The questions we have to ask ourselves in any strategic view of the Thames are, do we want a non-tidal river? And how much would it cost to achieve it? The attractions of Herbert's 'plentiful and quiet water' are obvious, as is the potential of harnessing the energy of the tides to reduce our dependence on conventional and nuclear sources of power, but Sir Jack Zunz raises a more fundamental and human question: 'Do we see the tidal mudflats as an eyesore or an ecological treasure?' Is the tidal nature of the Thames a positive strength? In his 1968 report into the viability of the Thames Barrier[29] Sir Herman Bondi wrote that the Thames at high tide was 'one of the great sights of the world, to be put well above Paris and in the same class as Leningrad'. He is right. To stand on the south bank of Lambeth Bridge and to see the newly cleaned Houses of Parliament, Barry's and Pugin's fairytale confection of cream stone and spires, dance on the surface of the water at high tide makes the spirits soar, but Bondi's delight contains within it a measure of ambiguity. The beauty of high tide can perhaps be loved the more because it is not constant but is rediscovered anew each day. There is a strong case for saying that it is the natural element of the Thames, including its danger and unpredictability, that is its unique contribution to London. In a city of concrete, where man has dominated everything on the earth, only the sky and the river remind us that we are mortals, weaker than the forces of nature.

The debate that has rumbled on for so long will continue. As Lord Lingren said when winding up a debate for the Government in the House of Lords on 20 December 1965, 'A Thames barrage scheme will always have attractions, and no decision on such a matter can ever be final.'[30] It is undoubtedly true that today's engineers could resolve the problems and tame the river by making it non-tidal. But, on balance, London would be the poorer for it, and the river should remain tidal. There are other important challenges for engineers in the capital, not least in crossing the river, whether by means of new tunnels or new bridges.

87

In considering the industrial and transport potential of the Thames it is easy to lose sight of one of the main reasons for the river's being a barrier between Angela Carter's two cities: the shortage of bridges. Until a modern bridge was erected at Putney in 1729, Old London Bridge and its predecessors had been the only bridge across the river for nearly 1,700 years. Five bridges were added in the eighteenth century,[31] a further nine in the nineteenth century.[32] Four bridges were replaced in the nineteenth century,[33] but only three have been added in the twentieth,[34] although eight have been replaced.[35] The result is that central London has only half the number of bridges, per mile, of central Paris and no bridge at all east of Tower Bridge. Not only is this a huge inhibition to mobility around the capital, it is a drag on economic growth. It was the building of bridges in the eighteenth century that opened up the development of west London on both sides of the river, with the pattern of expansion in areas like Battersea, Clapham, Balham, Wandsworth and Putney following the building of their bridges.

For the past forty years London has toyed with the possibility of a new bridge in the east of the city, an East London River Crossing (ELRIC). Such an initiative could have transformed the economy of the East End at any time, but, with the increase of traffic that is certain to come from Kent as a result of the opening of the Channel Tunnel, its potential today is hugely increased. In recent years the Department of Transport has been working on such a scheme, but its lack of urgency is extraordinary. Its proposal has been the subject of an official inquiry in 1985 that lasted for 192 days. Not content, the Government ordered a second inquiry in 1990, which ran from July 1990 to January 1991. The decision was finally announced in October 1991.[36]

There is no doubt that any bridge at this point in the river causes major environmental problems for wildlife in Oxleas Wood, which will not be easy to resolve. It is extraordinary that the Government seems determined to defy the European Commission, which has called in the plans. The change that is needed to our planning system is a statutory requirement to have an Environmental Impact Report. That would not solve all the problems, but it would provide a proper, objective framework within which the benefits of development could be assessed in relation to the need to conserve our natural environment.

In addition to the problems caused by the absence of an Environmental Impact Report and the ponderous progress of the bureaucrats, an opportunity has been lost in the design. If approved, this would be the most important bridge to be built in London since the war, the longest and most important bridge in Britain since the Humber Bridge in 1981. Its design could make a statement about London, about entering the city, about our new openness and enthusiasm for Europe, about how we value good design and the brilliance of our engineers. Brunel and Telford sent a message around the nineteenth-century world with their bridges over the Avon and the Menai Straits, as Freeman Fox & Partners did with the Humber Bridge.

In the same way ELRIC could trumpet Britain's civil engineering skills in the 1990s. Instead the Department of Transport has opted for a box-girder bridge. The Minister responsible decided that 'a review of alternative designs for the Thames Bridge has been undertaken, and the Department's consultants concluded that only a box-girder bridge met the criteria for the site'.[37] This is despite extensive evidence to the contrary from the London Rivers Association, among others, which argued that, in addition to the bridge being an eyesore, it would mean that a one-way working restriction would be placed on the river for large ships. The bridge was clearly designed for road traffic, threatening to impede any significant growth in river traffic.

The Government had been offered an escape from its lack of imagination by Stanhope Properties, the developers of the Royal Docks site north of the proposed route for ELRIC. Stuart Lipton of Stanhope had commissioned the Spanish architect and engineer Santiago Calatrava to design an alternative. Calatrava's spectacular concept of one white arch soaring across the river was precisely the dramatic gesture that the significance of the site demanded. Had it been built, it would have matched the beauty of his Felipe II–Bac de Roda bridge in Barcelona or his leaning suspension bridge in Seville for Expo 92. It would have instantly taken its place among the world's great bridges. Not surprisingly, the design was widely praised and was supported strongly by Newham, the borough council responsible for the north bank of the bridge. 'We don't want a black box,' Mrs Kate Jones, head of planning, said. 'It boils down to local prestige. There is support locally for upping the image of Newham, particularly the design aspect.' The Government objected to the fact that the Calatrava design would have cost between 10 and 15 per cent more than the estimated £85 million for the box-girder solution. For the sake of £5 million or £10 million we have lost a unique opportunity.

Aside from the controversy over the design, there is the additional problem that new bridges such as this will generate more traffic and so run counter to the overall policy, discussed in Chapter Two, of seeking to shift London away from private vehicles to public transport. That contradiction has to be faced. If the East London River Crossing goes ahead, with either design, it will make sense only as part of a transport strategy for the east of London that is weighted decisively towards public transport, together with the new rail route and the extended Underground line. In any other context new bridges will do more harm than good.

Whether or not we build more and better bridges, it is the opening up of the Thames as a public space that is most likely to capture people's imagination and to give the greatest pleasure. 'Pleasure' is a word that is not often used in public debate in Britain but there is no shortage of ideas about how it could be increased on, and beside, the Thames.

The priority for a strategy that opens up the Thames must be physical access. Although work on the Countryside Commission's Thames Path leaves only 10 miles of the 60 miles of riverbank paths in London not accessible to the public,[38] there still remains much to do to create continuous and effective access. There are some wonderful stretches of footpath. The route from Kingston to Putney Bridge, on the south bank, provides some of the most beautiful walking in London. Jonathan Raban describes it as 'a soft, suburban border country, more ambiguous and open to one's own impositions and interpretations ... It belongs to temporary people – floaters, drifters, visitors, and refugees, whose passage along it is far too rustic and diverse to endow it with any sort of stable character. Putney to Kew is a 7-mile walk along the extreme margin of city life, as rich and comforting a stretch of nowhere as it's possible to imagine.'[39] But this walk stops abruptly at Putney, where you are driven from the water's edge, and from there to Vauxhall Bridge only Wandsworth Park and a 1-mile passage between Battersea and Chelsea Bridge are walkable. On the north bank, going east from Blackfriars Bridge, access is patchy, and after Tower Bridge it ceases.

Some of this inaccessibility is caused by office and residential blocks, such as Crown Reach, but through London as a whole it is industrial sites that are the prime obstructions. The Countryside Commission is optimistic that solutions can be found; it rightly points to the raised walkway made by the GLC across the refuse station at Nickols Walk, Wandsworth,[40] and to the success of Greenwich Council's path past Angerstein's Wharf on the west side of Greenwich Peninsula. However, even the Commission accepts that the combination of the current economic recession and the variable enthusiasm of riverside boroughs means that the Thames Path will not be fully open when it is officially launched in 1994. To achieve that full accessibility would require a determined policy by a committed city-wide authority with strategic aims.

What is also needed is a coordinated, city-wide policy regarding information, both about how to get to the riverbank and what you will see once you are there. Here again Greenwich Council provides a model with its interpretation boards. Once you have overcome the problems of physical access and information, there remains only the question of what you can do. Some stretches, like Putney to Kew, need only a path, the water and trees. Others, in the centre of the city, need to offer opportunities to sit, eat or have a drink. When you compare the Thames paths with the Avinguda del Litoral in Barcelona or Rotterdam's Waterswand, it is clear that we have only just begun to explore the potential of the Thames.

Part of that potential is natural. The varying moods of the water need no enhancement to the constant shifts of the tide, but in parts the river bank is short of trees, shrubs and flowers. The greening of the Thames is a simple objective that must form part of any Thames strategy, as must the lighting of the river.

If the Thames is beautiful by day, it is ravishing at night. To stand on Waterloo Bridge, looking east over King's Reach, is to enjoy one of the great sights of London. As you view the floodlit buildings from Somerset House to St Paul's, around to the National Theatre, the Festival Hall, County Hall, across to Big Ben and back to Somerset House, the water is flooded with light. But there is no consistency in the type, quality or intensity of the lighting or even in which buildings are, or are not, lit.

Along the Thames in central London the Tate Gallery, St Paul's, County Hall and, above all, the Festival Hall are superb examples of how to light a building strongly but tactfully, but they stand out as exceptions. Others are over-lit, like Terry Farrell's office building over Charing Cross. Some, like the old St Thomas's Hospital, are barely lit, and there are many buildings that are not lit at all.

The same is true of the bridges. Suspended over the water, their potential for reflection makes them a lighting designer's dream, but, at the time of writing, Westminster, Lambeth, Vauxhall and Wandsworth bridges are all totally unlit. By contrast, Tower Bridge and the newly painted Albert Bridge are ablaze. The inconsistency arises in part from the fact that the road bridges are the responsibility of different local authorities. Every bridge has lighting, but Lambeth Council declares that Vauxhall and Lambeth Bridges are dark because their systems have fallen into disrepair and the borough has no replacement budget, while Westminster Bridge has had wiring problems for the past eighteen months and Westminster Council does not anticipate relighting the bridge for a further two years. Entrepreneurial Westminster is looking for private contractors who will do the job for little apart from the prestige of working on one of the most famous bridges in the world.

The position with respect to lighting the riverside roads and walkways is equally incoherent. In central London there are long stretches of festoon lighting between elegant dolphin lamp standards, notably between Westminster and Blackfriars bridges on the north bank and between Vauxhall Bridge and the National Theatre on the south. When lit, they are like strings of illuminated pearls, but whole sections of them have ceased to work. The broken bulbs are a reminder of the unnecessary state of disrepair into which London has fallen. Meanwhile London is missing a nightly light show that could be a glorious feature of the city and could draw people to enjoy the Thames. Here again coordination in a Thames plan is necessary to realize this potential.

In addition to these general policies of access, greening and lighting, the Thames has been central to the artistic life of the capital since the days of the Globe and the Rose Theatre. London has, on the South Bank, one of the finest concentrations of arts companies and venues in Europe. Where else could one find, side by side, a major concert hall, the Festival Hall, two excellent smaller concert halls, the Queen Elizabeth Hall and the Purcell Room, the three auditoria of the National Theatre, the new Museum of the Moving Image, the Hayward Art Gallery and the two cinemas at the National Film Theatre? Throw in platform performances at the National Theatre and foyer concerts at lunchtime at the Festival Hall, and you have a range of facilities that surpasses that of any other city in Europe.

But these delights can be enjoyed only once you have arrived there. You have several choices. You can add to the traffic problems of London by coming in a car, in which case you will be penalized, correctly if unintentionally, by streets that are impossible to park in and by open-air car parks that seem unchanged since their former use as disused building sites. Alternatively, you can arrive by Tube or bus and pick your way from Waterloo station through an imprecise forest of signs, or you may come from the north bank, from where you will have to brave the elements and walk over the ugliest bridge in London, Hungerford Bridge, deafened and shaken by the Charing Cross trains rushing past beside it. Your choices are all equally unappetizing. All lack any sense of occasion. They are like being offered fine food on a dirty plate. Worse, by 7.50 p.m., when all the evening performances have started, the area is as quiet and empty as a cemetery. Contrast it with Covent Garden, where the streets are alive all evening.

In the last two years architect Terry Farrell has presented two plans to redesign the South Bank Centre. This is not the place to discuss the merits of his designs, but his 1991 model has grasped the central point that the South Bank needs a setting that lives throughout the day and the evening. To achieve that, the tangle of walkways and levels has to be eliminated, and street life, in the form of cafés, bars, restaurants and shops selling a variety of goods at reasonable prices, has to be encouraged.

Beyond that, these venues deserve an entrance that offers a welcome and declares a pride in what they are offering. Why should the prelude to an evening of Mozart be a matter of stumbling over the pitted surface of a car park or battling with the windswept misery of Hungerford Bridge? This bridge follows the line of Isambard Kingdom Brunel's 'elegant suspension bridge', which he built for pedestrians in 1845 so that they could cross from Hungerford Market to Pedlar's Acre on the Surrey bank. Surely late-twentieth-century Britain can honour the memory of our greatest engineer with something better than this mess of iron netting?

Richard Rogers, in the Royal Academy's 1986 *London as it Could Be* exhibition,[41] offered an elegant design worthy of this important site, and Terry Farrell, in the Royal Fine Art Commission's Thames Study project of 1991, also proposed a new bridge.[42]

Capital Assets offered two other schemes for this stretch of the river, by Nicholas Hare Architects and David Quigley Architects, that involved new pontoons, islands and pedestrian walkways. Both incurred the scorn of the PLA. In his speech to the London Rivers Association conference[43] PLA's Chief Executive, David Jeffery, complained wearily, 'It is a cross that the PLA in particular has to bear that almost everyone, whether knowledgeable in a particular area of waterway management or ill-informed, thinks he knows what needs to be done to make better use of the river. What is said often makes good copy whether practicable or not.'

Mr Jeffery criticized both the Nicholas Hare and the David

Quigley proposals for, he claimed, ignoring the problems of navigation on the Thames. He concluded, 'Like so many embryo schemes, they appear superficially attractive but are likely to fail at the first hurdle since they do not appear to take account of the nature of the tidal river and its rises.'

Nicholas Hare believes that his proposal would allow river traffic to 'use the deep outer stream, and small boats [to] use the protected water south of the island'.[44] Whoever is right, if the PLA wishes to see the river play a fuller part in the life of London, it could begin to contribute more positively to the debate on such proposals. At present its attitude seems limited by the construction of the question that David Jeffery posed to the Working River Conference: 'Is it an acceptable or viable proposition to accommodate an ever-increasing amenity- and leisure-orientated use of the riverside and river at the expense of decreasing industrial and commercial activities?' It is a question that he believes reflects 'the reality of the world in which the PLA has to exercise its responsibilities'.[45] It scarcely seems to reflect the realities of the world in which most Londoners live, wanting to see a wider general use of their river for industry and commerce, for transport *and* for leisure amenities. Such negative attitudes on the part of the PLA can only impede the achievement of such a mixed and balanced development of all aspects of river life.

It is difficult to see, moreover, how the PLA can view increased activities *beside* the river as affecting commerce *on* it in any way, and, in the case of the South Bank, the riverside walkway could certainly be enhanced. Here is a stretch along which you can walk from County Hall to Blackfriars Bridge and beyond as the river makes a magnificent arc around King's Reach. With one sweep you can take in the Houses of Parliament, the gardens along the Embankment, Shell House, Somerset House, the Temple and the Inns of Court. It should be one of London's outstanding walks, but there is little evidence that any thought has been given to its design, which consists of nothing more than a straggling line of benches and trees. There is a handful of second-hand bookstalls outside the National Film

Theatre. On really hot weekends two vans arrive to sell ice-cream, and the Festival Hall kitchen puts a trestle table outside to offer food. At the eastern end is the temporary market of Gabriel's Wharf. That's all. Contrast the care and thought that David Mackay and Oriol Bohigas, together with Josep Martorell and Albert Puig-domènech, have put into the Avinguda del Litoral in Barcelona, and imagine how a comparable effort could transform this wonderful walkway with covered areas, shrubs and flowers, clusters of seats, children's play areas, a variety of places to eat and drink, fountains, sculptures, toilets, viewpoints and information boards, all helping to form a relationship between the buildings and the walkway and the walkway and the river.

Further to the west Barn Elms Water Works and Reservoirs, no longer in use, offer an opportunity to create a riverside park of out-standing interest. Situated beside Harrod's Depository on the south bank, east of Hammersmith Bridge, the reservoirs are a Category I Site of Special Scientific Interest, being a bird sanctuary, used partic-ularly by wintering wild fowl. On the eastern side of the reservoirs are Barn Elms Playing Fields and Sports Centre, which lead through to Barnes Common. Linked together, redesigned and with addition-al tree planting, these sites would make a park of wonderful variety, but to achieve that would require a city-wide authority that could bring together the various owners and interested parties, notably Thames Water and the local authority. To the east of the city, where the need for parks is considerably more acute, there are sites on both banks. The development of Greenwich Peninsula offers pos-sibilities, but across on the north bank, where the River Lea curls round Bow Creek to flow into the Thames and where the Green-wich Meridian crosses the river, the benefits of a new park could be even greater.

New riverside parks do not have to be on such a major scale as Barn Elms or Bow Creek would be. Oriol Bohigas has proved that a series of small initiatives can have a major impact, and there are sites all along the river for such projects. The area in front of Bankside Power Station descends in terraces to the river. Opposite it the dome of St Paul's peers over the top of a flight of steps. Bankside's terraces cry out to become a handsome garden or small park, and the demand for it would be overwhelming if this huge building of Gilbert Scott's were linked to the City by a pedestrian bridge and put to some cultural use – perhaps a Museum of Modern Art, a new home for an enlarged Design Museum, a Museum of Architecture or a Museum of the Thames.

The streets beside the river offer opportunities too. In *London as it Could Be* Richard Rogers proposed that the existing gardens along the Embankment should be linked into one major park, with the traffic being diverted underground, as has been done in Paris at several points along the quays beside the Seine. Alternatively, Nicholas Hare's plan extends the terrace of Chambers's Somerset House over the roadway to form a fine, albeit reproduction, garden and piazza overlooking the river.

It is extraordinary that no one in London appears to be responsible for resolving the impasse over Battersea Power Station. Now gaping open to the sky and to the weather, Gilbert Scott's great structure risks falling into such disrepair that it will be fit only for demolition. If the current owner, Mr John Broome, cannot find the finance to complete his elaborate scheme for an Alton Towers pleasure park in London, the city's strategic authority ought to have the power to coordinate a rescue package, either to prevent further damage pending a sale or, if necessary to acquire it through a compulsory purchase order. It would be a tragedy if this building, which has provided London with power for so long, were reduced to rubble.

In truth there are plenty of good ideas, as the Royal Fine Art Commission's 1991 Thames Study demonstrated. Some of them are simple (Siddell Gibson's plans to light the bridges), some ambitious (Tom Jestico's Brentford Lagoon), some highly practical (Panter Hudspith's floating walkway to connect Cannon Street with London Bridge), some more expansive (ORMS's Live Wire overhead funicular joining Twickenham and Kew). Some would need major investment (Dave King's and Rod McArthur's Festival of

Energy); another by Kim Wilkie demands only minor reshaping to recover the avenues and landscape lines around Richmond that were created in the seventeenth and the eighteenth century by Alexander Pope, Batty Langley, Sir William Chambers and John James and connected Richmond Hill, Marble Hill House, Orleans House, Ham House and Strawberry Hill.

Once London set itself on a Grand Projet to revive the Thames, schemes such as these would not be in short supply. If London invited, by means either of competition or of commission, designs from international architects such as Manuel Solà-Morales, I. M. Pei, or Hans Hollein, as well as from British ones, or encouraged proposals from Claes Oldenburg or Nigel Coates, the possibilities would be exciting, and the city would benefit.

Riverside locations could be used for outdoor concerts of all types of music, at the Jubilee Gardens, Bankside or St Katherine's Dock; there could be Son et Lumière performances in Parliament Square (closed off on weekend evenings) or at St Paul's. The potential of drama performances on a waterside site was demonstrated by the Keith Khan production that the London International Festival of Theatre produced in 1991 on the canal at Paddington Basin. All initiatives of this kind could be brought together in a major arts festival, as envisaged by the River Thames Group and its chairwoman, Judy Hillman.

Such festivities would go with the grain of the river's history, for it has always been a place of pleasure. Charles II established the Vauxhall Gardens, where, as Pepys records in his diary for May 1667, 'It is very pleasant and cheap going thither, for a man may go to spend what he will or nothing, all as one. But to hear the nightingale, and the birds, and have fiddles, and there a harp, and here a Jew's Thrump, and here laughing, and there five people walking, is mighty diverting.'[46] Mighty diverting too was the Gardens' Rotunda orchestra house, whose walls were decorated by Hogarth and where Handel, Dr Arne and, in 1764, Mozart at the age of 8 all performed their works.

So popular were the Gardens that they were copied all over

Europe. Paris had a Vauxhall Gardens, as did Moscow, while Copenhagen's Tivoli Gardens were modelled on them. Since then the Gardens have had a chequered time. Cut off from the Thames by the railway line into Waterloo, they went into decline and were built over for cheap housing. Those homes were demolished about twenty years ago, and there is now an open space, Spring Gardens, which Lambeth Council cannot afford to develop properly. These once great gardens are now home to the local homeless and alcoholics. In 1991 there were two murders in the area.

On the other side of the raised railway line Vauxhall Cross is little more than a huge island of billboards around which traffic races. Beside the river a coach park occupies land that was once Vauxhall's rival, the Cumberland Gardens, which 'consisted of an open space toward the Thames, laid out in grass plots, and surrounded by open boxes and tables for refreshments, after the style of old-fashioned suburban tea-gardens'.[47]

The whole area, either side of the railway line, needs a design plan to reawaken it and to 'put the pleasure back into Vauxhall Gardens', in the words of the Vauxhall St Peter's Heritage Centre director, Zoë Brooks. With Terry Farrell's new government building for MI6 about to be completed on the north edge of Vauxhall Cross, there could not be a better time for tackling this important site in the centre of the city and so close to Parliament. It is likely that, had it been on the other, more fashionable, bank, it would never have fallen into this condition.

However, even if its revival is achieved, this and other projects will have only limited impact unless they are part of a coherent strategy to revive the Thames. What all such initiatives have in common is that they envisage, and use, the Thames and its surrounding areas as public spaces, as parts of the public domain. Once that is done, the responsibility for strategy and for administration follows, and the principle is reinforced that the development of the Thames has to benefit everyone and all aspects of London life. As Burgomaster H. B. Cools has said in relation to Antwerp's plans, 'No city can leave such large-scale redevelopment to private enterprise. City, developers, academics, planners, architects and citizens must all work together."[48]

We need a city-wide authority to establish a Thames Plan that covers both the economic and the cultural life of the river and seeks coherent, rather than piecemeal, development. The plan should be based on the principle of the mixed use of sites, including housing (both for sale and at affordable rents), offices, shops, leisure and arts venues, with particular attention being given to those elements (access, lighting, greenery) that create a sense of unity along the length of the river.

Within that framework there will be plenty of opportunities for the private sector and for industry to contribute financially. Although the public purse will have to underwrite the key infrastructure for transport, police, safety and other services and for social housing, through both central and local government, there may be a case for funding some or all of this through dedicated forms of taxation such as a hotel tax. From the private sector there is likely to be little shortage of investment for the variety of projects that will arise. Some, such as protecting the ecology of the river, will continue to need public investment, and rightly so, since this is of vital importance, both in its own right and as an educational resource for London's schools. By contrast, the potential for sports on the river, enhanced by schemes like Tom Jestico's lagoon and marina at Brentford, could be financed jointly from both public and private resources.

But, whatever the balance of financial sources, the whole process of reviving the river should involve as many people as possible. If we are truly to make the Thames the centre of London again and turn the city to face it, not only physically but emotionally, then people must be involved at every stage of the plans. Listening to what people want must be the starting point. Information must be provided at a Thames Centre modelled on Paris's Pavillon de l'Arsenal, where plans can be considered, models examined, options compared, and where there can be a forum for discussion.

If we achieve that, people will be proud of the river once again.

We will have taken a major step towards renewing London, and the Thames will be seen not as lying, according to Angela Carter's description, 'between Brixton and glamour like a sword'[49] but as a ribbon drawing the city into one magnificent whole.

From the top of the Cesar Pelli tower in Canary Wharf, looking west to the City (*above*) and east across hundreds of acres of development land on Greenwich Peninsula and, beyond, to Woolwich and Thamesmead (*below*). This is where London must develop in the 1990s.

Sir Horace James's Billingsgate Market (*above*), built in 1875 and restored in 1989 by Richard Rogers but still unlet as trading floors. Surely we can find some better use for this beauti-ful riverside building than filling it up with faxes and filing cabinets?

The Victoria Embank-ment (*right*), passing Somerset House. The Embankment was one of the largest and most ambitious of Victorian London's investments in infrastructure. Stretching from Blackfriars Bridge to Waterloo Bridge, it relieved traffic conges-

tion in Fleet Street and the Strand. Sir Joseph Bazalgette's 1864 plan was a defence against the Thames flooding, while beneath it was run the new underground railway and a trunk server.

Above ground it gave people access to the river front and is notable for the quality of its design: the granite wall, benches decorated with camels, festoon lighting and Timothy Butler's elegant

dolphin lamp posts. Today the Embankment is blocked with vehicles, but a redesign of traffic flow could allow it to be one of the most elegant and exciting linear riverside parks in Europe.

It is almost impossible to see St Paul's Cathedral from the Thames, as views are blocked by some indifferent buildings. This gap on St Paul's Steps (*above, left*) is the only glimpse you can get of Sir Christopher Wren's masterpiece. These buildings also prevent people from sitting beside the river unless they are prepared to perch.

The closure of London's docks (*below, left,* and *above*) has left several thousands of acres of derelict land along both banks, even right in the centre of the City, within sight of Tower Bridge. These sites offer London magnificent opportunities to turn itself to face, and to enjoy, the Thames once again. If these developments are to benefit all areas of London life, and all its people, they must be balanced with a mixture of uses: residential, industrial, office, retail, leisure and cultural.

Britain has always provided fine civil engineers, and over the past 150 years London has been distinguished by some beautiful bridges, such as George Rennie's original Waterloo and London bridges (both now demolished) and R. W. Ordish's Albert Bridge. Isambard Kingdom Brunel's Hungerford footbridge was replaced in 1863 by John Hawkshaw's grim, trussed iron structure (*below*). This is not dissimilar, in the poor quality of its design, to the Department of Transport's box-girder bridge for the proposed East London River Crossing, which the Government has chosen in preference to the elegant design of Spanish engineer Santiago Calatrava (*above*).

In developing Greenwich Peninsula's 350-plus acres of development land (*above*) with new houses, jobs, parks, we must not forget that wharves such as this at Limehouse Basin (*below*) remain an important part not just of London's history but also of its current economy.

Docklands, looking from South Quay towards Millwall Dock. We must not repeat the mistakes of Docklands, which is as poor an example of British planning as it is of British architecture.

CHAPTER FIVE

Designing Public Space

Public spaces are the emblems of cities. Times Square, Red Square, the Piazza San Marco, the Via Veneto, the Bois de Boulogne, the Rajpath: it is these squares, streets and parks that evoke New York, Moscow, Venice, Rome, Paris and Delhi.

London is rich with such places. Parliament Square, Piccadilly Circus and Trafalgar Square are known throughout the world. They have always been the backdrop to great public events, the places where people meet to protest, about the poll tax or nuclear arms, or to celebrate election victories, royal weddings or simply the start of a new year. They embody and express part of London's character and identity. If a city is about people coming together, then these places are the city.

London's public domain is all around us: outdoors in its streets and squares, rivers and canals, parks and playing fields, churchyards and cemeteries; indoors in its libraries, museums, schools, bus stations, hospitals and government buildings. Going to work, taking a walk, shopping, we cannot avoid it; it is where we live. Consequently its quality, whether it is safe, clean, attractive, welcoming, well maintained, affects every day of our lives. Yet we give it little thought. When it comes to buildings everyone notices them and has strong opinions, but the spaces around and between them are strangely ignored.

In London the central public places are invariably full, even crowded, but in the main people are moving, going somewhere, walking with a purpose. Strolling is not a common London activity. The explanation offered is the weather. It's too cold and unreliable, apart from in mid-summer, for pavement cafés or for hanging about. But those who live in Amsterdam or Paris or Copenhagen wouldn't agree, and their weather is not significantly better. Indeed, the few pubs and cafés in London that do keep chairs and tables outside well into the winter seem to do good business. A more likely explanation of why Londoners don't live in these places lies in their design. These public spaces are thoroughfares, not made for lingering, for leisure. Where are the seats in Piccadilly Circus or Oxford Street? That's the nub of it: design. Being man-made, all public spaces are designed, though some are designed by default. If we are to improve the quality of urban life, there can be no better place to start than with those spaces and with the signs, railings, benches, litter bins and kiosks that fill them. Design improvements here are not simply a matter of appearance; they depend on understanding how a space functions, what it is for, how it is used, by whom and when.

But although bad design is an enemy of the public domain, it is by no means the only or, indeed, the most important enemy. The volume of traffic, poor street cleaning and maintenance, the fear of being mugged, lack of access if you have a disability – all conspire to limit our use and enjoyment of public spaces.

So too did dirt and smog until the 1950s, when the Clean Air Act (1958) transformed London and every other industrial city in Britain. For two hundred years London had lain under a pall of coal dust, grime and periodic fog, celebrated by every writer from Cole Porter to Dickens, who in *Bleak House* described London thus: 'Smoke lowering down from chimney-pots, making a soft black drizzle with flakes of soot in it as big as full-grown snowflakes – gone into mourning, one might imagine, for the death of the sun.'

When the sun shone again London was revealed as a city whose colours were green, cream, white and red, not grey and black. Buildings could be cleaned, revealing the architectural beauties under the dirt on the Houses of Parliament, St Margaret's and Westminster Abbey. No one, not even Nikolaus Pevsner, appreciated what a wonderful building, by Alfred Waterhouse, lay under the black and lowering exterior of the Natural History Museum until cleaning revealed its pastel blue and brown terracotta tiles.

However, to tackle the problem of traffic's impact on London's environment will require more than one wand-waving Act of Parliament. Today traffic dominates those central London spaces. Trafalgar Square, Piccadilly Circus, Hyde Park Corner and Parliament Square have become little more than roundabouts, where traffic frequently grinds to a standstill. Anyone who attempts to use the centre of these places, to sit at the feet of Eros in Piccadilly Circus or to feed the pigeons in Trafalgar Square, risks lead poisoning, as they are surrounded by a wall of traffic.

Consider the condition of Trafalgar Square. It occupies a pivotal position, the point at which the streets coming from the City, from Westminster, from Buckingham Palace and from Soho and the West End, all meet. John Nash understood the Square's significance and drew up a masterplan, which, sadly, was never built.

Trafalgar Square has always had to maintain a balance between pedestrians and vehicles. People come to it to visit buildings, whether the National Gallery, the church of St Martin-in-the-Fields, the shops and offices, or simply to meet each other. For that people need places to wait and to sit, which is perhaps why the steps and portico of James Gibbs's beautiful church are so popular. But the layout of the Square, whose centre is cut off from the surrounding buildings by cross currents of traffic, puts the needs of pedestrians second. A balance is needed, but at present that balance is wrong. How could it be restored?

If traffic were rerouted from the northern side of the Square, a piazza would be formed and the shape of the Square would change. Railton's Nelson's Column (1842) is inevitably its focal point, but it lacks at present any clear relationship with the National Gallery. It was to correct this that Richard Rogers's design for the National Gallery extension proposed, in the north-west corner of the Square, a tower to balance the elegant tower and steeple of St Martin-in-the-Fields and so make the base line between them of a triangle whose apex would be the Column. An apron piazza leading down the slope of the Square from the National Gallery would achieve much the same effect, that of bringing the whole space together.

This is particularly desirable in the case of Trafalgar Square, since the setting is everything. None of the buildings around its edges is especially distinguished, apart from James Gibbs's church, although they achieve some unity by means of their similar scale, colour and materials. What gives Trafalgar Square its special distinction is the grand openness of its space, its slope and the dominance of Nelson's Column, surrounded by Landseer's lions (1867) and Lutyens's fountains, which were not added until 1939. Remove the Column, and the Square loses the grandeur that makes it so popular. However, its popularity has been achieved in spite of the fact that there is little to do in the Square except feed the pigeons and take photographs. If it were transformed into a piazza, it would not be hard to design cafés, set against the drop wall below the National Gallery, between the two sets of steps. (To achieve this, however, would require amending the Trafalgar Square Regulations (1952), which expressly forbid almost every form of man-made pleasure.)

The other central spaces are also buckling under the weight of traffic. Hyde Park Corner was created in the early nineteenth century. It was recognized as a key site in the capital, the meeting point of Hyde Park, Piccadilly, Green Park and the gardens of Buckingham Palace. It was both the entry to the heart of London from the west and the link with Thomas Cubitt's grand development of the Grosvenor Estate in Belgravia, which was then approaching completion. The problem facing the architect, Decimus Burton, was how to make it work both for pedestrians and for its prime user, traffic.

The only given elements were the gardens of George IV's new residence at Buckingham Palace, which itself was in the process of being transformed by John Nash; Apsley House in its original form, as designed by Robert Adam for Baron Apsley; and the edges of Green Park and Hyde Park.

Burton's solution was to design two substantial structures that would define the northern and southern boundaries of the Corner, a long, open and delicate screen (1825) of Ionic columns as an entry to

Hyde Park and, opposite it, the solid mass of Constitution Arch (1827), heavy with Corinthian columns, as the gate to the grounds of Buckingham Palace. The rest of the corner was shaped, on its western side, by Sir William Wilkins's St George's Hospital (1827–9) and, to the north-west, by the new façade that Benjamin and Philip Watt put on to Apsley House in 1828–9. Together these four structures made a fine neo-classical setting for Hyde Park Corner.

Although there have been changes since – the Arch was moved to the top of Constitution Hill in the 1830s, and the statue of the Duke of Wellington on top of it was replaced in 1912 by the Quadriga, a vast bronze chariot driven by the figure of Victory – such alterations maintained the spirit of the original design. However, by the 1950s the increased volume of traffic demanded the restructuring of the roads. Engineers drove new routes through the Corner with no apparent regard for what the Victorians had achieved. The Arch is now isolated and without meaning, an entry to nowhere, while Burton's screen is bypassed, stranded between two streams of traffic. It is likely that, even if the accommodation of today's traffic had been approached as a design problem, there would have been no easy solutions. But if we care about the appearance of London, we could put the redesign of Hyde Park Corner out to competition with a brief to landscape the area again, to light it at night and, if necessary, to add new structures to bring together the main elements of the Corner and give it shape and coherence. Such a brief could make it once again a focal point of the city.

We would profit by a similar reconsideration and redesign of both Piccadilly Circus and Parliament Square. Nash's original scheme for Piccadilly, as a junction between Regent Street and Lower Regent Street, was destroyed in the late nineteenth century. Its replacement by Norman Shaw, and later by Reginald Blomfield and Aston Webb in 1905, has led to a hopeless confusion of advertising hoardings, people and traffic that fails in almost every respect, whether as a start of the Quadrant as it sweeps north up Regent Street, or as the culmination of Piccadilly and of Lower Regent Street, or as a space that welcomes the many pedestrians who come there to visit the shops and theatres.

In Parliament Square the problem is different. Here Church, in the form of Westminster Abbey and St Margaret's, and State, in the form of Whitehall's offices of government, come together in a square that ought by right to pay tribute to the heart of our democracy, Sir Charles Barry's Houses of Parliament. Instead there is a patch of grass and a stream of traffic in front of the Commons and a squalid triangle of a car park in front of Westminster Abbey in which coaches attempt to drop off visitors. This great church, in which our monarchs are crowned and whose building tells the story of British architecture from thirteenth-century French Gothic, through English Perpendicular to Hawksmoor's eighteenth-century West Towers, has a car park and a souvenir shop at its entrance. Would the French treat Notre Dame in this way? Of course not.

One reason for this is that the French have a well-established tradition of symbolism in their public buildings and spaces. They understand the meaning that places convey. Pei's Pyramide tells a story about the archaeological treasures hidden beneath it. La Défense was built at the end of the historic axis that runs across Paris, linking the Louvre with the Arc de Triomphe. The Arche de la Défense, as a building, marks the end of that axis with a huge white monument, visible for miles, but its shape (a cube without a centre) is set at a slight angle to the axis and so, deliberately, does not quite close it. Lewis Mumford described this conscious symbolism in a building as 'the attempt to use the constructional forms in such a way as to convey the meaning of the building to the spectator and user, and enable him, with a fuller response on his side, to participate in its functions – feeling more courtly when he enters a palace, more pious when he enters a church, more studious when he enters a university, more businesslike and efficient when he enters an office, and more citizenlike, more cooperative and responsible, more proudly conscious of the community he serves, when he goes about his city and participates in its many-sided life'.[2]

This is no new concept. Churches, with their spires soaring to the heavens and, in medieval times, their vast size in relation to surrounding buildings, told of the glory of God, His great and awesome power and man's smallness in relation to the Almighty. In the nineteenth century there were the works of the great railway engineers, such as Isambard Kingdom Brunel. He built Paddington Station, with its three vast vaulted sheds of wrought iron and glass held up by cast-iron columns, as the grandest statement he could make about the arrival of his Great Western Railway in London, bringing a new freedom and mobility to people. Likewise today the best airports, like Charles de Gaulle in Paris or Norman Foster's Stansted, express the excitement of taking off into the skies. In short, all good buildings and spaces convey a message to the public, although sometimes that message becomes garbled. For commercial reasons, many airports and stations are now more about shopping, buying and selling than about travel.

When that happens, and the original purpose of a building or place becomes confused or forgotten, the result is disruption. Lamarck's great theory that form follows function is distorted, as when Parliament Square becomes a roundabout for cars, not a meeting place for Church and State. Conversely, when the proposition is observed the result is invariably efficient and often beautiful. The finest works of engineering in London – R. W. Ordish's Albert Bridge (1873) or William Heywood's Holborn Viaduct (1863) – are elegant precisely because they convey and fulfil their function, that of transporting vehicles across space.

Today's vehicles are outgrowing the city, and this domination by traffic is not confined simply to the famous central spaces. Shopping and residential districts all over the city are being damaged by the noise and vibration of cars and the sheer volume of traffic. We have already discussed the general presumption in favour of roads and of vehicles in relation to the general future of London. With regard to public spaces, the consequence of this is that traffic has an environmental right of way. Pedestrians come a poor second.

We have to rethink that balance and to provide more pedestrian areas and more traffic-calming schemes. In order to do so local authorities should give greater consideration, in their Urban Development Plans, to the needs of pedestrians. To be effective, initiatives can be as modest as wider pavements, as introduced in Bedford Square, or a different proportion between pavement and street, as in Barcelona's Rambla Sant Josep, where cars are allowed to travel in both directions but are confined to a narrow single file, while the much wider area in the middle of the street is for pedestrians and for cafés, stalls and street entertainers.

We should look for opportunities to close streets like the Embankment at the weekends, so as to create a riverside linear park as a pilot scheme for the permanent park envisaged by Richard Rogers in the *London as it Could Be* exhibition. Charlotte Street, which is lined with restaurants, could be closed to traffic in the evenings after 6.30 p.m.

We should have more streets in London from which private cars are banned and which only pedestrians and buses are allowed to enter. Piccadilly would respond well to such treatment. Some squares and streets, such as Manchester Square, the home of the Wallace Collection, and St Martin's Lane, with its theatre, restaurants, cafés and cinema, should become permanently pedestrianized. Indeed, whole areas, like Soho, or Bloomsbury around the University of London, would benefit from traffic calming or a complete ban on vehicles.

The criterion should be whether there is sufficient street-level activity to demand a pedestrian solution. By this yardstick some squares, which are swamped with parked cars, would not qualify – St James's Square, for instance, since, apart from the London Library, most buildings in the square are offices. Overall we have to reverse the trend of recent years, which has been to encourage cars in London to use new freeways like Westway, and reassert the virtues of walking and the interests of the pedestrian.

There are also wider effects on the public domain for which we all must share some indirect responsibility. As consumers we have conveyed to retailers both our desire to be able to park by food stores and hypermarkets and our strong preference for surface, rather than multi-storey, parking. Retail chains have responded by seeking for new stores far larger areas of land beside major roads and away from existing shopping centres. This, in turn, has ripped a hole in those centres and so has contributed to the decline of the public, shared areas in the middle of communities.

The consumer boom of the 1980s, fuelled by the relaxation of restrictions on personal credit, led to a huge expansion of shopping malls and hypermarkets that have done more to change our urban landscape than anything else. Apart from stimulating – indeed, generating – the use of the car, many of these new shopping complexes have privatized land in city centres that used to be public. Private security forces patrol their precincts and decide who is not welcome. People who simply want to sit are treated with suspicion, and groups of lads are frequently banned 'as a precautionary measure'. We are witnessing a new generation of enclosures, which may have an effect as long-lasting as those of the eighteenth century. Now, as then, people's right of access to public space is being taken away.

Further enemies of public spaces are simple neglect and underfunding. Squares and piazzas that are not maintained, and in which there are inadequate levels of supervision, become dirty and unsafe. All over London these are the conditions with which many are faced when they go outside their front doors. The elderly feel trapped. Parents are nervous about letting their children go to the local corner shops (even if they exist). Women daren't go out at night by themselves. London is not yet New York, but there can be no revival of public spaces until these issues are tackled, and all of them have at their root the level of investment that local authorities decide, or are allowed, to make in them. While councils are so constrained by government legislation, and while competitive tendering for local services requires local authorities to accept the cheapest solutions to problems of maintenance and repair, there is little prospect of progress.

However, we cannot simply blame others. Improvements in the quality of our built environment depend on us, as individuals and as communities. At the moment we are too complacent and apathetic. Perhaps our response to a decade in which even the notion of 'society' was dismissed has been to lower our expectations of any part of our lives that is public. We have to reassert the importance of concepts like civic responsibility, civic pride, civic quality – indeed, of the public domain itself. We have to remember that almost everything we have has been hard-won.

Most people agree that prime among London's glories are the variety and beauty of the city's parks, both royal and municipal. But there is a tendency to take them for granted, to forget how they came to be public parks, how 'what had been the delights of the nobility, are now the delights of the people'.[3]

The city's parks have developed from two separate sources, crown lands and common land. What are now the Royal Parks were originally hunting grounds outside the city walls. Henry VIII increased these considerably when he, in the words of Jacob Larwood, 'drove the monks from their snuggeries and claimed the church lands',[4] confiscating Hyde Park from the Abbot of Westminster in 1536 and exchanging its 600 acres for a priory and an estate at Hurley in Berkshire.

But Henry and his successors intended the parks for their personal use, and it was not until the reign of James I that there was even occasional public access to the Royal Parks on public holidays, when fairs and booths were set up. Perhaps it was a desire to staunch this conspicuous enjoyment, perhaps the need for capital, that led Cromwell's Parliament to resolve, in 1652, 'that Hyde Park be sold for ready money'. The Park was bought by speculators who planned to build on it and, in the interim, charged the public for admission. John Evelyn, the diarist, was outraged that, on 11 April 1653, he 'went to take the air in Hyde Park where every coach was made to pay a shilling, and horse sixpence, by the sordid fellow who had purchased it of the State, as they called it'.

After the Restoration Charles II bought out the speculators and, having a somewhat personal interest in maintaining popularity, opened the Parks permanently. So committed was he to this gesture of magnanimity that he would take a morning swim, naked, in the new canal in St James's Park while his subjects promenaded past.

Access to common land, such as Hampstead Heath, Wimbledon Common and Blackheath, has also not been secured without problems. Notwithstanding its name, common land was owned privately by the local lord of the manor; on it the people had the right to graze their livestock, to gather firewood and to dig gravel. These rights are described in a seventeenth-century Act of Parliament relating to Hackney Common. The copyholders were able to 'lop and shred all such trees as grow before their houses ... upon the waste ground and the same convert to their own use, without any offence, so the said trees stand for the defence of their houses, yards or gardens; and also may dig gravel, sand, clay and loam, upon the said waste ground, to build or repair any of their copyhold tenements ... so always as every of the said copyholders do fill up so much as shall be digged by him or them'. As land values rose such rights over common land were whittled away, most particularly by the enclosures of the eighteenth and early nineteenth centuries. Over 7 million acres of public land were expropriated in England until the Metropolitan Commons Act put an end to such practices in 1866.

Although access to the Royal Parks had been established, it was not guaranteed, and, just in case people felt that they had any absolute right to be there, the Parks were set about with railings and gates. Lord Palmerston fought a long-running battle with the Chief Commissioner of Works, Lord John Manners, who was responsible for the Royal Parks in Parliament, asking 'when the noble Lord intended taking the people of the metropolis out of irons, so far as related to the parks' and when he would 'remove those abominable iron hurdles which now disfigured the parks, and prevented the people of the metropolis from the free enjoyment of them, although they were maintained at the public expense simply for the public recreation'. The railings are still there today in some parts of the Royal Parks, although there is no consistent policy, since Green Park and St James's Park can be entered at any time.

But access was only a beginning. There remained the question of what people were allowed to do in the parks. Was music permissible? The Archbishop of Canterbury thought not and, in 1856, put pressure on the Prime Minister until bands were forbidden in Kensington Gardens and Hyde Park on Sundays. Could people have the effrontery to eat there? Not if the Duke of Cambridge, Ranger of the central London Royal Parks, had his way. In 1883, confronted by this issue, he wrote a letter to the Queen's Private Secretary, Sir Henry Ponsonby, to protest that 'I have invariably, as Ranger, set my face against the erection of any places of Refreshment in the Royal Parks.'

If singing and drinking were suspect, it is hardly surprising that public meetings were not encouraged. One, in 1855, called to campaign against the high price of food, attracted 150,000 people. Sir Richard Mayne, the first Commissioner of Police, banned further meetings, but a Reform League Rally on 23 July 1866 challenged this decision. When confronted by 1,700 police guarding the locked gates of Hyde Park, the crowd ripped up the railings and entered. In court the League contested the police's action on the grounds that the park was public property, 'kept up and maintained out of the public purse'. In doing so it raised the whole question of who actually owned the lands and on what terms. The League's lawyer, Edmond Beales, argued, 'This park is either the property of the nation, as there are strong reasons for contending it is, under the transactions which have taken place between the people and the Crown, through Parliament respecting it; or it is still Crown property, though kept up and maintained out of the public purse. If the former be the fact, where is your authority for excluding the public from that property? If the latter be the case, then show me that you are acting under the express authority of the Crown, as claiming to be the exclusive owner of the Park.' Not surprisingly, he won and so established that the League and others could continue to meet in Hyde Park in order to listen to speeches, thus forming the origins of Speakers' Corner.

In spite of this the question of what controls and limitations the Crown puts on the use of the Royal Parks remains a live issue to this day. In 1990 the flying of kites in Kensington Gardens was banned, and although Royal Permission was given for the concert by Luciano Pavarotti in July 1991, remarkably few events of that kind have taken place over the past thirty years. It would seem that the terms on which the Royal Parks are public land are still conditional. Our ancestors struggled to achieve the quality of parks that we have today. It would be a tragedy if our complacency allowed them to decline, but the privatization of many of the services in the Royal Parks, such as the provision of deckchairs and other services, as proposed by the Government's recent Working Party, set up to consider the future of the Parks, may do just that.

If complacency, the pressure of traffic and general neglect are the main enemies of the public domain, what are the remedies? Before anything else we need to raise our expectations. Too many of us tolerate standards of interior design and urban design in the places where we work and in public buildings that we would never tolerate in our homes. Why accept the shabby condition of our hospitals when architect Richard Burton, with the help of more than two dozen artists, has shown in his new St Mary's Hospital in Newport, on the Isle of Wight, that hospitals can be both efficient and beautiful? Why put up with squalid bus and railway stations when the renovation of stations such as the Waterloo Tunnel Terminal and Reading, which Jane Priestland achieved in her period as British Rail's Director of Architecture and Design,[5] demonstrate that it is possible to have stations that express pride in public transport? Why endure the tawdriness of most London Underground platforms when the work of artists can transform an underground system, as it has in Stockholm?

If we have failed to set our sights high enough in London, other cities have been less timid. Birmingham has rebuilt its city centre, bringing together a new convention centre, Symphony Hall and the repertory theatre in a large, pedestrianized square, Centenary Square. To mark this achievement the council commissioned the artist Tess Jaray to design the pavements, light fittings and benches. Cardiff, Carlisle, Newcastle-on-Tyne, Wakefield, Ipswich, Plymouth and Winchester are among other British towns and cities to have created new pedestrian areas.

However, change need not be on a grand scale to be effective. We could begin by making more of what we have got. All over London are statues and friezes, mosaics and railings, stained glass and carved lettering, all bearing witness to the care devoted to the city over generations. As more local authorities develop public art policies, they could begin by identifying and highlighting the riches that are already all around them.

We should care for, and open up, the network of 'private' squares that is unique to London. That great lover of London, the Danish writer Steen Eiler Rasmussen, draws a distinction between the French or German Baroque square and the English square. The former 'was intended to be a monument for Absolutism and consequently must have a climax in some monument or other; it had to lead the eye to some public building, a castle, a church or whatever'. The English square 'was merely a place where many people of the same class had their homes'.[6]

From the first seventeenth-century London squares, Covent Garden and St James's, right through to those of the golden period between 1700 and 1850, when almost all the great squares were built, it was this motive, to make places 'where many people of the same class' could have homes, that led the aristocracy and the major landowners like the Grosvenors, the Bedfords, the Cadogans and the Portmans to develop their estates in the form of large squares. The shape of the squares may have changed over the years, but the twin motives of profit and privacy have remained constants.

The search for privacy meant that many squares were originally gated. Indeed, the Bedford estate did not remove its gates, which restricted access from both Euston Road and Oxford Street, until compelled to do so by Act of Parliament in 1893. Semi-private or public, these squares, of which there are more than 150 in London, are a precious part of the city's environment that must be preserved and enhanced; any neglect, of their trees or of their shape, would diminish London's character. But why should so many of them, like Belgrave, Chester, Eaton and Thurloe squares, remain locked? Local authorities should be encouraged to enter into negotiations with the owners – particularly those of locked squares that are on thoroughfares (Cadogan, Bedford) – to secure their opening to the general public. Think how much poorer London would be if squares such as Grosvenor, Berkeley, Hanover and Soho had remained private and locked.

We could make better use of the city's parks. We have a glorious variety of parks in London, ranging from the formal, picturesque elegance of Nash's and Repton's design for St James's Park (1828) to the splendours, both botanical and architectural, of Kew Gardens, the history of Greenwich, the open space of Richmond and the wildness of Hampstead Heath and Epping Forest, but their very variety and quality are making us complacent. In the past fifty years we have created only two major new parks, Haggerston and Burgess (the latter is far from being completed), and we give too little thought to what goes on in the parks we have. As a country we spend £450 million a year on maintaining civic parks and gardens, cutting grass and bedding plants but scarcely anything on the activities that go on within them.

We should certainly not forget that many people value parks precisely because they are places of quiet and peace. The Glass Inquiry undertaken for the GLC in 1969[7] found that 86 per cent of those questioned wanted simply to sit and to walk in parks, with 12 per cent wanting children's activities, 6 per cent sports and only 3 per cent arts and entertainments. This could be interpreted as the rejection of any active uses for parks – there is no doubt that they offer a unique respite from the stress and pressure of city life – or it may reflect the extent of people's expectations, since peace and quiet are all that is on offer in most places. When, by contrast, a park like Battersea offers a range of activities, the take-up is enormous. Fortunately, we do not have to make hard choices between active and passive uses for our parks, since good design can allow us to accommodate both, separating incompatible uses by time and by area. What is clear is that our parks are spaces that we could use for a far wider variety of events and activities, all of which would enhance the life of our cities.

We would be doing nothing very revolutionary, merely returning to a Victorian view of civic parks. When Sir James Pennethorne laid out Battersea and Victoria parks, and Joseph Paxton redesigned Kensington Gardens and created Birkenhead Park, Kelvingrove in Glasgow and the People's Park in Halifax, they rejected the eighteenth-century approach of trying to recreate for real the landscapes of Claude Lorrain and other artists as inappropriate for municipal urban parks. Paxton considered that these new parks should be primarily places of public activities, whether walks along paths between beds of flowers or sports such as cricket, bowls and archery. In that he was, consciously or not, returning to the days when Pepys recorded seeing races between 'running footmen' in Hyde Park, and Evelyn noted coach racing. In the days of the Commonwealth there had been hurling matches, with fifty Cornishmen a side, and prize-fighting took place in Hyde Park, as well as in the Pleasure Gardens, until the reign of George III.

Paxton's parks were instantly popular. Visiting Birkenhead in 1850 to seek ideas for the new Central Park that he was about to build in New York with Calvert de Vaux, Frederick Law Olmsted declared, 'All this magnificent pleasure-ground is entirely, un-reservedly and forever the people's own. The poorest British peasant is as free to enjoy it in all its parts as the British Queen.' So successful were Paxton's parks that their mix of formal paths, shrubs, bedding plants, open lawns and bandstands became effectively the template for all the new parks that sprang up during the rest of the century, although Olmsted, notwithstanding his praise for Birkenhead, was considerably more ambitious in designing Central Park, with its variety of levels and clever separation of traffic and pedestrians.

Since then new ideas in British park design have been so hard to detect that when George Lansbury, as First Commissioner of Works in the new Labour Government of 1929, approved a swimming lido on the Serpentine in Hyde Park, so that women and children, previously excluded, could at last have the opportunity to swim there, it stood out in this desert of ideas as an oasis of innovation.

Today, in London, Battersea is a model of a well-used and well-loved park, with numerous activities for all ages, its sports areas blazing under floodlights every night of the week. But generally more could be done. Birmingham, Oxford and Leicester all run summer arts festivals in their parks. Why does London have no equivalent of the Yorkshire Sculpture Park? The Arts Council's Serpentine Gallery actually encounters some resistance from the Royal Parks authorities when it places sculpture outside. There is the Open Air Theatre in Regent's Park, but we could be more ambitious. That is as true of education as it is of the arts. Some parks, such as Epping Forest, do have education officers and programmes, but as an educational resource and as wild-life habitats London's parks could be explored more positively. It is good that a new park is being established on a Site of Special Scientific Interest at Barn Elms, on the river between Barnes Common and Harrod's Depository, but existing parks could do more to develop specialist areas for flora and fauna. It is possible that what is needed is a London Parks Council, not as a heavy-handed bureaucracy to administer the parks but as an enabling body to coordinate initiatives, to promote the parks collectively, to provide information and to link up with existing health, sports, education and other bodies. However, there is also a case for larger actions.

When Prince Albert determined that the profits from the 1851 Great Exhibition should go towards creating a district for education and culture, an 83-acre site between Kensington Gardens and the Cromwell Road, he set in train a process that has given London an area unlike any other in Europe. The energy that set up the Great Exhibition was transferred to the new museums district, as was the imagination that inspired Paxton's monumental glass building in Hyde Park, covering 18 acres, and Albert's insistence on quality.

Sir Henry Cole, a member of the Great Exhibition Committee, was put in overall charge of the development, and he commissioned some of the best Victorian architects, led by Captain Francis Fowke. Before his early death Fowke himself built the Albert Hall (1867–71) and the quadrangle of the Victoria and Albert Museum (1856) and made the original drawings for the Natural History Museum, later recast and completed by Alfred Waterhouse (1873–81). Sir George Gilbert Scott designed the Albert Memorial, Norman Shaw the blocks of flats named Albert Hall Mansions (1879–81) and Albert Court (1890) and Thomas Calcutt the Imperial Institute (1887–93). A second wave of activity saw Aston Webb finish the Victoria and Albert Museum, with a new façade on the Cromwell Road (1899), and build the Royal School of Mines, while Sir Arthur Reginald Blomfield added the Royal School of Music (1889–94) and Sir Richard Allison the Science Museum (1913).[8] But the demolition of all of the Imperial Institute except Calcutt's tower, and the addition of a jumble of new buildings to house Imperial College, have negated the original sweep and scope of Albert's plan, which could and should be reasserted. One solution, as proposed by architect Philip Gumuchdjian, would be to move some Imperial College buildings, erect others and so create two major new piazzas that would restore the original axis of the whole site, running from the Albert Memorial to the Natural History Museum.

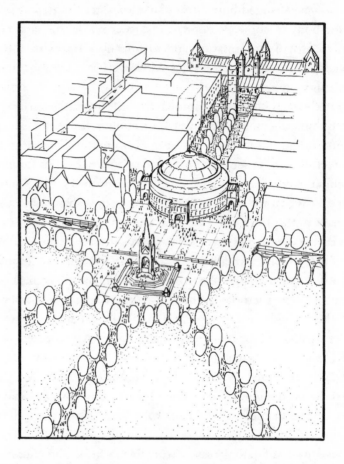

Although a plan like this would involve more reshaping than new building, it is ambitious and might be achievable only under an umbrella of initiatives to celebrate the millennium. However, there are many more immediate opportunities for improving London's public domain. Barcelona's programme of small actions could serve as a model, as could what Dundee has achieved in the Blackness district of that city. There work funded jointly by the Scottish

Development Agency, the Scottish Arts Council and the two local authorities has revitalized what was once a low-income, run-down area. The artists employed have worked closely with the community to ensure that any sculpture or mural becomes 'part of every-day surroundings rather than an expensive, jewel-like addition'.[9] Sixteen projects in the first three years, 1981–4, cost £90,000, which indicates what can be achieved, given thought and time. And in London Lewisham is setting an example that could be studied by other local authorities. Under a scheme called 'Lewisham 2000' a team of engineers, urban designers and landscape architects are working with the sculptor John Maine to reshape the town's centre.

Another area of London's public domain that should be developed is its network of canals, running through the north of the city for 54 miles. Like the Thames, these were once at the heart of London's economy but are now run-down and, in some cases, derelict. British Waterways, which is responsible for them, recognizes the opportunities they offer and the contribution they could make to the life of the city. There are several sites with considerable development potential, such as Paddington Basin, City Road Basin and Limehouse, and there are possibilities for extending and improving towpath walks and leisure activities on the canals themselves.

All these initiatives seek to bring new life to public spaces and to streets. It will not be enough to restrain or remove traffic. In many places, particularly shopping centres, there are attractions in animating street life. Why are the police and many local authorities so hostile to buskers? Most, if not all, of their music increases pleasure rather than diminishing it. In Covent Garden street performers are rightly popular, showing that public places can be improved not only by designers, architects and sculptors but also by the ephemeral and the transitory, whether that is represented by Free Form's hoardings on building sites or the performances of groups like Welfare State and Alternative Arts. Why do local authorities not give more support to restaurants and cafés that apply for glass pavement extensions in the winter? Why do not more local authorities adopt Stoke-on-Trent City Council's Green Street Scheme, through which private companies jointly finance the landscaping of streets?

There is no doubt that London's population has the necessary skills – whether among performers to enliven the streets, artists and designers to make better street furniture and street landscapes or architects to contribute better buildings. It is up to us to create the circumstances in which these talents can be put to good use. One-off initiatives can inspire and give a lead, but to improve the state of the public domain city-wide new policies and new thinking will be needed. We could profit by learning from abroad. On the Continent there is a word for the issues that affect the built environment, 'urbanism'. It incorporates a concern for urban design, not just in contributing to the appearance of the city but in doing what design does best, solving spatial problems. 'To me it's not decoration,' the Japanese landscape architect Isamu Noguchi has said. 'I despise decoration. It's the creating of space, not the cluttering of space.' Urbanism also involves a coordinated relationship between the elements (traffic, housing, land use) that determine the public domain. To implement it effectively demands planning and a concern for quality, both in major schemes and in such details as a coherent and efficient approach to public signs and to the lighting of streets and buildings.

Until about ten years ago few private buildings in London were floodlit at night. But improved lighting techniques have created new interest and new possibilities. Nicholas Grimshaw's *Financial Times* printing works has mercury vapour lighting, revealing the huge working presses as you drive past at night. The blue lighting of Richard Rogers's Lloyd's Building has been copied by others. But, inevitably, private buildings are lit at the whim of their owners, so that London at night is a random hotch-potch of darkness and light. The major public buildings offer an opportunity to create some coherence and order, but the Government offers no guidelines to Ministries or to public bodies. Some buildings are superbly lit, notably the Tate Gallery and Westminster Abbey; others, like Buckingham Palace, not at all. The absence of any coordination can be seen in Trafalgar Square. The portico of Gibbs' St Martin-in-the-Fields is beautifully lit from below, and Wilkins's National Gallery is flooded with a warm yellow light, but on one side South Africa House follows suit, while Canada House on the other is in darkness.

Going down Whitehall, the finest building, Inigo Jones's Banqueting Hall (1619) is unlit, as are the Cabinet Office, the Treasury and the Foreign and Commonwealth Office, but the Scottish and Welsh Offices blaze with light. In response to Parliamentary Questions the Minister responsible at the Department of the Environment, Sir George Young, was unable either to identify which government buildings were floodlit or to say how much such lighting costs. Central London at night is already a fine sight. Ministerial guidelines for the lighting of all government buildings would turn it into a real spectacle. We should give the capital that coherence.

Some government support and enthusiasm for public art and Percent for Art policies could also pay dividends. Over forty local authorities in Britain have formally adopted these policies, but, compared with their counterparts in the United States, where cities have been working in this area for twenty-five years, our councils are inexperienced. As they begin to appreciate the contribution that public art, at its best, can make, it is becoming clear that artists must work as closely as possible with communities and be involved with planners and architects at an early stage. The success of Richard Burton's St Mary's Hospital owes much to the fact that Burton was able to plan for, and work with, his chosen artists from the earliest stages of designing the building, so that they were making works for particular, pre-determined, locations within the hospital. Burton was no doubt assisted by having given much thought to the best ways of cooperating with artists, as an architect, while chairing the Arts Council's Steering Group on Percent for Art. Overall the major difficulty for local authority art and architecture departments is to gain the active cooperation of all other council committees, such as housing and education, so that opportunities for public art can be identified and grasped and, above all, have the support of the planning and finance committees. Without that, progress will be impossible.

Many of the opportunities for Percent for Art initiatives come from private-sector developments. These are vulnerable to the vagaries of the economy, but several leading developers are showing what can be achieved. Stuart Lipton and Stanhope plc at Broadgate and Olympia and York at Canary Wharf have paid particular attention to the quality of landscaping and of works of art and to the overall urban design of their developments. But even if developers and local authorities are showing greater interest in public art, their efforts will need to be supported by national policies and by central government's setting a good example in its allocation of the £3 billion it spends each year on new building and renovation.

Above all we need a clear policy to favour the pedestrian over the driver in the inner city, led by a variety of initiatives to plant trees, calm traffic, create play streets for children, close certain streets to traffic, limit access to some streets and areas and totally pedestrianize others. The presumption has to be in favour of reclaiming the city for people, so that they can walk in it, meet, talk, travel. Put together, such a programme would amount to a new urbanism, arising out of a liking for, and enjoyment of, the city and relying on the talents of artists, designers, engineers and architects to set high standards in the design of spaces and in the detail of street furniture.

All this will require investment. In almost every initiative there is potential for co-funding through planning gain, and it is clear that the private sector can, and will, contribute if central and local government give a lead. But, finally, if we want improvements in London's public spaces, we will have to pay.

We will be more than repaid if these policies make London a more enjoyable place by attending to its public spaces, all of them. For although it is the grand and the famous places that give London its international fame, it is the quality of streets and squares all over the city that most touches the lives of all its people. Unless we can improve those in Lambeth, in Hackney and in Barking, as well as in Chelsea or Fulham, we will not be changing London, merely gilding it.

London is one of the greenest cities in Europe, with several thousands of acres of public parks and squares offering everything from sport in Battersea Park (*above*) to a place for lunch in Russell Square (*below*).

London needs to pay
greater attention to
urban design in order to
transform public spaces
that, like Waterloo Bull-
ring (*above*), are bleak,
unwelcoming and, at
night, frightening.
Broadgate (*above, right*)
and Covent Garden
(*below, right*) show how
design and activities can
make spaces animated
and enjoyable.

London has a unique heritage of over 150 squares. Almost all of them began as private spaces, but many, like Covent Garden and Grosvenor, Berkeley, Russell (*above*) and Soho squares, have been opened to the public. From others, such as Bedford Square (*right*), the public remains barred.

London's reputation for great architecture has faltered somewhat in the twentieth century, with a few notable and welcome exceptions such as Alison and Peter Smithson's *Economist* building (1964) in St James's Street (*above, left*), Charles Holden's stations for London Underground, such as Arnos Grove (1932–3) (*below, left*) or W. Crabtree's Peter Jones department store (1936) in Sloane Streeet (*below*). As important as the buildings themselves are the spaces around them, and Cesar Pelli's tower in Canary Wharf (*above*) has been placed by North American developers Olympia and York in a setting that displays solid and serious attention to urban design.

The Conservative Government's reluctance to take architecture seriously has meant that London has relied on private companies to commission the few exciting and distinguished buildings that have been designed in recent years, such as Nicholas Grimshaw's *Financial Times* printing works in East India Road (*above*) and Ralph Erskine's Ark (1991) at Hammersmith (*below*).

CHAPTER SIX

Regenerating Communities

'Before the war my dad used to take me to Shoreditch Town Hall on Friday nights to the boxing. It was the grandest and most beautiful building you've ever seen. The brass on the handrails gleamed, the floors were all marble. It was something.' Those are the memories of Terry Edwards, the present chairman of the Hackney Federation of Tenants Associations.

Today Shoreditch officially no longer exists, having been absorbed, like Hoxton, into the borough of Hackney. The Town Hall is shabby, the brass begrimed, the marble covered by cracking lino, the panelling by plastic and veneer and the grain of the oak doors by a thick coat of civic paint. The condition of the building is not simply a matter of neglect or lost facilities; it is a symbol of lost pride. In remembering its glories Terry Edwards isn't indulging in sentimentality for the past; he is expressing a real anger about the present.

It is a feeling sharpened by the sight of the multi-million-pound offices of Broadgate and the City, a three-minute bus journey to the south. For all the good that such splendours bring to the people of Hoxton, Broadgate might as well be 300 miles away. This juxtaposition is a reminder that, no matter how some parts of London prosper or are renewed, the prosperity will profit us little unless it extends to all areas of the city. There is an echo of the words of Tom Paine: 'The contrast of affluence and wretchedness continuously meeting and offending the eye is like dead and living bodies chained together.'

The problems of Hoxton, as the poorest part of the poorest borough in London (Hackney), are acute, but there are areas like Hoxton in boroughs all over London – in Lewisham, Wandsworth, Brent, Haringey, Lambeth, Tower Hamlets, Newham, Southwark, Barking, Islington and Greenwich. Indeed, they exist in every major industrial city in Britain and in cities all over Europe.

These areas share a number of environmental and social problems: inadequate housing, poor amenities and services, low income, high unemployment, endemic racism, rising crime rates. Houses and flats are in need of repairs. Where local shops exist, they are often of below-average quality and charge above-average prices as supermarkets siphon off custom. The businesses that have survived are clinging on rather than expanding. Commercial and retail properties stand empty. There are high levels of vandalism and, often, drug abuse. It is hardly surprising that the morale and optimism of residents is low. Their circumstances are summed up by a London estate officer: 'There is poor delivery and poor information on repairs. The district heating is inadequate and expensive. The design of the estate is unsuitable. There is a high level of break-ins. Most tenants want to leave. It's an unstable community. Because of all the problems, it's hard to let to a balanced community. Rent arrears are very high. There are many social problems but lack of support from social services, a department even more beleaguered than housing.'

Differences do exist between these areas, particularly in the type and history of the housing. Some are estates built in the 1950s and 1960s, as governments and local councils replaced urban slums with concrete high-rise blocks of flats. Some are cottage estates, with lower densities of population and lower-rise properties but no less pressing problems. Some, like Hoxton, are older areas, containing some high-rise blocks of flats that have been added to existing terraced housing dating from the nineteenth century.

Whatever their housing make-up, all these areas have become, or are in danger of becoming, 'sick' estates into which only desperate or 'difficult' families are moved by many local authorities. They are sliding down a spiral of decline that leads either to apathy and misery or, occasionally, to anger and riot.

It is a process that is both wrong and self-defeating. As Professor David Donnison said in his evidence to the Archbishop of Canterbury's Commission on Urban Priority Estates in 1985, 'We make things worse by placing some of the most vulnerable people in some of the most expensive environments created by progress ... Then they call these neighbourhoods not "hard to live in" but "hard to let" or even "problem estates" – as if their difficulties were somehow the fault of the tenants.'[2]

The reasons why the problems of persistently poor housing and high-crime areas intensify is a matter for debate. Different experts give different emphases. Oscar Newman has explained the relationship between social and physical factors in terms of the type and size of family and the type of housing.[3] This concept of 'defensible space' links crime and loss of community with other factors such as security arrangements and relationships with neighbours. Newman includes in this diverse package problems that arise out of the design of estates, but others, like Alice Coleman, have identified design as the major contributor to the undermining of a sense of security and privacy among tenants.[4] Coleman's is a view that has been widely criticized for the weight it gives to design and other physical factors rather than to social and economic problems[5] such as poverty, unemployment, illiteracy and, in many inner-city areas, including Hoxton, racial prejudice and intolerance.[6]

What is certain is that there can be no new London unless these areas are renewed. If strategic plans for reviving the city are not relevant to such estates, they will have failed. We can transform the Thames, clean up London's streets, embark on a generation of great architecture, even reshape London's transport system, but unless we tackle the poverty and neglect of districts like Hoxton we will not only undermine our achievements but may actually intensify the problems, as the gap between rich and poor widens and people living in such areas see that they have been further marginalized and ignored.

The scale of the task is daunting. In London 253,000 homes were classified 'unfit' in a 1990 Department of the Environment survey.[7] Unemployment levels reach 20 per cent[8] in boroughs such as Hackney, though unemployment on particular estates can be double that, and 654,900 people in the capital are on income support.[9] Crime levels are three times higher than those in better-off areas.[10]

As these problems have intensified over the last ten years, the Government has tried various approaches, but, particularly under the Thatcher administration, there was a tendency to ignore them and to hope that they either could be contained by tighter policing or would eventually go away if swept out of sight under the political carpet. How this would happen, or how restricting the finances of local authorities would help, was never made clear.

The Government put its faith in the process of 'trickle-down'. This presumes that major investment, almost invariably by the private sector, as in the new enterprise zones such as Docklands, will trickle down to those who live in adjoining, poorer areas. In practice there is little evidence that 'trickle-down' works except to create a relatively small number of cleaning, catering and other semi-skilled and unskilled jobs. There is a fundamental mismatch between the requirements of companies in places like Docklands, whether for individual employees or for service companies, and what neighbouring areas can supply.

In 1991 the Government introduced a new element, competition. The Department of the Environment's City Estate Action Programme offered capital investment to problem estates, for which they would have to compete with each other. The sum provided by the Government was finite and was reallocated from existing departmental budgets rather than being 'new money'. As a result, no matter how great the needs or how good and creative the proposals, only some were successful. The scheme was open to bids from all over the country, and in the event only thirty-five estates in London received help, although 106 applied.[11] The Government's intention may have been to stimulate the ideas and inventiveness of housing authorities, but to require estates with enormous problems to enter such a beauty competition in order to catch the Secretary of State's eyes and gain his favour is no way to address their difficulties. What is needed is not gimmicks or the recycling of money but a coherent strategy, which should have three basic elements.

First, what is needed is increased investment, by both central and local government, in infrastructure, particularly housing, transport, education and training. Second, there must be an emphasis on quality rather than cheapness if, for example, the present housing-maintenance problems are not going to be repeated in the future. Estates such as these do not need less investment and less attention to quality than those in better-off areas – they need more. We should bear in mind the words of Alfred Doolittle in Shaw's *Pygmalion*: 'If there's anything going and I put in for a bit of it, it's always the same story: "You're undeserving; so you can't have it." But my needs is as great as the most deserving widow that's ever got money out of six different charities in one week for the death of the same husband. I don't need less than a deserving man: I need more.'[12] Third, and most important of all, the strategy must provide opportunities for people living on these estates to help themselves and manage their own futures. The Priority Estates Project, introduced as a pilot scheme in 1979, has had some success in this respect, but it is clear from Anne Power's analysis[13] that decentralization and tenant involvement are not necessarily cheap options or cure-alls. They may well save money on centralized bureaucracies, but they need proper funding, training, premises and facilities, if their potential is to be realized fully. Overall any successful strategy must involve a revolution in the way that not only local residents but all experts (politicians, planners, social workers, architects) approach such areas.

To see the scale of the problems and the difficulties in the way of solutions, we looked in greater detail at Hoxton, invited to do so by Brian Anson, director of the Hoxton Trust until 1991 and a community architect and planner of great experience. The existence of a young and enthusiastic team of officers in the planning department of the local authority was an encouragement, as was the acquaintance with the area that Richard Rogers had established when working briefly on plans for a new community college on the Shoreditch Secondary School site in 1988. But the scale and intensity of the problems facing the area were alarming.

The facts about Hoxton are not hard to establish. They stare at you from the street. There is a high proportion of elderly infirm and of single parents and their children. One in five households contains only pensioners. Incomes are low; unemployment is high; health standards are poor, with a high incidence of arthritis, skin complaints, lumbago and senile dementia. In winter heating is a major problem. Heating systems, where they exist, are old. Disconnections for non-payment are above average and have risen since the local Electricity Board closed its showroom in Hoxton Street in 1987 and moved to a shopping centre in the north of the borough. The elderly suffer from damp-related illnesses and, in cold winters, from hypothermia.

The area itself is a strange mixture, parts of it having hardly changed since the nineteenth century. Hoxton Square is at first glance an elegant London square shaded by mature plane trees in the middle, with wrought-iron railings and a merciful lack of parked cars. A second glance explains the parking spaces. Most of the buildings are empty, and those that are occupied are run down. A few businesses cling on. Others have gone bankrupt or have moved elsewhere. Hoxton also contains several large housing estates, including the Arden Estate, dating from the 1950s. Tying the various parts together is Hoxton Street, which runs north–south and is the location for Hoxton Market, a street market that has slowly reduced the number of days on which it operates.

The condition of the area comes into focus when you listen to people who live there. 'We've been bombed out of Hoxton.' 'People don't feel things can change.' 'For two pins I'd move out. I never thought I'd say that.' 'I'm frightened for my children, even during the daytime. Frightened to send my ten-year-old across to the shop. Myself, I take the dog when I go to the park.' 'People don't talk to each other any more.' These are the voices of Hoxton people, two mothers, a pensioner, a housing officer, a social worker. A resident who has come from St Lucia is baffled to observe, 'There simply aren't many people on the streets.'[14]

There are few basic amenities. Hoxton has had no police station since the one in Old Street closed; there is no secondary school; and there has been no local hospital since all major departments were shut at St Leonard's on Hoxton Street. Groups of youths hang about the estate at night. One resident sympathized with their predicament: 'There is little in the area for them, so they are attracted to the pubs. They need a place of their own, a shed, a hut, a small plot of land. In fact, the estate has plenty of unused huts and garages, but they need to be converted into basic community spaces or even workshops for small businesses.' Young mothers complain that, of the three children's playgrounds that used to exist, one is locked up, one is closed and the survivor has just one swing and a climbing frame. No wonder people feel that, in addition to all the normal problems of the inner city, such as drugs, racial prejudice, police harassment and eviction, the heart is being pulled out of Hoxton.

Compared with some areas, Hoxton has not been significantly vandalized. However, a study of the Arden Estate, conducted in 1987 by a group of architects including Brian Anson, Geoff Hague and Chris Billson (Robin Moors, Allmott and Partners), revealed that residents were frightened and dissatisfied.[15] As one said, 'Imagine, you look out and see a stranger looking right in … they do things outside your bedroom window,' while a young woman recalled, 'The man put a knife to my throat in the lift. But he did nothing … I was terrified.' There are some parts of the estate, such as the Osric Way short-cut from Hoxton Street to Pitfield Street, that have become no-go areas for many people after dark.

The result is a cycle of neglect. Unlit streets, incidents such as those described above and groups of teenage lads loitering on corners have made people nervous and apprehensive. This has encouraged residents to stay indoors in the 'safe' environment of their homes. It is this withdrawal from the public parts of the estate that has made streets and paths further neglected and 'hostile' and left them as the territory of those pushing drugs, or sleeping rough, or drinking, thus confirming people's feeling that the public areas of the estate do not belong to them. The idea that such public areas should be positive and enjoyable elements in local life has been lost. The community has ceased to use these areas, and, having no space to share, has ceased to operate fully as a community. In the words of

Jane Jacobs, the Arden Estate has ceased to have 'community eyes'.[16]
It is no surprise that people's expectations that things can change are
low. 'There have been so many promises, and nothing has happened' was one comment.

However, in some respects Hoxton is more fortunate than newer
areas consisting of large estates. There are some fine nineteenth-
century streets and buildings, notably a magnificent church, St
John's. Buttesland Street has a late Georgian elegance. Aske Square
and gardens front the classical façade of Aske College, and there is a
solid red-brick Victorian public library, the Passmore Edwards. The
district has a rich history going back to medieval times, when
Hoxton was the market garden for the city. James Burbage built
London's first theatre here in 1576, and it is said that early plays of
Shakespeare were performed there. More recently it has been a
major area for music hall and vaudeville, Marie Lloyd making the
Empire her local. Other districts would be envious of such riches.
Several of the post-war estates, like Hobbs Lane and Royal Oak,
opened by Nye Bevan, are solid blocks in good open spaces with
grass and trees. Nevertheless residents feel angry and frustrated. In
trying to identify a way forward it may be useful to look at what
other comparable areas have achieved.

Further to the north-east, in Hackney, the Lea View Estate presented a gloomy prospect in 1980. Built in 1939 as one of two
blocks, each with 300 flats containing modern kitchens and all mod.
cons. and sharing a community hall, tennis courts, a bowling green,
porters and a resident caretaker, Lea View was described as 'Heaven
in Hackney' and, by architectural historian Nikolaus Pevsner, as
'uncommonly well designed'. But over the years the bowling green
was concreted over, porters and caretakers were not replaced and
the estate declined until, in 1980, the tenants demanded action.
Architects Hunt Thompson were appointed, but when the residents
of Lea View were informed that further Government cuts meant
that they could not be rehoused during renovations, they protested
and insisted on a proper say in the development. Hunt Thompson
opened a site office, initiated a series of meetings and redesigned
their plans in the light of residents' comments.

Rod Hackney describes the improvements in his book *The Good, the Bad and the Ugly*.[17] The building was 'completely restructured internally, making ground-level "houses" with gardens and front doors facing on to surrounding streets. Internal staircases were … wallpapered and carpeted, elderly tenants (were) housed in sheltered accommodation, some flats were … designed specifically for the disabled, and everyone could choose how their place would be decorated. Externally the courtyard was … landscaped, lift towers … built with decorative brickwork, there (were) pitched roofs, and all windows were … replaced.' As an exercise in community involvement it was a huge success. Whereas before the work 90 per cent of Lea View tenants wanted to move out, after renovation 'Every single person said they were very happy.'[18]

The regeneration of Broadwater Farm in Tottenham presented more complex problems, which long pre-dated the riot of 1985. Some of these problems had their roots in the original design of the estate. It was sited directly over the course of the River Mosell, and the state of the surrounding marshy land, always prone to flooding, led the architects to decide that the twelve blocks should be built on stilts. The life of the estate was intended to be led on the first-storey walkways that linked the blocks, and the street level was abandoned to car parking under each block, without even the addition of pavements. It was literally an estate fit for cars to park in, although few of the tenants actually owned them. To compound these problems there was no community hall, no social centre, no pub, no youth club, no playgroup, no sports facilities, no surgery for a dentist or a doctor. It was a community as short on amenities as it was flush with parking.

Structural faults appeared quickly, along with the seeping water and the cockroaches. The waiting list for repairs lengthened. The lifts didn't work; security was poor; burglary and vandalism were rife. Broadwater Farm became the subject of a Department of the Environment report on 'difficult to let' estates, which concluded, 'At best the local authority can hope to make it tolerable for the next decade or so, but eventually, because the estate is so monolithic and comprises such a large proportion of their housing, the possibility of demolition is one that will have to be considered.'[19] The experts in the Ministry had moved from praising it to considering its demolition within the space of five years.

The causes of Broadwater Farm's decline are a complex mixture of physical, social and economic problems. Having been badly planned, badly designed and badly built, it was provided with few community amenities and had allocated to it a large number of tenants with social problems. Chief among these were poverty and unemployment. Experts and residents disagreed about which of these factors was most significant and about the solutions. Some wanted better security arrangements, with stronger locks on front doors; others wanted a higher police profile on the estate. Almost everyone wanted more community facilities. Whatever the differences, there was a consensus that something had to be done and that only residents on the estate could provide the organization that was necessary. The result was the foundation of the Broadwater Farm Youth Association (BWFYA) in 1981.

While unemployment in London generally was 10.8 per cent, in Haringey it was 18.2 per cent,[20] and of the young people on Broadwater Farm 43 per cent were without work.[21] In founding the BWFYA the residents of the estate had begun not only to address the needs of bored and unemployed young people but also to tackle the estate's problems from within. The BWFYA formed a co-operative limited company (the Co-op) 'to promote economic activities and to create employment for local residents'.[22] They also formed the Broadwater Farm Panel to act as a forum at which residents could 'express their interests, concerns and demands'. In July 1986 they conducted a survey that identified security, estate appearance, internal improvements, building maintenance and new facilities as the priorities, in that order. The survey was 'part of a wider effort implemented by the community to get tenants involved in the decision-making process with regard to the management of our estate'.[23]

With money from the Government's City Estate Action Programme the Co-op launched a series of projects: the Remembrance Garden, the Nations' Square, better lighting and murals by local artists. One principle behind these Co-op schemes was that, whenever possible, the work should be done by people living on the estate, so that the community was involved, benefiting itself and increasing its skills and so that the income earned stayed on the estate. The council had set up a Building Design Service team in an office on the estate, and, working with the Co-op and the Panel, the team of architects developed a strategic action plan. Its main aims were to sort out the flow of vehicles, diverting through traffic around the perimeter of the estate and creating pavements; to add further gardens, starting with Time Garden in 1991, and generally to green the environment; and to renovate the high-rise blocks, installing a concierge system with controlled entry. Meanwhile work was proceeding, with the aid of a £2.5 million grant from the local authority and the Government, on a community centre and twenty-one Community Enterprise Workshops, built by the Co-op and sited under the walkways.

This brief catalogue of achievements would be misleading if it gave the impression that Broadwater Farm is now without problems. The money to complete the Building Design Service action plan is by no means secure. The community centre will open with no staff and without any revenue finance, all of which will have to be self-generated. Unemployment remains high and incomes low. The estate is still desperately short of facilities, and most of the existing shops have gone out of business. The Co-op and the Panel depend on the active involvement of an inner core of twenty or thirty activists and 100 semi-activists out of an estate population of over 3,000. The estate remains on stilts.

Despite all this, the experience of Broadwater Farm demonstrates that estates with major problems can turn themselves around. Design, for ill and also for good, is a factor. Investment is essential, as is an estate-based office to organize improvements, caretaking and repairs. But above all the lesson of Broadwater Farm is that the community has to be consulted, involved and, finally, persuaded to participate in the regeneration of its estate. The same message has come out of the Priority Estate Project schemes around the country. As the Archbishop of Canterbury's report, *Faith in the City*, says, 'How property is managed, as well as its physical condition, is important, for it affects how people make decisions. To believe that you have no control over one of the most basic areas of your life is to feel devalued.'[24]

Involvement and participation are fine aspirations, but they are not easy to achieve. However, the decline in the morale of tenants and the decay of housing stock demonstrate that changes are needed. Among many authorities neglect of the environment is growing. Rent arrears are rising. Housing estates are, in Anne Power's phrase, 'running to stand still'.[25] It is no wonder that people are unhappy. Indeed, many in London hate the conditions in which they are required to live.

Involvement and the self-management of estates present substantial challenges both to local authority housing staff and to residents. Residents are unlikely to underestimate the problems that arise once they become involved in making decisions for the future, particularly when such decisions necessitate hard choices and differences of opinion with neighbours. For this reason they are often nervous of taking over responsibility from local authorities. Similarly those authorities cannot view tenant initiatives as relieving them of responsibility. Their intervention remains essential to many parts of an estate's life, such as combating vandalism and crime, providing children's play facilities and enforcing basic standards.

As Broadwater Farm shows, decentralization is one of the keys. Estate-based offices can lead to improvements in the relationship between tenants and council. Housing officers gain a greater understanding of the community they serve and become more involved. In the words of one London officer, decentralization can 'expose officers to the public, make them accountable to tenants, and give them an idea of tenants' priorities'.[26] Assessing one such estate office, a Hackney official said, 'I think tenants actually now believe that results are obtainable simply because pressure can be applied locally, whereas in the past it was very difficult for them to affect decision-making.'[27]

However, as a London Director of Housing warned, 'There are no automatic advantages to local housing management. More is required – localization must be comprehensive, well managed and allow decision-making on the front line.'[28] Cuts in budgets, frozen posts and the turnover of staff can all threaten the success of such initiatives. Where local offices can help particularly is in improving the position over lettings and repairs. London has a poor record on the speed of lettings. The Audit Commission's 1986 survey showed that, on average, London local authorities took nineteen weeks to allocate homes, compared with the Audit Commission's suggested good-practice benchmark of six weeks in London, three weeks outside London. But speed, though important, is not everything. Lettings policies have a wider impact on communities.[29] Local lettings schemes must operate as part of wider policies to avoid problems of discrimination, but they can also be buffers against a council that operates a policy, however covertly, of 'dumping' difficult tenants on the least popular estates and so creating unmanageable ghettos.[30]

Giving responsibility for repairs and maintenance to local estate-based offices is essential. Indeed, one London housing manager said, 'Unless there are estate-based [local] repairs, and control of caretaking, it is not worth having a local office.'[31] Equally, in order to make rational decisions, those offices should have control of their own budgets.

The final area for increased involvement of tenants is in the security of estates. Apart from making representations through Police Consultative Committees, there is little that residents can do to influence the number of police on the beat, but, as Broadwater Farm shows, changes in the design of entry systems and the introduction of resident caretakers can improve tenants' sense of security.

Any decentralization initiative should involve full consultation and dialogue, so that trust can be established both among the community and among council officers and elected members. Tenants' associations and forums can play a part, but progress towards complex and complete forms of self-management, such as estates management boards, with powers delegated by the local authority, is unlikely to be fast. Above all councils, and the Government, must accept that such developments would need proper resources, in the form of training and basic facilities for tenants' groups, such as an office, a phone, access to a photocopier, a budget for newsletters and visits to other estates. In Sheffield and Glasgow, these expenses are paid for by a tenants' levy, but paid for they have got to be.[32]

Even when all these conditions are met, there must remain questions about whether self-management is a viable option on estates or blocks with above-average problems, such as the Sara Lane flats in Hoxton. Sara Lane was built in the early 1960s and is, in the opinion of Brian Anson, who has worked in Belfast, 'almost as bad as the infamous Divis flats, commonly regarded as the worst housing in Europe'. Those windows that aren't broken or boarded up have unpainted frames that are falling to pieces. Below the flats is a two-storey car park, which, until part of it was recently converted into a lock-up storage business, was a tip for old mattresses, furniture and rubbish and a centre for the selling of drugs. On its flat roof what had been intended as a community area is derelict, the remnants of concrete plant pots filled with muck, the wooden benches smashed, puddles on the ground. But it isn't until you go inside and climb the staircases, filthy with litter, excrement and used condoms, that the misery of living there really hits you. The corridors on each floor have no windows and no natural light. Their length of painted concrete is broken at intervals only by three steps and a metal rail that lead up to the front door of each flat. The doors have no handle, no knocker, no letter-box, only a keyhole and a number. The more cautious tenants have made their doors secure with metal grilles and bolts. A landing in a prison would be as welcoming. Who can have designed a place so lacking in humanity? Who could call this home?

It's not surprising that the residents hate it. 'It's not a home, it's a cell.' 'It stinks.' 'I've been waiting for repairs to my sink for weeks.' 'Kids come and piss in the lifts. I'd rather use the stairs, shitty though they are.' 'They [the council] just think we're vermin.' 'We had no water on four occasions over Christmas last year.'

Sara Lane demands major rehabilitation, gutting and redesign. Daylight should be brought into each corridor by eliminating one of the central flats. There must be an extensive programme of repair, which should include new window frames and the landscaping of the flat roof. As at Lea View, the tenants should be fully involved in the changes, but if processes like self-management are introduced before the renovations are completed, tenants will be handed liabilities rather than assets.

Studies by Anne Power and others demonstrate that even the most difficult estates can revive themselves[33] – but not without investment. While central government artificially constrains local authorities' expenditure and refuses to allow them even to spend their own capital receipts, let alone attempt to borrow money in the market like any other landlord, we will make little progress. We need a long and sustained period of investment in inner-city housing by a partnership of local authorities, housing associations and the private sector, not simply to house the homeless but also to renovate the 253,000 homes that were declared 'unfit' in 1990.[34] That partnership will have to be financed in part through increased government investment in housing associations through the Housing Corporation, in part by a National Housing Bank, which could lend money to council housing departments, and in part by an unfreezing of local authorities' capital receipts, although this last will have to be progressive and gradual if it is not to lead to a sudden distortion of prices. Private landlords will have to be encouraged back into the market, as will private developers, so long as they earmark a percentage of their schemes for rent as well as for sale.

Important though housing is, the regeneration of the Hoxtons of London must be led by improvements in the local economy and in employment. Unless jobs and an increase in levels of income come to an area, recovery will be impossible. This will depend to some extent on the general state of the national economy, but there is much that central government can do to open up the potential of the poorer areas of London. Government investment in the city's infrastructure, particularly transport, is one of the keys to attracting corporate finance into parts of the city that at present have no such investment. Moreover, it is a more effective use of taxpayer's money than is forgoing tax in the form of fiscal incentives in enterprise zones, which concentrates new economic growth rather than spreading it throughout the capital.

In the same way that new transport links, like the extended

Jubilee Line and the Channel Tunnel rail terminus at Stratford, will create huge opportunities for the east of London, so the extension of the east London Underground line would bring jobs to Hoxton if it were pushed north from Broadgate and the City, along Kingsland Road, the eastern edge of Hoxton, and up to Dalston.

To make certain of deriving the full benefits from such government investment, there needs to be synchronization with local development strategies. Already Hoxton's closeness to the city offers the council and residents the prospects of both income and capital in the form of land development. At best this could bring Hoxton, through capital receipts and planning gain, the amenities and regeneration the community needs, particularly since the community, through the council, owns so much of the land. But, conversely, it could flood the area with offices and gentrified housing, forcing land values up and local people out.

To prevent that sort of impact development policies need to identify a range of opportunities for investment both by the local authority and by the private sector. Hoxton is not short of such sites. Apart from the 7 acres of the former Shoreditch Secondary School and a 3-acre site around Hoxton Square, bordering on Old Street and the City, there is, at the top end of Hoxton Street, St Leonard's Hospital – or what used to be the hospital before it was closed. People resent the loss of those services and the fact that they now have to travel for medical attention. In spite of the site's potential development value to the health authority, which owns the hospital, the Authority displays no sense of urgency, no coherent ideas about its future use, and there is no indication even whether it would be a willing partner in any Hoxton-wide strategy. The site is a key one, bounded by Hoxton Street to the west, Sara Lane to the south, Kingsland Road to the east and a large housing estate on the other side of Nuttall Street, the hospital's northern edge. A hostile or thoughtless development could do as much damage as a constructive one could do good. All over London health authorities own comparable, unused, sites, which they must be encouraged to develop, either by incentives or by penalties.

Throughout the capital similar sites and similar possibilities exist, waiting to be developed. But development alone will not provide the answer. We need a wide range of initiatives, social and cultural as well as economic: local health centres and chemists within easy reach; child-care facilities and adult education classes; public libraries, with books in reasonable condition, and access to information services; community and leisure centres; Citizens' Advice Bureaux; local markets, pubs and parks. It is these places and opportunities that bring city districts to life by satisfying people's everyday needs and wants. To establish just what those needs are we have to ensure that people are not just consulted but able to play an active part. Regeneration should not – indeed, cannot – be a gift from government. It must be an act of self-assertion by the whole community.

After Mrs Thatcher won the 1987 General Election she declared war on inner-city problems as her overriding priority. Five years on it is a war that we are far from winning. The problems of poverty continue to exist, and the powerlessness and despair that people feel grow greater every year.

Hoxton and places like it have every reason to believe that they are ignored and that until the experts, whether in government or in the professions, are, in Brian Anson's words, 'suitably shocked' by such areas, nothing is going to change. It matters little whether a change of attitude is the product of self-interest, which led to the great nineteenth-century reforms and investment in infrastructure, or comes about because London recognizes at last that the continued existence of blocks like Sara Lane is an affront to any society that claims to be civilized. Either way, now is the time to start planning for recovery and re-establishing confidence in local people that things can change, as Barcelona did in the early 1980s. People want to take the same pride in their local community as the young Terry Edwards took in Shoreditch Town Hall: 'It was the grandest and most beautiful building you've ever seen ... It was something.' Unless we can give people the opportunities and resources to re-capture that pride we will have failed London, not renewed it.

PART THREE

Ways Forward

CHAPTER SEVEN

Planning Changes

One hundred and thirty-four acres of derelict land and marshalling yards at King's Cross present a crucial challenge to London's planning system. It is a development that could greatly enhance the city or blight it. Just as cities all over Europe are finding that their docks are redundant, so too are they recognizing the potential of alternative and additional uses for some of their central railway stations. In Paris the Gare d'Orsay has been converted into an art museum. The land around Barcelona's old Vilanova Station, or Estació del Nord, has been transformed into a park in the Plaça de les Glòries that will be the setting for the new National Theatre of Catalonia and a concert hall. By contrast, the plans for King's Cross have become paralysed, a special preliminary Act of Parliament being required before British Rail's part of the development could even begin.

The potential of this site is enormous, not just for reconstructing the surrounding area but for the whole of London. To its immediate community it could offer jobs, a new park, the renovation of this stretch of the Regent's Canal, new housing and, above all, hope. To London it could offer an example of how to employ the thousands of acres of unused or under-used land that make up part of the legacy left to the capital by its nineteenth-century railway network. In doing this it could signal a new attitude towards the recovery and design of public space in London. Is there the political will to grasp this opportunity? Can our planning system cope?

The history of the site gathers together much of London's industrial past. Beside the vast complex of railway lines from the Midlands, the east coast, the suburbs and London's Underground network is the Regent's Canal, whose freight role these lines largely usurped. A former gas works, a granary, a potato market, a smallpox hospital and a burial ground for infected horses complete the site. By these last, and by coke residue, the land has been severely contaminated.

On it are a number of historic buildings of great value – the granary by Cubitt, Grunling's German Gymnasium, Gilbert Scott's St Pancras Hotel, Barlow's King's Cross and some amazing train sheds and gas holders. Around the site lives an embattled community with low incomes, few jobs and poor housing, in an environment described by the architects Foster Associates, in their masterplan submission, as 'inadequate and brutalizing'.[1]

No one disputes the importance and potential of the site, which brings together this community, the local authority (Camden), the developers (the London Regeneration Consortium – LRC) and a panoply of national bodies, including English Heritage, the Royal Fine Art Commission and the Victorian Society. All have different interests and objectives, forcefully held and often mutually exclusive.

The community groups want more social housing, more jobs and fewer offices. The developers wish to press on with a £6 billion scheme that will, they believe, provide £171 million of planning gain in new facilities to the local community and 25,000 jobs, of which at least one quarter will go to local residents.[2] LRC maintains that the new 34-acre park, one of the few to be created in London since the war, will be a major local resource. The community believes that public access to it and to the canal development will be restricted. Camden is torn between the desire to respond to the community it represents and the need for development. The architects are convinced that they are setting new standards in urban design.

Can these interests and viewpoints be reconciled? Can our planning system take into account social and commercial ambitions, the pressures on the environment, the desire to conserve our heritage and to create our future, the wishes of local people and the needs of London and of Britain? After four years of surveys, discussions, meetings, legislation, negotiation and adaptation, the scheme still hangs in the balance. It is a crazy situation, benefiting nobody, frustrating everybody and in sharp contrast to the speed of Barcelona's development of the Olympic Village. What this unhappy saga illustrates is the total inability of our planning system to determine applications within a reasonable amount of time. That is not simply a matter of regret. Almost every idea for regenerating London needs, rightly, to pass through the planning system, to be scrutinized and to gain approval. If that planning system is deficient or ineffective, then London's future is shackled, no matter how good the proposals or how strong the will to improve the city's environment.

There is little dispute that, at present, Britain's planning system is ineffectual. It does not reconcile conflicting interests, and it is cripplingly slow. Decisions can take months, sometimes years, leading to both frustration and expense. Developers' capital, which in central London can run to tens, even hundreds, of millions of pounds, is tied up, generating nothing except bank interest charges. Any gains from the proposed development in terms of jobs, services, facilities or economic activity, are frozen. The local authority loses income from the business rates on the new buildings. When land lies idle or is poorly used everyone pays a high price.

Our planning system is failing to deliver. In London the effects of this are particularly severe because, in addition to the general faults of the system, there exists no city-wide strategy within which to assess the significance of any scheme, nor adequate mechanisms by which to forge consensus. Each planning battle is fought afresh and in isolation. It is easy enough to blame the lack of a strategic local authority to take responsibility for the shambles and to draw up an agreed strategy for the city, but these real defects, which are inhibiting London's future, shroud a basic confusion about what planning is and what it can achieve.

'For most people in our country, planning has two functions,' writes John Delafons, a former senior civil servant at the Department of the Environment, in a report arising out of his period as a Nuffield and Leverhulme Travelling Fellow (1989–90). 'One is to decide where development should or should not take place; and the other is to control its design or appearance.'[3] Both involve recognizing the interests of at least three sets of people – those who live on or use the site, those who own the land and the architect, who is expected to design a building and an environment that fulfil everyone's expectations and are both beautiful and economically viable. Decisions concerning 'where development should or should not take place' – that is, those connected with land use – operate on two levels: macro-decisions about the shape of a city, its transport, infrastructure, population, economic development, and micro-decisions about specific applications for individual buildings or groups of buildings. Although related, the two raise separate difficulties.

'Every city must have a vision and a dream,' maintained David Mackay in an Arts Council lecture at the Tate Gallery in 1991,[4] and it is that wide sense of London's future that ought to run through the planning debate. What sort of city do we want? We have a choice, either to set about creating a strategic plan or to continue with the existing *laissez-faire* approach. The advocates of *laissez-faire* deny that such strategic planning is possible for a city as vast and complex as London. Many believe that it is not desirable. These people question the usefulness of any structure plans, and their influence on government can be seen in the Department of the Environment's *The Future of Development Plans* (1986) and in the move to abolish such plans. In the case of London they support their argument by pointing to the city's history, which, as Edward James and Christopher Woodward note in the introduction to their book *A Guide to the Architecture of London*,[5] 'has always resisted a systematic reconstruction (unlike, say, Haussmann's Paris or Cerdà's Barcelona) ... London is notable for its looseness of structure.' With regard to street planning they have a good case. Much of London's charm and character derives from the haphazard way in which it has evolved, but it is somewhat misleading to claim that London was entirely unplanned. Although the city lacks either a formal grid pattern, such as Daniel Burnham's for Chicago and Cerdà's for Barcelona, or a unifying planning concept, like Haussmann's Paris, large areas *were* planned, notably the great estates owned by the Grosvenors, the Bedfords and the Portmans. There is indeed a 'looseness of structure', in that these planned estates are not united by a coherent framework, but such arguments miss the central point that the problems currently facing London and other cities today are not primarily those of street structures. They concern transport and pollution, rising energy consumption and declining industry, population density and balance, poverty and homelessness.

Problems of this complexity demand strategic planning within which they can be addressed, as has been acknowledged throughout this century in the writings of Patrick Geddes and Lewis Mumford, in the work of Daniel Burnham in Chicago and of Herbert Baker and Edwin Lutyens in New Delhi or in the eight regional plans that Thomas Adams drew up in the 1920s and 1930s for the areas around London. That a wider and more fundamental approach is necessary is confirmed in the opening paragraph of the European Commission's *Green Paper on the Urban Environment*,[6] which reviews the future of all European cities. 'This means addressing not just the proximate causes of environmental degradation, but examining the social and economic choices which are at the root of the problem.' The paper goes on to warn, 'Treating each of the factors threatening the city environment in isolation leads to short-term solutions – mere palliatives or simply delaying action.'

The most recent attempt at a strategic view of London was the 1984 Greater London Development Plan, which updated the 1976 document. By the time this was drawn up Mrs Thatcher's Government had determined to abolish the Greater London Council and had already passed the London Regional Transport Act (1984), which removed responsibility for the city's transport system from the GLC and passed it to central government. Lacking control over transport and over the financial heart of the capital, the City of London, the document was severely weakened even before the prospect of the GLC's abolition turned it into little more than a despairing parting gesture.

Before that by far the most influential broad-brush view of London was Patrick Abercrombie's *Greater London Plan: 1944*.[7] He

149

recognized the difficulties and uncertainties of shaping the future of a metropolis that was, in his words, 'a living and organic structure'. This book does not attempt to be a new Abercrombie, but it does assert the need for such a work and the desirability of starting from many of the same premises, particularly Abercrombie's insistence that successful planning cannot be imposed from on high but must be rooted in the community, using it as 'the basic planning unit'. In those words he emphasized that, although buildings and public spaces give physical form to a city, it is people who bring a city to life.

Even if the scale is broad and the approach begins from the premise that people's views should be canvassed and considered, there can be no guarantee that strategic planning will resolve all difficulties or that it will inevitably produce successful cities. Brasilia, Le Corbusier's Chandigarh and the grandiose urban masterplans ordered by Mussolini and Hitler for Rome and Berlin demonstrate the inadequacies of strategic planning when it is imposed from above. What is certain is that failure to share David Mackay's vision and dream will mean that the city's future will be piecemeal and without coherence. When we come to the specific contents of that vision, however, consensus is less easy to establish, even about such basic issues as the shape of London, its position within the surrounding region or how it should respond to technological change.

The history of twentieth-century planning is the history of decentralization. In his book *Cities of Tomorrow* Peter Hall considers a 1925 article by Clarence Stein and observes, 'The new technologies were making New York, Chicago, Philadelphia, Boston and the rest into "Dinosaur Cities", which were breaking down under the weight of congestion, inefficiency and escalating social cost, and finally complete physical collapse. The result was that these cities were fast becoming the least logical place to locate industry.'[8]

The response of Lewis Mumford and the other members of the influential Regional Planning Association of America (RPAA) in the 1920s, and of most planners and architects in Europe since then, was to look to the region, dispersing both population and industry. The RPAA's special edition of the magazine *Survey* declared in its editorial, 'Planners, builders and rebuilders, have tried to remould cities in conventional ways and, finding the task a labour of Sisyphus, have pinned their faith boldly to the new concept of Region.' Mumford's further thoughts followed immediately in the magazine's first article entitled 'The Fourth Migration'. Having characterized America's past as consisting of three migrations – opening up the west, establishing new industrial cities and creating financial centres, 'the cities where buildings and profits leap upwards in riotous pyramids' – he continued by declaring, 'we are again in another period of flow' in which 'the technological revolution that has taken place during the last thirty years' is 'a revolution that has made the existing layout of cities and the existing distribution of population out of square with our new opportunities'.[9] Mumford christened this 'period of flow' the Fourth Migration.

The effects of the Fourth Migration were certainly apparent in London. Mumford singled out as a prime factor 'the tendency of the automobile ... to disperse population rather than to concentrate it',[10] but he could have added the impact of the telephone and improved rail services for both passengers and freight.

As Ebenezer Howard predicted and exhorted in his book *Tomorrow: A Peaceful Path to Real Reform*,[11] people should, could and would move out of inner London to garden cities such as Unwin's and Parker's Letchworth and, later, Welwyn and to garden suburbs like Hampstead, Ealing or Bedford Park, for such a move would mean a better quality of life. Mumford insisted that 'no form of industry and no type of city are tolerable that take the joy out of life. Communities in which courtship is furtive, in which babies are an unwelcome handicap, in which education, lacking the touch of nature and of real occupations, hardens into a black routine, in which people achieve adventure only on wheels and happiness only by having their minds "taken off" their everyday lives – communities like these do not sufficiently justify our modern advances in science and invention.'[12] But if dispersal could help people attain happiness, there was a price to be paid. The move away from inner cities tended to sidestep urban problems rather than to resolve them. Indeed, for those on the lowest incomes who remained, the problems could often grow worse, in spite of lower levels of population density. Areas of deprivation, such as Hackney, Lewisham, Brixton and Tower Hamlets, bear witness to the fact that decentralization has left a hole of poverty and homelessness in the heart of London.

Jane Jacobs, in her book *The Death and Life of Great American Cities*,[13] was among the first to recognize this when she attacked the Garden City movement, claiming that its 'prescription for saving the city was to do the city in'. She was less than fair to attribute the unhappy consequences of inner-city depopulation solely to the influence of the garden cities. However, she was right about the general impact of a steep drop in population density. Furthermore, in many cases the despair felt in such areas was given a vicious twist by their closeness to districts of great affluence. It has always been thus in the inner city. The grand houses in Inigo Jones's seventeenth-century Covent Garden were next to the appalling, overcrowded living conditions of the Rookeries; the slums of Brownlow Hill ran up to the elegant Georgian terraces of Liverpool; the Plaça Reial in Barcelona was surrounded by the sewerless alleys of the medieval city. In London today the wealth of Notting Hill Gate, Barnsbury and the City knocks against the poverty of North Kensington, North Islington and Hoxton. Garden cities offer no solutions to such inequalities.

Today we have the worst of all possible worlds: huge energy and transport costs, increasing demand for inner-city services between 9 a.m. and 5 p.m. and low income from residential taxation. If, as a society, we take no action, the centre of London and of other cities will become increasingly polarized. The City and the West End will continue to attract investment and to turn a smiling and inviting face to the international capital essential for their survival. Other areas, like Hoxton, Dalston and Peckham, will decline further and faster. Demand for education, health and other services will fall. More schools and doctors' surgeries will close, forcing people to travel further. The quality and variety of local shops will suffer. The cohesion and spirit of the city will evaporate. To reverse this cycle we need a higher level of population density, for both social and economic reasons. Only that will ensure sufficient income to provide decent services, both public and private, as well as the variety of people and skills necessary to make a lively community.

If we are to reject the accepted wisdom on which urban planners have based their theories for nearly a hundred years, namely, that low population densities are in themselves good, we need to consider what constitutes an acceptable level of density. Jane Jacobs has proposed a level of 100 dwellings per acre or 200-plus people. This compares with current levels in London that range from fifteen dwellings per acre in inner London to six in outer London.[14] While 100 dwellings per acre would be both unnecessary and unlikely in London, there is clearly scope for a significantly higher density. Elkin and McLaren, in *Reviving the City*, suggest 'a level equivalent to the typical three- and four-storey urban street: a level at which it is still possible to provide each dwelling with its own front door on to a public street, and to provide gardens for all family dwellings'.[15] Defining densities solely in numerical terms runs the risk of being too simplistic, since the right densities in a city will vary from district to district. Indeed, 'decentralized concentration' between a number of centres should mean that each centre finds the level of population that suits its needs and circumstances.

Elkin's and McLaren's prescription has limited relevance to Britain, where two-storey terraces are more typical than 'three- and four-storey' streets. Implicit in their view is the assumption that houses, not flats, are the ideal, yet Anne Power's work on the Priority Estates Project has shown that such housing, in the form of cottage estates, is neither more nor less prone to crime, vandalism and other social problems than estates of tower blocks. It is the density of housing, rather than its nature, that is important. Undoubtedly we should continue to avoid the levels of density that led the Milner-Holland Committee in 1965 to identify overcrowding as a major problem in Islington, where there were over 300 people per acre in some wards,[16] but a target of between 150 and 225 would be sensible.

To achieve that it is vital that we attract people back to live in the centre of London. We need a Fifth Migration, which will happen only if we provide more job opportunities, better houses, better schools, better health care, better cultural facilities and a better urban environment in the form of streets, squares and parks. Central London must become a more enjoyable place in which to live and bring up children. Quality, in services and in the environment, must be our overriding aim.

By a nice inversion, technology, whose rise has contributed so much to the migration from cities, could now provide one route back to a better quality of urban life.

As long ago as 1915, in his book *Cities in Evolution*,[17] Geddes maintained that in a 'neotronic' future the new technologies of electric power and the internal combustion engine would cause city populations to disperse. However, the service industries, such as banking, insurance, advertising and broadcasting, which replaced London's industrial sector, continued to demand concentrations of staff. The computer and fax machine have meant that financial services, in theory, can operate anywhere at the end of a telephone link – and, indeed, satellite stock exchanges in Manchester and Glasgow have expanded. But in practice bankers and brokers find that they need to stay in close touch with one another, and, far from declining, employment in financial services in and around the City boomed even before the deregulating Big Bang.

Ian Miles, of the Science Policy Research Unit at the University of Sussex, observes, 'Many of the forecasts of substantial change in the spatial distribution of activities, for example, are based on the assumption that NTS [New Telematics Services] can substitute perfectly for traditional means of communication – including telephony and face-to-face contact. But that is far from always the case. It is sometimes said, for instance, that the major use of the mail is for individuals to establish mutually convenient times when they can talk on the telephone.'[18] Perhaps we have overreacted and must now ensure that telecommunications become the servant of cities, providing new and better services, rather than being a cause of their decline. Yet, even if we do, there is no doubt that high-technology companies will continue to favour greenfield sites outside London, such as Swindon or Milton Keynes, for their headquarters. This pull in two directions, with high-tech companies moving out and people needing to be attracted back in, makes the need for a strategic regional view most urgent. Paris has recognized this regional dimension by encompassing five *départements* within the scope of its *Livre Blanc*, but even this may be too narrow an ambit as companies and jobs move out further to cities such as Orléans.

Since there is no easy answer to this problem and there is a limit to how far cities can throw a planning net, it may be better to view the regional context not as a matter of strategy but as an issue for liaison. The growth of industry and population inland from San Francisco has led the towns and cities in the region to form a body called the Association of Bay Area Governments precisely to address these problems. Such an initiative may seem a simple matter of pragmatism and good sense, but it is a distant dream in most parts of Britain, where there is little tradition of regional thinking, let alone action. When London boroughs have difficulty in cooperating, what hope is there that local authorities throughout the south and southeast, leaving aside East Anglia and the Midlands, will work with London to implement the regional planning advice developed by the Standing Committee on South-East Regional Planning?

Apart from the shape of the city, its population density and its position within a wider region, there is one further macro-political problem facing London: the city is dangerously unbalanced. In its geography and economy, in its infrastructure and its social structure, in its cultural life, the resources of London are out of kilter. As has been noted in previous chapters, many cities in Europe have, as a legacy from their industrial past, a tendency to have a west–east imbalance in favour of the west. In few of them is such maldistribution as acute as in London. Whatever yardstick is used, house prices, land values, unemployment or income levels, the poorest boroughs, such as Hackney, Newham, Tower Hamlets, Southwark, Lewisham and Barking, are in the east. Again, for historic reasons, there is an imbalance, less pronounced but still real, between the north and the south of the river.

These imbalances are more than geographical; they go deep into the social and economic bone of the city. It is not simply a matter of the widening differentials between rich and poor, although there is at present a painfully sharp disparity between the 18 per cent of the city's population who comprise London's professional and managerial classes, with average incomes in excess of £25,000, and the 28 per cent who are unemployed, on income support or on basic pension and whose income is between £2,000 and £5,000 a year.[19] Nor is it only the growing differential in land values, with the £60,000 cost of the freehold of an average terraced house in Newham or Barking contrasting with £175,000 for that of a similar property in Camden or Fulham. The imbalance can be seen only too starkly by comparing the dishevelled streets of Hackney or Lambeth with the immaculate squares of Belgravia, the plight of the homeless sleeping out in Waterloo's Cardboard City or in Lincoln's Inn Fields with the opulence of the penthouses rising up along the banks of the river. If this polarization continues, the city will split apart.

Any strategic plan that does not seek to bridge these divisions will fail and will deserve to do so. What use a refurbished Leicester Square if we turn away from the problems of the Aylesbury Estate in Peckham? To avoid this it is essential that London reviews its future needs, economic, social and environmental. Professional efficiency demands that there should be coherence and integration of planning and investment. At the same time the people of London need to ensure that their representatives have some sense of what David Mackay called 'a vision and a dream'. Unless the plan is one to which they can relate, it will be hard for them to endure the many physical disruptions that the regeneration of London will entail.

Strategic planning documents like the *Livre Blanc* can be valuable in identifying problems and the infrastructure needs that arise out of them. However, their scale is too large and diffuse for them to be effective in prescribing development action for specific areas or sites, such as the Olympic Village in Barcelona or the ZACs in Paris. At present our planning system is also unsatisfactory on this micro, or local, level. In Britain local plans have not in the past been a statutory requirement, although more local authorities are beginning to recognize the benefits they can bestow. H. W. E. Davies reports that 440 local plans were adopted between the early 1970s and 1986 and a further 250 deposited for adoption.[20] (The virtues of local plans, it should be noted, do not extend to increasing the general speed of the planning system, with local plans taking an average of fifty-two months to prepare,[21] while between forty-eight and sixty months are needed for a structures plan.)[22] Yet we still lag behind Europe, where many cities are developing detailed plans and are then commissioning architects to turn these local briefs into reality: Bohigas and Mackay were appointed to design the whole Olympic Village in Barcelona and have also won the competition to reconstruct part of Aix-en-Provence; the Taller de Arquitectura of Ricardo Bofill has been awarded the contract to extend Montpellier north of its medieval centre; in Berlin the municipal authority has commissioned a number of architects to advise on various parts of the city, including the Potsdamer Platz, the crucial site where East meets West.

One consequence of such local plans is that architects are increasingly turning their attention away from individual buildings and looking at the streets, the squares, the parks, the spaces between those buildings – in short, the wider urban context in which communities live and the use which they make of it. In doing this they are addressing problems of land use and landscape, of balance and of urban design.

Planning at this level raises the question of appropriate land use and zoning. Since the 1940s there has been general acceptance of the idea that a community's various activities should be kept separate, that workplaces, shops, homes, places of entertainment should not be mixed. The out-of-town shopping centre and the industrial park are the latest manifestations of this belief. Undoubtedly few people want to live next door to a rubber or chemical plant or a factory with a night shift. Zoning is the best way to isolate activities that involve noise or air pollution or stimulate heavy traffic. However, cities such as Baltimore have shown that certain mixtures of uses can happily coexist. Shops, offices, hotels, restaurants, cinemas, theatres, museums, libraries and housing can all positively benefit from being mixed. The variety of activities keeps streets alive throughout the day and into the evening, long after the last office has closed. Hence streets not only offer more to people; they are also safer places. We must reconsider the advantages of mixing the uses of districts and rethink some of the rigidities of zoning, which may go against the grain of London's villages as both residential and economic communities and of concepts such as 'decentralized concentration'.

The classic case for zoning was put by Robert Murray Haig in his 1927 Regional Plan for New York, where he wrote, 'Zoning finds its economic justification in that it is a useful device for ensuring an approximately just distribution of costs.' However, there is little evidence that it has been effective in achieving such a redistribution; indeed, there is persuasive evidence that inflexible zoning increases transport costs and hence both energy use and pollution. That a more sophisticated approach to zoning is practicable is demonstrated by some American cities, such as San Francisco, where 'appropriate use' is determined block by block, thus actively promoting mixed uses of land within districts. In London we need to take that sort of positive approach to zoning, with a presumption in favour of a balance of uses and amenities wherever possible. To achieve this will require changes in the laws that determine planning permissions and in the ways in which they are implemented by local authorities. An overhaul of planning law is required.

In 1965 Richard Crossman, the Minister for Housing and Local Government, published a Government White Paper, *The Housing Programme for 1965–70*. It concluded, 'Three major defects have appeared in the present system. First, it has become overloaded and subject to delays and cumbersome procedures. Second, there has been inadequate participation by the individual citizen in the planning process, and insufficient regard to his interests. Third, the system has been better as a negative control on undesirable development than as a positive stimulus to the creation of a good environment.' Since then there have been three major pieces of legislation, dozens of minor, 575 departmental circulars that relate to planning and, at any one time, an average of fifteen ministerial guidelines, but the same complaints, that the planning system is slow and bureaucratic, that it is negative and reactive and that it excludes the public, are commonplace today.

It was not always so. The 1947 Town and Country Planning Act was received with rapturous enthusiasm by both planners and architects. With its approach of positive, rather than reactive, planning the Act made possible the reconstruction of post-war Britain and followed the legislation on new towns (the New Towns Act 1946), described by Leslie Lane as 'the greatest conscious programme of city building ever undertaken by any country in history'. The Act consisted of two main elements, the requirement for each local authority to devise development plans, indicating the land use proposed for every area, and the need for planning permission for each intended development. 'Whatever its shortcoming,' wrote Nan Fairbrother in *New Lives, New Landscapes*,[23] 'no one can doubt that the system has worked. It has checked irresponsible development and encouraged appropriate use of land, and the fact that the spread of built-up areas has been halved despite our vast expansion is indisputable proof of its effectiveness.'

The unqualified triumph of the Act has been its contribution to the retention of Britain's tracts of unspoilt countryside, not just remote areas, such as the Lake District, the Broads or the Yorkshire Dales, but also those like the Sussex Downs or the Kent Weald, which, because of their closeness to London, might appear to be at greater risk. Much of the credit for this must go to the Council for the Preservation of Rural England and the Civic Trust, but it was the planning system that allowed us to establish a clear distinction between town and country. A glance at the valleys of Switzerland or at the Dordogne, with their half-plot developments scattering suburbia at random, shows that success in preserving beautiful countryside is not automatic. Nor has rural preservation been the only success of the Act. Land reclamation, traffic control, pedestrian schemes, constraints on advertising billboards, the cleaning up of the urban mess caused by cat's cradles of wires and lines that zigzagged across streets, all these have improved the quality of urban, and rural, life considerably and have helped to make cities places fit for people to live in.

In view of this catalogue of benefits, how and why was this brave new system, described by Nan Fairbrother as the 'Magna Carta of planning', transformed into the butt of the 1965 White Paper's criticisms and of the present widespread dissatisfaction?

As concrete estates proliferated and tower blocks rose, the system's failures became only too apparent. Slums were cleared, but communities were broken up. The common characteristic of all these actions and strategies was that the impetus came from the top, from the State. The fine aspiration of 'planning for people' became blurred and obscured. Even when, in 1968, planning participation was made a statutory element in planning law, there was little effective improvement. The new opportunities for individuals and for interest groups to voice their objections did not mean that these were actually listened to, let alone accepted.

Blame should not be attributed solely to the planning system. The scale of the task of rebuilding Britain between 1945 and 1960 meant that speed of executive decision and action was a high priority. The result was a planning system that became increasingly autocratic. Planning came to be seen as part of the problem, not part of the solution or, as George Nicholson, former Chair of the GLC's Planning Committee described it, 'the problem of solutions'.[24]

Attempts were made to close loopholes and rectify faults, but these led only to greater complexity. Today it is possible that eighteen[25] different planning applications may be necessary for a single development. Nationally the proliferation of circulars on specific issues, and of statutory and non-statutory guidelines, makes planning a legal nightmare. The number of bodies that can raise objections has also risen. For a riverside development in London more than fifty agencies now have such rights, including the Port of London Authority, the Thames Passenger Services Federation, the National Rivers Authority and the Metropolitan Police Thames Division.

Into this bureaucratic shambles, described by Prince Charles in his June 1987 speech to the Royal Institute of British Architects as a 'spaghetti bolognese of red tape', the Tory Government introduced two new elements – the ideology of the free market and its twin, hostility to local government. Throughout the 1980s the Thatcher Government saw planning as a burden on enterprise and an obstacle to growth. Its response to the complexity of the system was not to reform it but to bypass it. Rather than trying to identify the causes of inefficiency it created areas within which planning regulations either didn't apply or were neutralized.[26]

The London Docklands Development Corporation (LDDC) was set up in 1981 specifically to demonstrate that free-market economics, in the form of Thatcherism, could provide the answer to the problems of inner cities. The aim was stated more prosaically in the LDDC's stated policy: 'to maximize investment and development in Docklands and support the Corporation's broader regeneration objectives by acquiring and/or servicing derelict land and under-utilized land as necessary and marketing it to potential investors and developers'.[27] But it was the political symbolism of huge new commercial buildings rising out of the wasteland of derelict docks that captured Mrs Thatcher's imagination, not least because the 8-square-mile site adjoined two of the poorest Labour-controlled boroughs in London.

To ensure that the development market was not so much free as positively favourable, incentives were offered in the form of 100 per cent capital allowances for new buildings, no development land tax, exemption from local rates for new commercial and industrial buildings until 1992 and an Enterprise Zone on the Isle of Dogs. The Government has resolutely refused to quantify the cost of these fiscal incentives, borne by the tax-payer, but they are likely to exceed £1 billion. Perversely, it has been these conditions, intended to demonstrate the miraculous power of capital to transform, that have undermined the scheme and prevented its success. 'Freed' from any obligation to involve local people, whether through jobs or social housing, in an area where unemployment at times was between 20 and 30 per cent, housing conditions were poor and homelessness rife, the LDDC has failed to find a role or an identity. In its designs the editor of the *Architect's Journal* was of the opinion that it had 'lurched drunkenly from suburban business park, to pseudo Amsterdam, to miniature Manhattan and finally complete visual chaos'.[28]

A brief that allowed companies to build what they liked, where they liked and how they liked has resulted in a district with inadequate transport facilities, no schools, no green spaces, no civic amenities and no community. A scheme that should have enriched London and begun the regeneration of the eastern boroughs has succeeded only in polarizing the city. If the many and frequent calls to return to Victorian values had been heeded and understood by those who made them, Docklands could have learned from the great nineteenth-century developments in London like De Beauvoir Town or Norman Shaw's Bedford Park. Instead, by a nice irony, its deficiencies have led to the re-emergence of the conditions that originally led to public regulation and a strong voice for local-authority planning departments. Docklands is a sadly wasted opportunity, but it is an extreme symptom, not the cause, of problems whose roots go back over thirty years. In particular its 'visual chaos' is only one example of the failure of Delafons's second function of planning, namely, design.

The Town and Country Planning Act 1990 mentions 'external appearance' once[29] and 'design' once.[30] Apart from these two references, planning legislation has been a design-free zone. However, numerous ministerial circulars have given guidance,[31] and Delafons estimates that 'about a third of all planning appeals involve matters of design, as either a primary or secondary consideration',[32] while 50 per cent of planning permissions include design conditions.[33] Design aesthetics are clearly a major consideration and have been for decades before Prince Charles's interventions,[34] with commentators such as Ian Nairn deploring the poor quality of British landscaping and design since the Second World War.[35]

Ministerial advice in circulars has been vague ('Local authorities should reject obviously poor designs ... they should confine concern to those aspects of design which are significant for the aesthetic quality of the area,' and 'Planning authorities should recognize that aesthetics is an extremely subjective matter')[36] or cautious ('Where design detail is acceptable authorities shall think twice before seeking to improve it.'[37] 'They should not therefore impose their tastes on developers simply because they believe them to be superior').[38] These warnings, however, have not deterred planning officers and planning committees from making decisions on the most minute details of proposed buildings – the size and dimensions of windows, the positioning of balconies, whether a doorway should be arched, whether the materials used should be brick or stone, tile or slate. When they are confronted by the macro problems of planning, which are so complex and interrelated, it is perhaps inevitable that planning committees should latch on to those details about which it is somewhat easier for lay people to have opinions.

Two things result: the planning system is bogged down in detail, and buildings, good and bad, are revised piecemeal by people who are not architects. Of the estimated 21,000 people working in planning departments only about 4,500 are qualified town planners or have been trained as architects. It is right, and democratically essential, that planners, preferably well qualified and trained, and councillors should decide on land use and on a strategy for the development of the urban environment of their communities. The future of a town, not to mention the value of an individual's property, is at stake and should be decided in a democratic forum. But once those decisions are made, is it the best use of a planning committee's skills that it should spend time determining architectural detail? Would an arts committee seek to decide the artistic programme of a regional theatre that it grant-aided? Would it be well advised to go through the script of a new play and delete lines and add speeches? Yet this is what planning committees do when they reject details on aesthetic grounds and ask for specifics such as smaller windows or a greater use of brick.

Few buildings end up as they started in an architect's plans, and there is no evidence that the changes benefit the public or the buildings. This isn't the way to encourage architects to build buildings that express something about a community or a generation. Apart from competence, decisions concerning detail demand a coherent aesthetic taste among twenty or so individuals. How can that be possible? Aesthetics are, by their nature, subjective and changeable and always have been. Even those whose lives are devoted to thinking and writing about aesthetics have been capable of coming up with some bizarre and eccentric judgements. William Morris, craftsman, artist, printer and founder of the Society for the Protection of Ancient Buildings, believed that the eighteenth century was 'quite unconscious of its tendency towards ugliness and nullity', thus writing off in a sentence Robert Adam, John Nash and Sir John Soane. At the same time he claimed that the nineteenth-century railway stations of Brunel and Scott were 'the horrible and restless nightmare of modern engineering'.

Decisions of detail are profoundly subjective. There can be no 'right' or 'wrong' about whether a roof should be of tile or slate. It is a matter of personal preference. To allow for that we must return to a more liberal and generous attitude towards style. The battle between Modernist, Post-Modernist and Classicist generates heat but not light. Advocates of all three are contemporary architects whose taste has been formed today. If they can find clients, public or private, who share that taste, they should have the opportunity to build. Our life will be the better for the variety that is introduced into our cities. Let our children decide which buildings of our generation should be kept and which replaced.

David Mackay, in bringing together thirty architects to contribute to the Olympic Village in Barcelona, acknowledged that this group encompassed as wide a range of ability and flair as it did of age. Such potential variations in quality didn't worry him. 'A city is made up of many buildings,' he said in a lecture on the subject at the Tate Gallery in 1991. 'Some of them will be indifferent. Why not? That's in the nature of things.'[39] It is a generosity of attitude we should heed.

In doing so we must adopt a more relaxed planning regime that frets less about detail. Circular 22/1980, issued by Michael Heseltine when he was Secretary of State for the Environment, counselled local authorities to cease to try to impose their aesthetic on architects. The circular said that, even in conservation areas, councils should not be 'over-fastidious in such matters as, for example, the precise shade of colour of bricks. They should be closely advised in such matters by professionally qualified advisers. This is especially important where a building has been designed by an architect for a particular site.' Unfortunately, local authorities employ comparatively few 'professionally qualified advisers', and the majority of all planning applications are submitted without plans drawn up by an architect.

These are not the only reasons why this well-intentioned circular has not been more effective in restraining local councillors from pursuing their careers as aesthetes, and it is doubtful whether the wording of the new draft Planning Policy guidelines will have any greater effect. These guidelines again exhort local authorities 'not to impose their taste on applicants for planning permission simply because they believe it to be superior' and not to 'interfere with the detailed design of buildings', but in the very next words local authorities are given an escape clause, 'unless the sensitive nature of the setting for the development justifies it'.[40]

To reduce the emphasis on aesthetic debate in our planning system would not involve adopting the more radical position on effective non-planning advocated by Reyner Banham and others in *New Society* in 1969, when they wrote, 'The whole concept of planning (the town-and-country kind at least) has gone cock-eyed ... Somehow everything must be watched: nothing must be allowed simply "to happen". No house can be allowed to be commonplace in the way that things just ARE commonplace.'[41] It could, however, help both to speed up and to simplify a system that is at present in no shape to respond to the new generation of building that will be essential in London and elsewhere if we are to tackle the problems of homelessness and housing conditions in the 1990s.

Faced by these substantial imperfections in speed, clarity, participation and aesthetics, how can we improve our planning system? For once, looking abroad offers only limited assistance. H. W. E. Davies warns that 'to a considerable extent, any strict comparison and evaluation of efficiency and effectiveness in five such different countries and control systems is highly problematic. Even if comparison between the five countries [France, the Netherlands, Germany, Denmark and England] is possible, comparability does not necessarily imply transferability.'[42] Apart from involving legally binding plans and building regulations, all five regimes differ, reflecting the countries' legal systems. In general most European countries, whose law stems substantially from the Code Napoléon, are prescriptive and rigid, while the English planning system, rooted in common law, is discretionary and adaptive. The corollary of such differences is that European planning law has a clarity and a certainty that the English system lacks, with the result that planning decisions in

England are unpredictable. Although this is true in principle, in practice it is not as simple as that, since most European systems also incorporate a considerable degree of negotiation.

A study of the authoritative *Planning Control in Western Europe* leads to the conclusion that no system is perfect. The consequences, both social and financial, of all planning decisions are of such importance that planning law is bound to be complex and, to some degree, not totally satisfactory. In France a highly centralized political tradition meant that central government controlled all planning until 1983. Since then powers have been devolved to mayors and communes, under the general guidance of the national government's Code de l'Urbanisme. This consists of three parts: the laws passed by Parliament, the regulations and procedures to implement them and *arrêtés*, or ministerial orders, comparable with British circulars. It is in practice a code that contrives to be both complex and vague, and it has been described by John Punter as 'at best an inconvenient and at worst an impenetrable system'.[43] Local authorities are required to draw up structure plans, Schémas Directeurs d'Aménagement et de l'Urbanisme, in conjunction with more detailed documents on land use, the Plans d'Occupation du Sol (POS). Although this hierarchy is not dissimilar to Britain's, its precision means that applications that adhere to the local plan are asssured of authorization, although appeal procedures do exist.

The Netherlands has in many ways the antithesis of the comprehensive, and at times complex, French system. Dutch planning is totally devolved to local authorities, which are required to formulate structure plans. The Minister[44] has a national responsibility, which he fulfils with the assistance of three national planning agencies,[45] all created under the Physical Planning Act 1985. However, the Government's powers are essentially supervisory, and in practice planning decisions are made at provincial and municipal level. Here too there is a substantial body of advisory agencies. In Rotterdam Riek Bakker's Urban Development Department is responsible for drawing up the city's structure plan, but a number of outside bodies have to be consulted during the planning process, including an aesthetics committee, a committee of landscape experts, the Central Environmental Control Agency and even a committee of agricultural specialists. It is a system that contains all the virtues of consensus and consultation, but it is not designed to promote decision making, and it is likely that Rotterdam's Kop van Zuid scheme owes its shape and existence more to Riek Bakker's personal dynamism and perseverance than to the city's planning system.

There are obvious cultural and legal differences between France, the Netherlands and England, but the structures of their planning systems have much in common, particularly the division of national and municipal responsibility. Accordingly it is tempting to look for models that are radically different, and the USA, home of free-market capitalism, might be seen as providing such an alternative. Indeed, it is instructive to study planning in American cities, but for the quality, scope and intention of their regulation rather than for the absence of such regulation.

With the exception of Houston, every major American city has planning controls that are considerably more detailed than anything in Britain.[46] San Francisco's planning regime is generally considered to be among the best. The city has a natural environment worth protecting, its plunging, precipitous hills looking west out over the Pacific and east, inland, up a majestic bay 45 miles long. Since the earthquake of 18 April 1906 the city planners have created a built environment worthy of this location. Three substantial documents[47] form the basis of the planning regime operated by the Planning Commission, consisting of seven (lay) members, and by a strong, professional Planning Department, headed by Dean Macris. The Ordinance designates six conservation areas and several hundred buildings that should be protected, but its approach is not negative. It treats the city not 'as an architectural museum but as a living organism that must adapt to change and can be enhanced by new development and by the conversion of old buildings to new uses', comments John Delafons.[48] In this it is more akin to the French system, under which the law that creates a conservation zone within 500 metres of any important historic site has been used to enhance, not to ossify, the quality of contemporary architecture in cities. Alongside it the San Francisco Downtown Plan contains general objectives for the area (on pedestrianization, harmonization with nearby buildings, streetscape, etc.) and detailed policies to implement them, in the form of design guidelines covering height, bulk, street-level activity, wind speeds and overshadowing.

All three documents are covered by a general exhortation that 'the guidelines establish minimum criteria for neighborhood compatibility, not the maximum expectations for good design'. Informed by that spirit, the design guidelines seem to succeed in avoiding the meddling interference in aesthetics that disfigures the British system. Instead they are concerned with urban rather than architectural design, in particular with the relationship between groups of buildings and between buildings and their surroundings. Hence they provide a detailed urban brief rather than an architectural handbook.

San Francisco extends the obligations that developers already have to the built environment into the social sphere. All new office buildings have to contribute a proportion of capital costs to the city's social housing ($6 per square foot), public needs ($5), open space ($2), general welfare ($1), public art (1 per cent). When contributions to disabled access are added the total charge is between $18 and $20 per square foot.[49]

Other American cities achieve comparable results with incentives rather than tariffs. Portland, Oregon, requires new developments to include crèche facilities, retail at street level, cultural amenities, landscaping, with fountains and roof gardens, and public art through a Percent for Art scheme. The incentive is that those who comply to the satisfaction of the Commission can increase their floor/area ratio by up to a factor of two.

On the level of strategic planning too San Francisco is worth studying. While the Downtown Plan covers only the built-up central area, where development is restricted to 0.5 million square feet a year, the Bay area is expanding from its current population of 6 million to a proposed 7 million-plus in 2020. Here too development is planned in detail. In Mission Bay, a 300-acre site not dissimilar to London's Docklands, a mixed community has been ensured by insisting that the plans include schools, fire and police stations,

68 acres of recreation space and 2,200 homes at affordable rents, as well as a 500-bed hotel and 5,800 homes for private sale.[50]

What can we learn from this mix of social planning and free enterprise? Do these fine-grain, and socially conscious, systems work? As San Francisco's has been in existence in this form for only six years, it may be too early to come to conclusions. Could design guidelines of this type apply here? Judy Hillman, in *Planning for Beauty*,[51] thinks so. John Delafons is more cautious, but both are agreed that the work of Dean Macris in San Francisco, and that of other US cities, merits closer scrutiny.

Whatever lessons we do or do not learn from abroad, we have a major task in improving the speed, clarity, fairness and quality of our planning system. We need not rush into new legislation. The Thatcher and Major Governments have shown how our planning system can be significantly altered by circular and guideline, and Robin Thompson, Chief Planning Officer of Kent County Council and a former President of the Royal Town Planning Institute, advises that 'The adaptive nature of planning should be exploited rather than deplored.'[52] However, in the medium term new legislation will be needed, and some things must change. To reduce the emphasis on aesthetics, and the detailed amendment of building designs, greater weight should be put on proposals for land use in local plans and at all earlier stages of the planning process. We should consider whether the American type of design guideline is at all appropriate in London, but, even if it is not, we should place more emphasis on those elements, present in San Francisco's guidelines, that are quantifiable, such as height and bulk.

This would reduce, but not eliminate, the range of decisions over which planning committees have to use their judgement, and, to help them in this task a wider range of advice and expertise could be made available in the form of co-opted lay members, as on American planning commissions and as on local-authority education committees in this country. Broader-based committees such as these could be the basis of a new three-way partnership between local authorities, private-sector developers and the public. Further, the adoption of Environmental Impact and Social Impact reports, as part of the

new Planning Consultation Regulations, would give the public considerably more information on the effect of a development on traffic
levels, public transport, zoning, housing, child-care provision and
other factors. These reforms should improve both the clarity and the
quality of planning decisions.

After the planning mistakes of the 1980s there are welcome signs
that we are beginning to move in a more positive direction. The
Planning and Compensation Act 1991 indicates several significant
departures from past practice. In future local plans will be mandatory
for all local authorities. Nationally this will improve the planning
system, but it will have little effect on London, which will still be left
with thirty-two borough plans, and the City of London's, but no
city-wide plan. The Secretary of State for the Environment can,
but is not obliged to, create that strategic framework, and the present
Secretary of State shows no sign of doing so. The case for a strategic
authority, capable of forming such strategic plans, remains overwhelming.

Of even greater significance is the demise of the presumption,
when considering planning applications, in favour of development in
relation to the local plan.[53] This should bring the British system closer to the French POS, but before celebrating unreservedly this
remarkable change of heart by the Conservative Government it
would be wise to see how the Secretary of State responds to the
consultation exercise on the planning policy guidelines that ended
on 29 November 1991 and how he, and the law courts, interpret the
new Act.

Even so our planning system will still depend greatly on the
nature and effectiveness of the appeals procedures. In the 1980s
ministers made hugely increased use of appeals and found invariably
in favour of developers and against local-authority planning committees. The Chief Planning Inspector's Report (April 1990–March
1991) shows appeals rising from 19,856 in 1986 to 32,281 in 1989.[54]
In doing so they skewed the entire system, since local authorities
against whom costs were awarded began to grant approval to
schemes that went against local plans rather than risk the Secretary of
State's judgement. We need now to reform the appeals system, so

as both to simplify and to speed it, and to correct the imbalance of the 1980s.

With regard to speed, we should look again at the pilot scheme run by the Department of the Environment in 1990 in conjunction with three West Country planning authorities to assess the use of Oral Sessional Hearings. The planning authorities, appellants and inspectors all approved of the scheme, and only the Council of Tribunals had 'substantial reservations'. More general adoption of such a fast-track approach would be constructive. There is also a case for abolishing the automatic right of appeal, abused by some developers, and replacing it with a right to seek leave to appeal. However, such a change would almost inevitably lead to a large number of applications, bogging the system down further; it would be more effective to award costs against any unsuccessful appellant who had flown in the face of the local plan and the new presumption in its favour.

These changes by themselves will not transform our planning system or improve the quality of development and design overnight, but they are likely to help considerably. In pursuing them we should not lose sight of Abercrombie's axiom that planning must be rooted in the community. For that to be more than a pious wish we have to improve the quality of consultation and information available to the public.

CHAPTER EIGHT

Involving People

In its first year[1] the Pavillon de l'Arsenal was visited by 60,000 people. They came to see exhibitions or films, take
part in discussions or study the development plans and projects that
will shape Paris over the coming years. Almost all went away
enthused, but they were also better informed.

In Britain we have nothing comparable with the Pavillon de
l'Arsenal, and so debate on planning and architecture lurches from
controversy to controversy and is invariably limited to wrangles over
style. Whether the subject of the public row is the extension of the
National Gallery, the National Museum of Scotland, Spitalfields,
King's Cross or the plans before your local council for a by-pass, discussion would benefit from better information. A purpose-built centre with interactive technology enabling people to tap in on-line, or
simply to visit, is what is needed.

That need is being recognized by the Royal Academy, which is
planning an exhibition of London's built environment by the Royal
Institute of British Architects (RIBA) and by the newly formed
Architecture Foundation. The RIBA announced in 1989 plans to
establish in its Portland Place headquarters 'the centre of architectural learning and debate in Great Britain'. The Institute already has
a superb collection of drawings and an excellent library, matched
only by those of the Canadian Centre for Architecture and
Columbia's Avery Library, but the then President, Max Hutchinson,

believed that 'It is not enough for a learned society like ourselves to be a mere repository of knowledge – we must also be the propagators of knowledge.'[2] The RIBA plans to bring together all the collections of its library, including the drawings that are housed separately at present, and so provide a unique resource for its architect members and for academics. But its buildings, even when extended, will not be ideal for a public centre. Furthermore, the extent of the public facilities in the new centre would be a bookshop, a reception area and an information service on the ground floor, in addition to a new gallery already planned. It will be a collection of amenities and services that, though welcome and useful, particularly for professional architects and planners, could not attempt to replicate the role of the Pavillon de l'Arsenal.

By contrast the Architecture Foundation has more comprehensive ambitions but no buildings. At present it can only plan a series of exhibitions, at the *Economist*'s offices in St James's Street, but it sees its eventual aim as both to 'show what London has to offer' and to 'offer Londoners a window on the world'.[3] More specifically, it will give 'a new resource to London which – in the absence of a metropolitan authority responsible for planning – will engender a comprehensive debate and increase our collective awareness of architecture in its social, economic and cultural context'.[4] It will also mount exhibitions of 'contemporary and past masters – from the UK and abroad – and explore the work of emerging designers of talent'.[5] These are aims that mirror those of the Pavillon de l'Arsenal and the German Architecture Museum in Frankfurt, both of which have representatives on the Foundation's Programme Council,[6] and that will synchronize well with the more academic and profession-oriented RIBA Centre. Both are needed, and both would add something to London, but neither is likely to succeed without some public finance.

The RIBA Centre requires an extension to its Grade II listed building, which is likely to cost substantially more than the 1989 estimate of £12 million. The Foundation's proposed annual budget will be at least £800,000, exclusive of leaseholding requirements, which is almost identical to that of the Pavillon d'Arsenal. This supports an Arsenal staff of fifteen, a building of 16,000 square feet, four major and numerous smaller exhibitions a year, a permanent model of Paris, videos, conferences, publications, conferences, events, a reference library and a photographic collection. The German Architecture Museum is a similar size, the difference being that, while the German museum is funded largely by the local authorities, 80 per cent of the costs of the Pavillon's running costs are met by development companies. At the moment the British Government is showing little interest either in the RIBA's Centre or in the Architecture Foundation, but without greater government support it is hard to see either opening in the near future, although they will continue to produce more modest exhibitions within their existing space.

One advantage they have is to be able to learn not just from the examples of Paris and Frankfurt but also from the many other major museums all over Europe and North America, such as the Centre for Canadian Architecture in Montreal, Stockholm's Swedish Architectural Museum and the Finnish Architectural Museum, and from exhibition venues both large (the Urban Centre in New York) and small (Bordeaux, Graz, Copenhagen). There are two ways in which we could improve on the services they offer. The first is to make a major centre linked to a network of smaller, local venues. The second is to strengthen a centre's educational work.

Entry to the Pavillon de l'Arsenal is free; its location is reasonably central; and, as a building, it is inviting and approachable. Good though the attendance figures for the first year (60,000) are, though, they show that it is not attracting a wide general public. The right site, good publicity and word of mouth could well produce a larger attendance at a London centre, but to capture people's interest and concern fully, a link would have to be made between London/international issues and proposals for specific neighbourhoods. The Pavillon de l'Arsenal's permanent exhibition, 'Paris, the City and Its Projects', has a 36-square-metre model of the city (scale 1:2,000). Connected with this is a laser programme that can summon up details and stills on a video screen of developments, not just on the Grands Projets but also on individual, neighbourhood ZACs. This is an excellent use of technology, but in London such a programme would have to be extended by a network of smaller exhibition centres that would stimulate interest and provide information locally. There is certainly an overwhelming case for one in east London, perhaps in Newham or in the Royal Docks, as the construction of the Channel Tunnel link, the East London River Crossing and the development on both sides of the river transform that landscape.

Such local centres do exist – there is the Emerald Centre on Hammersmith Broadway and the Coin Street Design Centre – but they would benefit from being coordinated and from sharing resources and information, not just with each other but with similar centres that ought to be established in other major British cities such as Birmingham, Cardiff, Manchester and Glasgow. From such a network, specific exhibitions and information could be put into public libraries and other community venues. We are never going to improve the quality of the public debate about urban design and architecture until people are given the opportunity to see what is already there around them and what is being planned for their city's or their community's future.

Given a range of centres, museums and venues, we could look forward to a time when all national, and even some local, newspapers carried regular articles on architecture and design and when these matters received fuller coverage on radio and television. The audiences for programmes on our heritage and on conservation, and for Prince Charles's *Vision of Britain*,[7] show that there is an interested public waiting for more information, debate and education.

That education ought to begin in the classroom. Only if we educate our children better than we have been educated will we progress. At present the built environment hardly features in the classroom at all. As a subject it slips down in the gaps between the increasingly rigid subject-demarcation lines in the school curriculum, always just off the edges of Craft, Design, Technology (CDT), of fine art and of social geography. With notable exceptions, such as that of Cambridgeshire, most education authorities and most schools do nothing to rectify this. The result is that children can leave school at 16 without ever having read or talked about architecture or urban issues. How can we call that a comprehensive education? The question is doubly ironic when you consider that education about the built environment is a wonderful medium for developing so many areas across the curriculum: our history and our future; technology, ecology, culture; gathering and recording information; designing and making. It is a compleat subject.

In the 1970s the Schools Council, before its demise, was beginning to do work in this area, but at present the RIBA and the Building Experiences Trust (BET) are ploughing a lonely furrow with the support of only a handful of education authorities, advisers and inspectors, and, more generally, the excellent work that the Design Dimension Foundation is doing in design education. The BET has published a teacher's handbook for using the built environment in the education of primary school children at Key Stages 2 and 3.[8] It is a model of its kind and builds on similar work being done abroad, notably in the United States and in Denmark,[9] expressed in *The Things Around Us: Architecture* by Lars Hegelund, but its scope ought to be extended to all stages of schools education. Unless we educate the people who will use and shape the urban environment of tomorrow, we run the risk of repeating all the mistakes of the last fifty years.

So many of these mistakes were the result not just of people being uninformed but of their never being consulted about, much less involved in, planning decisions. Early ideas about planning, whether those of Howard, Geddes and their disciples in Britain or of Daniel Burnham and others in the United States, were drafted on clean sheets of paper and realized, usually, on greenfield sites. Regardless of whether they were visionary or misguided, the early planners saw people as the objects of planning, not its subjects.

Although Patrick Abercrombie recognized that 'the social arguments for community planning are now fairly generally accepted' and believed that, in his plan, 'we have used the community as the basic planning unit', his concern remained essentially paternalistic.[10] Certainly the people who, in the following twenty years, implemented his plans, whether in the new and extended towns around London or in the Comprehensive Development Areas in the capital, did so at a speed that never allowed for listening to people or for discovering what were their wishes or priorities, let alone for acting on such views. Although there was some degree of public consultation over specific planning applications, the public were not normally allowed to attend their local authority's planning committee meetings at which final decisions were made.

This paternalism ran through every level of the planning system until the 1960s, when documentaries such as Nell Dunn's *Cathy Come Home* and the establishment of action groups such as Shelter (1966) began to put the human consequences of poor housing and planning on the political agenda. Criticism about the lack of opportunities for public participation grew, and finally the Labour Government set up the Skeffington Committee to consider these questions. The Committee reported in 1969, and its recommendation that public participation should be a right, and should be seen as an important and positive part of the planning process, was introduced as a new statutory provision in the 1971 Town and Country Planning Act.

The same rising tide, which increased social consciousness of women's rights and the rights of ethnic minorities, brought in new attitudes to community politics. Younger social workers, planners and housing officers supported demands for participation and consultation by newly formed community groups. The property boom of the 1960s and 1970s, and the local authority plans required by the 1971 Act, provided plenty of occasions for these groups to explore the new statutory rights. Publications like *Community Action* and *Undercurrents* were set up, and in 1972 Rod Hackney launched his campaign to prevent the demolition of Black Road in Macclesfield. Provoked by the appalling housing conditions revealed in reports such as the White Paper *Old Houses to New Homes*[11] and by the autocratic attitudes of central and most of local government, people were for the first time beginning to take a hand in changing their own environment.

In 1977 the Campaign for Homes in Central London was formed, and out of it came the beginning of the Community Areas Policy, adopted by the GLC in 1981. The election of a Labour administration in London led to the identification of sixteen Community

Areas[12] and support for over 100 projects in these areas, including community centres, land clearance, the acquisition of property and feasibility studies.[13] For the chosen few communities participation led to action, but most people in London probably saw little change. The workings of their local-authority planning committees remained as shrouded in mystery as ever.

This distinction between the successful campaigns of single-issue pressure groups and the perceptions of the general public is a problem that bedevils all areas of public life in Britain. Political parties, charitable bodies, the whole voluntary sector know that even the most 'popular' campaigns are organized and run by a small handful of people. We are a dangerously passive democracy, and it is this failing that undermines moves to improve consultation procedures in planning and to achieve genuinely wider involvement. How many people submitted comments to their local authorities in 1991 as their UDPs were drawn up? How many people were aware that such plans were being made or that there was a consultation period, in spite of considerable efforts on the part of boroughs to publicize meetings and plans? How many people even know what a UDP is? There are no easy or sure-fire ways to make certain that consultation is effective, but, whatever the techniques or networks, consultation is rooted in listening to people. Such an approach improves the chances of planning strategies growing out of people's experiences, their patterns of living and their needs.

In his introduction to a study entitled *Gaeltacht*, which he conducted for the Irish Government in north-west Donegal in 1981, Brian Anson describes this process as 'the identification and encouragement of community initiatives, on the premise that the most important resource of any area is the local community itself, whose energy and ideas (let alone knowledge) must form an integral part of any plan for the future'. Without processes similar to these, and the time and patience to see them through, it is no wonder that people are frustrated. Their frustration takes many forms, from cursing the local planners in the privacy of their homes to the public protests of Prince Charles, in his *Vision of Britain* television programme, when he lambasted some of the works of contemporary planners and architects. He pursued a similar line in 1991, when he resigned as a trustee of the National Museum of Scotland on the grounds that the public ought to have been involved in the process of choosing a design for the Museum's extension. Prince Charles's instincts were right. This is an important public building. The public ought to be involved. It is a sentiment that is correct to hold and easy to express but hard to promote. Prince Charles wanted, on the eve of the trustees' announcement of their decision, when the short list was to be published and the models and drawings displayed, to declare his position before a choice was made. But that still ducks the question of how individual members of the public, who have visited an exhibition of short-listed designs, can express their preference.

Sometimes there will be a clear consensus. When National Westminster Bank asked the public to comment on three designs for its new headquarters in London (a high-rise, a medium-rise and a low-rise building) the public chose, by a considerable majority, the skyscraper, which the bank then built. However, the experience of the National Gallery trustees, when inviting public comments on their short list for the extension in 1984, showed how difficult such exercises can be. Voting identified Richard Rogers's design as both the most liked and the most disliked of the plans. Not surprisingly, the jury was confused.

But, as interest in planning and architecture grows as a result of better media coverage and initiatives like architecture centres, so too will the demand for more active forms of consultation on area plans and on individual designs. If the existing formal planning procedures provide inadequate opportunities, if community action groups, however successful, only invoke relatively few communities, if voting is unsatisfactory and inconclusive, what can be done? It is a question that is going to have to be addressed, not only because of the desirability of the principle of planning for, and with, people but also because, by listening to what people want and how they live in and use buildings or neighbourhoods, both planners and architects will produce better work – and may even, at the same time, restore some of their tarnished credibility. As Richard Weston writes in *Schools of Thought*, his book on the architecture of Hampshire County

Council, 'The gulf between "professional", "educated" taste and popular taste in Britain is so vast that it may appear naïve to suggest that it can – or, some might even argue, should – be bridged. But if we are to have modern buildings worthy of the name architecture, some kind of reconciliation is vital, for the profession needs urgently to regain the public respect which – along with most other professions in contemporary Britain – has been largely destroyed in recent years, not least due to a sustained political assault on professional values which have a nasty habit of inhibiting the "free" operation of the Government's beloved "market forces"!'[14]

What can be done? How can architects and planners 'reach different people in ways they want to be reached'? That is the question posed by Lesley Gallery, who has done so much to improve public awareness of, and interest in, urban-design issues in the USA. There she has championed public urban forums in which to air and debate issues and specific training and education programmes to widen the experience of mayors and elected representatives.

In Britain increasing the opportunities for public debate will undoubtedly help, but it will not be sufficient. As the amount of information, consultation and participation increase, so too will expectations. As those expectations are thwarted, or are met only in part, new frustrations will grow. Quite apart from the vested interests that surround every urban issue (whether related to development or conservation), there is the need to find ways to mediate between the needs of a neighbourhood community and the needs of the wider London community in cases such as King's Cross.

Every politician hopes for decisions that hurt as few people as possible, and in London the amount of derelict or unused land offers sites for development that could provide pain-free options. But most development will involve unpopular decisions that cut across sectional interests, whether of conservationists, the local community, employers or the unemployed.

It is not hard to balance these arguments; it is hard to balance the necessary actions. Finally, developing the future of London will involve compromise and negotiation, which would be considerably easier to achieve if there were the same general presumption in favour of the future, and in favour of change, as exists in Barcelona, where people are enduring great physical disruption and, in some cases, the destruction of neighbourhoods. They accept, even approve of, the changes because they have become convinced that they, and their city, will in the end be enhanced.

Their conviction has been built up, not instantly by rhetoric but over a period of years, by the actions of the local authority, the Ajuntament, which has gained the confidence and the trust of the city's people. Unless we can generate a similar confidence in London, change will be hard both to achieve and to accept.

CHAPTER NINE

Inventing Tomorrow

The spiralling, tent-like roof of Stoke Park Infant School at Bishopstoke in Hampshire grows out of its site, half-sunk in sheltering mounds and surrounded by Forestry Commission woodland. It has a festive air, almost like the big top of a circus, yet its eaves come down low to gather in, and reassure, small children.

It is a building flooded with light, full of joy and designed by Hampshire County Council Architects' Department for this particular site. It sends one very clear message to both teachers and children: that education is so important, and they as individuals are so important, that only something built especially for them is good enough. In a better world every school – indeed, every building – would convey the same message. Why should we settle for less? Why are not all buildings designed with the same care and respect for people as this? As a society we have erected a mass of offices and shops over the past ten years, and even a few schools, but we have paid too little attention to the quality of their design. Stoke Park Infant School is an exception rather than the rule. Why?

It is a paradox that, although we train fine architects and live surrounded by great buildings bequeathed to us by previous generations, there are so many shoddy contemporary buildings in every town and city. No one group of people is responsible for this neglect. We have already noted the imperfections in the planning system that inhibit good, innovative architecture, but any blame must also be shared by developers and private builders, by local authorities, by central government and by architects themselves. Deep down, as a society, we don't value architecture, and so we don't promote architects in the way that the Victorians fêted their engineers. Then Brunel and Telford were household names; today their equivalents, star architects such as Norman Foster and James Stirling, can safely shop on a Saturday morning without fear of being recognized.

This lack of interest in architecture will continue until we begin to care enough to want to change it. In that process many groups can play a part, but central government will have a key role in setting out a policy framework for architecture and proving that it, at least, values this most inescapable and public of art forms.

As yet there is no sign of willingness, let alone enthusiasm to do this, even though there is good reason to believe that time is not on our side. Whichever political party is in government in the final years of this century will need to build. One effect of the obsessive antipathy to public expenditure that characterized the Thatcher years has been to dam up a desperate need for new buildings: new homes for the homeless, new hospitals for the sick, new libraries to provide books for new communities. The next few years are likely to see a building explosion, in both the public and private sectors, that will go a long way towards changing the face of Britain. We have a choice – either to put up good buildings, using the best architects to create a new generation of fine buildings, or to knock up the cheapest, fastest, and leave our children to pick up the maintenance bill in twenty years' time.

Government has yet to tackle this problem. When asked in Parliamentary written questions about their design policy, many Departments of State acknowledged no responsibility for this whatsoever. When questioned about their expenditure on architecture,[1] some, like the Department of Trade and Industry, passed responsibility to the Property Services Agency (PSA)[2] even though it ceased to be responsible for major government projects after 1 April 1988. Others, such as the Home Office and the Foreign and Commonwealth Office, said that such information was 'not available centrally and could not be obtained without disproportionate cost'.[3] The Government has no policy for architecture; worse, it appears to be unaware of this omission, which is curious when you consider that, in spite of the constraints on public expenditure, central government spent over £3 billion on new buildings, renovation, repair and maintenance in 1990/91.[4] However, all this expenditure was undertaken without coordination between departments and with little thought for the quality of architecture that resulted.

The scale of this activity indicates the real potential for the Government to promote high standards in British architecture and to set a good example to local authorities and private developers, both of which could be achieved without spending an extra pound. There are a few isolated examples to suggest that it, and certain publicly financed companies, are beginning to recognize this potential. Richard Burton of ABK, the designer of the excellent St Mary's Hospital on the Isle of Wight, has been commissioned to build the new British Embassy in Moscow. Terry Farrell's offices at Vauxhall Cross are nearing completion – even if the Government client is MI6. Nicholas Grimshaw is working on the Channel Tunnel terminus at Waterloo. London Underground is employing Will Alsop and Michael Hopkins on new Jubilee Line stations in addition to Foster Associates, who designed Stansted Airport. But, in the context of that £3 billion a year, these are only a handful of exceptions, and overall the design quality of most PSA-managed buildings is low. The PSA's policy and priorities were described by the minister then responsible, Patrick Nicholls, MP, in a letter:[5] 'Consultants are selected from those who have expressed interest in working with PSA, taking account of factors such as track record and experience in the type of project under consideration, and the resources they are able to offer. Since 1984, fee competition has become a major influence in the selection process. In essence, this means that a careful pre-selection takes place to produce a short list of about three firms judged to be capable of developing a satisfactory design solution for the particular project. The consultants are invited to submit tenders against a fully developed brief and the commission is normally awarded to the firm submitting the lowest bid.' '

No wonder that Richard MacCormac, President of the RIBA, wrote in his introduction to *Schools of Thought*,[6] a book about the architectural work of Hampshire County Council between 1974 and 1991, 'It was widely assumed, if not publicly declared, that to be socially and financially responsible, architecture could not afford to be an art. This is a view still deeply ingrained in "official thinking" about the environment, as the current procurement practices of government departments demonstrate.'

Apart from procurement, there are many possible initiatives that are open to the Government if it wishes to promote better standards of architecture, including the use of competitions, the encouragement of young architects and the publication of information and examples of excellence. In pursuing such opportunities British ministers could benefit from studying how their counterparts in Europe have fared over the past fifteen years.

Twenty years ago the French Government began to tackle a different, and more difficult, problem: that French architecture was of a conspicuously poor quality. There had been scarcely a French architect, or a public building, of quality since the Second World War. The first move to change this grim state of affairs was made by President Pompidou, when he decided in 1970 that the choice of architect for a new cultural centre in the heart of Paris should be made by a competition open to architects from all over the world. The following year over 600 architects submitted proposals, and the competition was won by the partnership of Renzo Piano and Richard Rogers. For the President to allow a competition of this national importance to be won by a non-French partnership was, in itself, significant, but Pompidou went further and backed the radical, much criticized, design personally. The era of open competitions was launched and was to continue for twelve years through to the competition for the Grande Arche de la Défense in 1983. In that period every competition for a Grand Projet was won by a foreign architect, but with people of the stature and calibre of I. M. Pei and Gae Aulenti working in France, it was inevitable that interest in, and debate about, new architectural ideas should be excited and that new standards were set for French architects.

High-profile international competitions could symbolize a new interest in architecture on the President's part, but, by themselves, they could not foster a new generation of young architects. In 1974 the creation of the Programme d'Architecture Nouvelle (PAN), under the direction of Robert Lion, began to address this need. Each year the PAN would organize a competition for architects under the age of 40 to design a specified project, such as a library, leisure centre or primary school, with a guarantee that the winning design would be built. Not only did this focus attention on new French talent but it began to build up a cadre of architects, and a body of work, around the country.

Of equal significance was the appointment, in 1978, of Joseph Belmont as Directeur de l'Architecture, with a brief to build on the PAN initiative and restore the quality and reputation of French architecture. Belmont was an experienced architect in his forties who had worked with Jean Pouvé. This won him the respect of fellow architects and the authority to set about this task. While the Assemblée Nationale passed a new Loi sur l'Architecture, Belmont assembled a small team and set up the Mission Interministérielle pour la Qualité des Constructions Publiques, at the centre of which was a Code des Marches Publiques, whose provisions applied equally to central and to local government. Under this Code the design of every new public building in France, above a certain size, has to be determined by architectural competition.

There are two scales of competition. For buildings whose architect's fees are between 400,000 and 900,000 francs (that is, buildings costing between, approximately, £0.5 million and £1 million) the competition regime is light, and juries make their decision without the aid of drawings, either from references, usually accompanied by slides of previous work, or after interview. References and slides are also used to help establish a short list for larger projects with fees of over 900,000 francs, but for these there has to be a full design competition, and all architects on the short list are paid. Belmont understood from the outset that one key to the success of this competition regime would be the quality of the briefs and of the juries. As an architect he knew that briefs could be too detailed. What was needed was a small package of key documents: a description of the site; the aims of the client, whether a local authority or a government department; the local planning regulations, the POS; and an outline of the urban constraints, the *Cahier des Charges et des Obligations Urbaines*. As for the juries, Belmont quickly came to the conclusion that they had to be uneven in number, to ensure that majority decisions could be arrived at, and that, with regard to size, the smaller they were, the better, with an optimum of nine members. This was the size of the jury originally appointed for the Grande Arche competition, but by the time the final decision was made, it had risen to thirteen. Some Grands Projets juries were even bigger, the one for the Bibliothèque de France being composed of seventeen and those for the Opéra Bastille and the Parc de la Villette more than twenty-five each. Whatever the number, Belmont stuck determinedly to the principle that one third of the membership of each jury should be practising architects and to the objective that designs commissioned under the Code should always be built.

It is inevitable that an architectural policy that seeks to encompass everything from major national buildings and public spaces, such as the Pyramide at the Louvre and the Parc de la Villette, to everyday buildings such as primary schools and police stations, must have considerable flexibility. But the basic elements – clear briefs, professional juries and some form of competition – are all constants, and it is these that have been so important in improving standards at regional and local level. The Government's instrument regionally has been the Conseil d'Architecture, d'Urbanisme et d'Environnement (CAUE), established under the 1977 Loi sur l'Architecture. This agency, with an office in each of France's 100 *départements*, is available to give advice to local authorities and their mayors, and to the private sector, not just on individual buildings but also on larger urban plans. These are formally outside the Code, but cities frequently employ competitions, *marches de définition*, to canvass ideas for complex sites. The fact that so many cities – Dunkirk, Lille, Nantes, Bordeaux, Nice, Nîmes, Montpellier, Aix-en-Provence, Dieppe – are engaged in major building and urban-regeneration projects demonstrates both the need for, and the effectiveness of, the work of CAUE, which also has the wider role of promoting debate and interest in local architecture by means of exhibitions and conferences, as does the Institut Français de l'Architecture nationally.

In choosing architects for shortlisting, mayors and other public bodies can turn to the *Album de la Jeune Architecture*. This book has been published every year since 1979 as a means of advertising the designs of the best young architects and is sent to every public body, institution and local authority.

The cumulative effect of these various initiatives can be seen in the Salon d'Architecture, held annually in La Villette in Paris. Here government departments, regional cities and public companies come to exhibit the models, photographs and drawings of their best new buildings in a highly competitive atmosphere.

It would be misleading to suggest that the way in which the French have approached public architecture is without problems. At this moment they are looking again at the operation of their competitions policy under the Code with a view to simplifying it. The very success of the Code meant that over 1,000 projects were submitted to some form of competition in 1991. Under such a volume of work the system is beginning to buckle, and high costs are entailed by both administration and architects' fees. Moreover, the pressure on architects, both those who compete and those who serve on juries, is intense and is beginning to result, in Joseph Belmont's words, in 'competition fatigue'. While retaining the principle of competition, it may be necessary to draw up looser regulations and to insist that more competitions should be decided on the basis of concepts rather than of designs.

Furthermore, the implementation of the policy has not always been perfectly smooth, particularly when it has come to building the designs of competition winners. The Grande Arche de la Défense nearly foundered when the incoming Chirac Government changed the purpose of the building from a broadcasting and communications centre to a commercial office block. The public institution that was to acquire a large part of the project, the Carrefour de la Communication, was disbanded in April 1986, and all government finance was

withdrawn with the exception of the sums necessary for the purchase of the land and for the (unlettable) roof, which amounted to
between 5 and 7 per cent of the total cost. Only the ingenuity
of Robert Lion, chairman of the holding company, the Société
d'Economie Mixte de la Tête-Défense, in raising the balance of the
2,777-million-franc construction costs and in letting the offices at
commercial rents, saved the project. And, on a smaller scale, in
Nantes a good design for a major government office building was
rejected by the local mayor (overruling the competition's jury) as
having the 'wrong image' for his town.

With the exception of occasional incidents such as these, however, it has been Belmont's guiding, even driving, hand that has
been essential to the success of the national strategy, in the same way
that the influence of Emile Biasini, the Secretary of State for Grands
Projets, has been central to the realization of the major buildings.
Without Belmont and Biasini the policy, by itself, would have been
far less certain of success.

No part of this policy, least of all the practice of competitions
under the Code, is a cure-all, but for France it has worked, at least in
the public sector. It must be said that, even after fifteen years and
more, there is little sign of this public example of good practice having an effect on the quality of most private-sector developers in
France, who are as liable to opt for Design and Build, or Concep-
tion/Construction (a system offering fast and cheap buildings), as are
their counterparts in Britain. However, it is possible to detect some
influence on the biggest and most prestigious private developments:
the new office tower to the west of La Défense, planned as the tall-
est and slimmest tower in Europe, was put out to a competition that
was won by Jean Nouvel, the architect of the Institut du Monde
Arabe.

In spite of these hiccups and imperfections the policy has achieved
its primary objective of shaking up French architecture, so that new
ideas and approaches are now sought by cities and by institutions as a
matter of course. In expanding higher education the Government is
building five new universities in a ring around Paris but is uncertain
about the best way to organize, or where to locate, a University of

the Twenty-first Century. Accordingly, it has put the design out to a *marche de définition* as a means of canvassing solutions for the different sites.

The greatest success of the policy, however, has been, by general agreement, the fact that a new generation of young French architects has been brought to the fore. The promotion provided by the *Album de la Jeune Architecture* and the opportunities offered by the PAN and by the numerous small *monuments du quotidien*, such as local schools, have established the basis of a career structure for French architects. In the ten years after he qualified from the Ecole des Beaux Arts in 1979 Dominique Perrault built a primary school, a college of technical education and two industrial buildings. All were decided by competition. In 1989 he won the international competition for the £720 million Bibliothèque de France and is now established as a major international architect. Behind him is a generation of French architects with experience and confidence. Had Perrault been working in Britain, he would not have been offered the same opportunities.

Witness the experience of Ken Armstrong and Jennifer Smith, who in 1990 won the competition for the new Japan Centre in Paris. Although slightly older than Perrault, these talented British architects had previously worked with Foster Associates but had never built any of their own designs before. Overall the policies adopted by French Governments over the last fifteen years have made a strong public statement: that architecture is important and that government, central and local, can play an important part in promoting quality, in conserving the architectural heritage and in commissioning exciting new buildings.

Not that France is the only country from which we could profitably learn. In the Netherlands the Government has recently published a White Paper on architecture as a joint policy statement of the Secretary of State for the Environment, J. G. M. Alders, and the Minister for Welfare, Health and Cultural Affairs, H. d'Anconca. Although criticized by Dutch architects as too timid and imprecise, it has some points of similarity with the French approach. Competition is proposed but not for all major public buildings and not within a coherent framework such as that of the French Code. Instead local authorities are encouraged to employ competitions on a voluntary basis. The Netherlands are not driving their policy forward by means of Grands Projets – indeed, their one venture in this direction, the Amsterdam Opera House, has been marred by confusion and controversy not dissimilar to that surrounding the National Gallery extension. However, the Dutch have a great tradition of urban design, the Berlago (1912) and van Eesteren (1935) developments in Amsterdam being models of their kind, and it is this new urban thinking, particularly in relation to social housing, that is noteworthy in the Netherlands.

The Government already has a national supervisor for building and architecture, a seconded senior civil servant with the title Rijksbouwmeester. Although this post is apparently similar to the position held in France by Joseph Belmont and is also held by an architect, to date his work has been concerned primarily with building and procurement. The position has not been upgraded by the White Paper, but its role in future is to be more concerned with the quality of architecture. To assist in that the Government has set up a new fund to stimulate innovation by subsidizing projects that could serve as an example and by supporting local government in developing its own architectural policies. However, these advances are somewhat undermined by the fact that the Rijksbouwmeester has only advisory, rather than executive, powers.

At a local level cities like Rotterdam have Departments of Urban Development headed by a supervisor who is able to take a wider view in much the same way as Oriol Bohigas operated through the Urban Design Unit in Barcelona. The different ways in which the French and the Dutch use the same elements of policy probably reflect their distinct approaches to politics and administration. French political life has tended to be directed strongly from the centre, unlike the more decentralized structures in the Netherlands. The Dutch White Paper is consensual, but at least, with its publication, the Netherlands recognize that this is an important issue. In Britain we have still to take that first step.

What can we learn from the French and the Dutch? First,

perhaps, that competitions can be a useful tool, although in Britain they would need to serve a different purpose. Unlike that of the French in 1975, our problem is not a lack of quality in our architecture; it is a lack of opportunity for our architects, and a greater use of competitions in deciding the design of public buildings could provide precisely that opportunity – if, and only if, these competitions were part of a wider policy.

The British Government ought to be encouraged by the private sector and by local authorities that are making increasing use of competitions. The RIBA has a competitions department that responds to approximately 500 requests for advice a year, but the Government neither provides any financial support for this work nor demonstrates any interest. Perhaps it feels that its own experience of competitions is not encouraging.

When Michael Heseltine became Secretary of State for the Environment in 1979, he brought to the Department an interest in, and enthusiasm for, architecture and, indeed, initiated a series of competitions. However, after five years only nine projects had been built, and competitions were in effect abandoned. The official view of the Department was expressed by Under Secretary of State Patrick Nicholls, MP, writing some years after Mr Heseltine had left the DoE: 'I recognize that the French have traditionally made extensive use of open competition, but experience in the United Kingdom in both public and private sectors has not made competition the first choice for a number of reasons ... Many competitions in the UK in the past have not produced a totally satisfactory outcome. Perhaps the major drawback with the competition approach is that the brief is normally prepared by a panel – and effectively denies dialogue between the architect and the client during development of the design.'[7] The true seeds of failure can be detected, though, not only in the writing of the brief but in the Minister's further description of the policy: 'On the initiative of Michael Heseltine ... a programme of competitions for Property Services Agency buildings was developed. They were launched singly during the period 1980–85. Various sections of PSA were asked to suggest suitable subjects, many of which were not investigated in depth due to obvious snags. However, fourteen of them were seriously considered, but only nine of them became the subjects of completed competitions.' Those abandoned included a National Library complex at Port of Spain, Trinidad, Harrow Crown Courts and a library for the Royal Military College of Science at Shrivenham.

However, even among the nine completed projects there are signs of a lack of commitment; the second stage of the competition for the Sir Joseph Banks Building at the Royal Botanical Gardens, Kew, was abandoned, as a further sift of the 270 entrants 'would have incurred too much delay', while only part of James Watson's winning design for RAF Tanin's control tower and related buildings was constructed. More crucially, 'When four of the five problematical competitions occurred sequentially, there was a minor hiatus.'[8] In total these nine completed competitions represented buildings worth no more than £7.8 million of the several billions of pounds that the Government spent on new building and renovation between 1980 and 1985.

What, in all probability, finally brought an end to the Heseltine initiative, however, was the high-profile disaster over the National Gallery extension. From the seventy-nine entries seven were chosen for the second stage. Inviting the public to vote on the designs established nothing, as the most popular proposal, by Richard Rogers, attracted 30 per cent of first preferences and at the same time proved also to be the most disliked (27 per cent of votes). The competition was abandoned, and the proposal by Ahrends, Burton and Koralek 'emerged' as the winner, at which point Prince Charles, in a speech to the RIBA at Hampton Court on 30 May 1984, described the winning design as 'a vast municipal fire station' and, in case anyone should be uncertain about his viewpoint, went on to say, 'What is proposed is like a monstrous carbuncle on the face of a much loved and elegant friend.' When the Sainsbury brothers offered to finance the extensions and initiated a new international competition, won by Venturi, Rauch and Scott-Brown of Philadelphia, the Government gratefully withdrew from any attempt at a concerted competition policy. But the Houses of Parliament resulted from a competition, as did Manchester Town Hall, the Law Courts, the

National Theatre and the Burrell Collection, all among the finest buildings in the land.

The contrast with France is clear. An enthusiasm for, even a belief in, competitions, which Michael Heseltine undoubtedly had, is not enough. What is needed is a policy that establishes ground rules for briefs and juries, a long-term commitment, the courage to stick with decisions even if criticized and a Joseph Belmont figure to hold all this together, as did Norman Shaw in Britain at the turn of the century. Only then will the public sector in Britain begin to realize the potential of that £3-billion expenditure budget and offer British architects the chance consistently to design major buildings at home as well as abroad.

However, as the experience of France also makes clear, there are likely to be many more opportunities for commissions in local authorities than in central government. Even in a climate of great hostility towards all local-authority expenditure in the 1980s, when municipal housing new starts in London in particular were reduced from 9,131 (1979) to 306 (1990), local councils in the UK still spent billions on new buildings. But morale in those authorities' Architects' Departments has ebbed catastrophically, their energies being directed to reducing the costs of projects rather than attempting to find the best solutions. Even in this unfavourable climate the example of Hampshire County Council shows that it is possible to develop imaginative policies.

Cutbacks in local-government expenditure had really started in 1975, when the then Secretary of State for the Environment, Tony Crosland, made it clear that 'the party was over', and both he and his successor, Peter Shore, began to reduce both central government's contribution to local expenditure and Rate Support Grant from 66.5 to 61 per cent. (Today it stands at 42 per cent.)[9] It was just before this, in January 1974, that Hampshire appointed Colin Stansfield Smith as County Architect. The department that he inherited was neither better nor worse than that of most other local authorities. Hampshire was a member of the Second Consortium of Local Authorities (SCOLA), together with Cheshire, Gloucestershire, Shropshire, Worcestershire, Dorset and West Sussex. SCOLA's hallmark was a school programme dominated by system-building, which, as Richard Weston notes in his book *Schools of Thought*,[10] mentioned above, 'was still seen by the Education Department as an efficient way of producing schools with the added advantage of severely limiting the architects' capacity to "interfere"'.

Colin Stansfield Smith set out to change this, making it clear at his appointment interview 'that the Council had to be sure if they appointed him that they wanted "real architecture"'. How he did so to such effect that in 1991 he received the RIBA Gold Medal for Architecture is, as Richard MacCormac says in his foreword to *Schools of Thought*, 'a record of an extraordinary collaborative venture to transform architectural practice. It raises crucial arguments about the objectives of public architecture today and about the context of local government and political opinion in which that practice takes place.'[11]

Colin Stansfield Smith applied no instant solutions – indeed, he later said, 'It took us ten years to understand what we were managing' – but one of his first steps was to establish a Design Centre within his department. Not only did this make a clear public statement about his commitment to innovation and to raising the quality of buildings and environments in the county, but it also offered a practical design service to other departments. The brief of the Design Centre was to generate new solutions and ideas. 'It seemed obvious to me,' he said, 'that the last chap you asked to design fire stations was the one who had been designing fire stations for the last ten years, because these buildings were designed by formula and pre-conception.'[12]

To raise both the expectations and the standards of his colleagues still further Stansfield Smith began in 1979 to introduce, as consultants, outside experts with national reputations. The structural engineer Tony Hunt was brought in to work with in-house architect Peter Galloway on the extension to, and remodelling of, Frogmore Comprehensive School in Yateley, where, by incorporating an inner skin of seasonally adjusted insulating panels, he was able substantially to reduce energy costs for what had previously been a typical flat-roofed SCOLA school. Hunt went on to collaborate with architect

Mervyn Perkins on designs for a new primary school, also in Yateley, named Newlands. Although here the double pitch of the con-
servatory roof is in glass, it anticipates many of the ideas and the scale
of the 'big roofs' that became a feature of Hampshire primary and
infant schools like Stoke Park at Bishopstoke. These roofs were not a
design signature but arose out of new thinking in the Architects'
Department about energy saving. Richard Weston explains, 'The
flat-roofed SCOLA schools were dependent on high, mechanically
produced, ventilation rates – with the consequent running and
maintenance costs and loss of heated air – whereas the large volume
of a school like Yateley substantially reduces the required ventilation
rate, which can be achieved naturally by inducing air-flow up to,
and through, the ridge.'[13]

Also in 1979 Stansfield Smith commissioned the first of a series of
distinguished architectural practices when he invited ABK to design
Portsmouth Polytechnic Library. In the 1980s Edward Cullinan
remodelled the SCOLA Calthorpe Park School in Fleet (1984);
Michael Hopkins was the architect for Fleet Infant School (1986);
and Richard MacCormac designed new county offices in Havant
(1987). Local architect John Browning, of Plincke, Leaman and
Browning, was also commissioned for the major redevelopment of
Winton Secondary School in Andover (1987–90).

If new ideas were being introduced through the work of these
distinguished architects and engineers, new energies were also being
harnessed by giving students, who were gaining a year's work experience before qualifying, some real responsibility on projects. Some
of those students remained for a further year with the department,
forming links that are likely to become even closer, particularly in
relation to Portsmouth Polytechnic, since Colin Stansfield Smith
was appointed Professor of Architectural Design at the Polytechnic.

However, it was not solely the quality of these design initiatives,
treating each project as a unique challenge, that really eased the way
for abandoning the SCOLA system-building. This was achieved
not by confrontation with the Education Department but by a gradual process of demonstrating that design, for new buildings or
grounds, could provide better solutions to the many problems facing

the Education Committee, whether those of falling rolls and spare capacity or the high maintenance costs of SCOLA buildings.

By the late 1980s Hampshire's 667 schools had 40,000 surplus places. Costed at an average of £400 a place, this represented a waste of approximately £16 million worth of ratepayers' money. In helping to tackle this problem the Architects' Department moved decisively into the management of the county's estate.

In total that estate consisted of 17,000 acres of land and 8,000 buildings with 2.3 million square feet of accommodation, approximately three times the floor space of all Marks and Spencer's stores in Britain. In the past the maintenance of these buildings had been tackled separately by different departments. The appointment of Andrew Smith as Head of Resources and Operations in 1985 altered that. He developed a 'Strategy for the Built Estate' that recognized buildings as representing both assets, in their capital value, and liabilities, in their running and maintenance costs. The audit he set in train allowed the Architects' Department for the first time to assess the existing use of a site and its potential as a public space. What was revealed was often surprising. SCOLA buildings, although accounting for only 25 per cent of the school estate, soaked up 50 per cent of Education's maintenance budget; a magistrates' court that needed £250,000 for immediate repairs was shown to be used for only three hours a week; infant schools were actually only open for 9 per cent of the year; at the same time as having 40,000 surplus places, Hampshire schools were still using over 1,000 temporary buildings, whose heating and maintenance costs were appreciably higher than those of permanent structures.

The design skills of Stansfield Smith's architects could help with all these problems – for instance, by remodelling buildings or by allowing joint use. In combining the twin responsibilities of design and estate management Stansfield Smith and Andrew Smith enabled the council to begin to anticipate and resolve its difficulties at source rather than simply reacting to their symptoms. In short, the local authority began to shape its own future and, by doing so, Hampshire offers a valuable lesson both to other local authorities and to the Government.

With school buildings in England and Wales worth over £30 billion and covering 150,000 acres on 24,000 sites, which are themselves worth a further £25 billion, the Department of Education and Science itself has a huge opportunity and an urgent need. But the Government has been intent on moving away from coherent management. Far from encouraging the PSA to develop in this direction it has, in the name of market forces, dispersed responsibility. Norman Lamont, the Chancellor of the Exchequer, explains the Government's thinking: 'Where Departments are free to use agents other than PSA for building and maintenance work, it is for them to decide on value for money grounds, and after the usual tendering and contract procedures have been observed, whether such agents, or PSA, should be employed.'[14]

Mr Lamont's phrases about 'value for money' and 'the usual tendering and contract procedures' have been given a new significance by the Government's proposal, outlined in the 1991 Queen's Speech, to introduce Compulsory Competitive Tendering (CCT) for building services and procurement, thus bringing these services into line with refuse collection and the many other civic activities that have been put out to the marketplace in recent years. The effect of CCT will, in the words of architect Michael Wigginton, be twofold: 'First, that in-house Architects' Departments in local-government and state-funded organizations will be disbanded, so that their services can be procured "in the market". Second, that projects organized and founded by government will be put out to tender, with the lowest fee obtaining the commission'.[15]

The damage that would result would be considerable. The whole future of local-authority Architects' Departments, like Hampshire's, would be in doubt, but deciding the design of buildings by lowest-fee bidding could have even greater implications. In any commercial contract a balance must be struck between quality and price, but CCT abandons the problems of finding that balance. Whatever its merits in determining contracts for services, which can, in the main, be objectively quantifed, it is inappropriate as a method of choosing designs, which, by their nature, are qualititative. The result will be that work goes to the cheapest architect, not the best. This is likely to lead to a generation of buildings, poorly designed and shoddily built, that in turn will produce higher maintenance and running costs in the future.

In Richard MacCormac's words, these are 'crucial arguments about the objectives of public architecture today'. What the experience of Hampshire makes clear is that there is not simply one 'correct' way to develop an architectural policy. We can argue about the relative merits of the French or the Dutch use of competitions, but Colin Stansfield Smith has employed a competition only once, exploiting instead the power of patronage. It is a method of selecting architects for projects that depends for its success on the taste and integrity of the patron. Consequently it would be dangerous to adopt it widely in a national-government context of hundreds of projects a year, since it could be open to abuse and misinterpretation while risking the adoption of a narrow range of styles. But on one element of a successful policy Hampshire is in complete agreement with Paris and Barcelona: strong political leadership is essential.

Stansfield Smith is the first to admit that none of what has been achieved would have been possible without the active support of the leader of the council, Freddie Emery-Wallis, just as the work of Bohigas and Mackay wouldn't have happened in Barcelona without the intervention of the mayor, Pasqual Maragall, or that of Belmont in France without President Mitterrand. All of them have done what is most difficult for politicians – they have taken a long-term view. As Stansfield Smith complimented Emery-Wallis in his Winchester lecture, the leader of the council understood 'that it cannot all be done in one generation'.

That is one of the reasons why Hampshire County Council has proved to be a model client, both for its own Architects' Department and for those outside practices it has employed, and the quality of clients, whether in the public or private sector, is vital if architecture is to prosper. In the case of the Lloyd's Building the commitment and determination of the Chairman of Lloyd's, Sir Peter Green, was as crucial a part of the design team as were the architects and engineers.

If clients are interested only in the cheapest possible solution, and value only an architect's ability to build the largest possible enclosed space for the smallest investment in the quickest time, then good architecture is impossible, regardless of what example the Government sets or what policy it pursues. SCOLA shows that system-building, using repetitive, formulaic ideas, is a false economy and creates problems rather than solving them, yet the Government is positively encouraging Design and Build schemes, through which the building contractor undertakes the design as part of a package. The Government's policy of competitive tendering for new buildings actually requires local authorities to put cheapness before quality. Dispensing with the services of an architect may satisfy the Government's preferred criterion of awarding contracts to the firm submitting the lowest bid, but it is unlikely to stimulate original or thoughtful design ideas. Similarly, rigid use of the Essex Design Guide[16] can constrict and stultify, preventing the individual consideration of sites and of the needs of those who will use a building. The Essex Design Guide may be a useful aid to the layout of an estate, but it has been responsible for some horrible results when misapplied or when applied with uncritical zeal.

In these circumstances short-term considerations will continue to dominate, and buildings will be judged on how they maximize the ratio of rentable space to gross space or the ratio of wall size to floor. The number of storeys that can be compressed into the given height of a building will become a significant factor. As a result we will live and work in structures that are little more than thin-skinned boxes, devoid of character, atmosphere or individuality. 'Non-rentable areas', such as gardens, trees, shrubs, fountains and sculptures, will become rarities.

Of course, there are developers who take a longer-term view and reject the simplistic equations that quantity plus economy equals profit, while quality plus investment equals loss. Such developers recognize that good design matters and is likely to pay eventually. Developers can make profits in many ways – by relying, for example, on a steady rise in land and rental values to increase their capital asset and rental income. In such an approach the market does the work regardless of the use of the land. Alternatively, a developer can add value to land by making it desirable or attractive through imaginative use or through the good design of the buildings and their surroundings, as the best developers in Britain have always done.

This was how the John Woods (father and son) created Bath as a piece of speculative building, how John Nash made money out of Regent Street and the crescents and terraces around Regent's Park and how, in the 1760s, the Adam brothers built the Adelphi between the Strand and the Thames, one of the most elegant eighteenth-century developments in London. Rasmussen describes this as 'not only a dream of antique architecture, it was just as much a finance-fantasia over risk and profit; the financier was an artist and the artist a financier'.[7] He is perhaps too kind to the Adams, as Adelphi's stark serenity didn't gain immediate favour, and the scheme would have collapsed, bankrupting the brothers, had not an Act of Parliament allowed the houses to be sold off by lottery.

In the meantime government could set a good example, in the commissioning of its own buildings and in its general valuation of our environment, but it is probable that only regulations or guidelines will be necessary. The point is demonstrated by the example of Manhattan, where it is regulation that has insisted that all commercial buildings should provide some public space at street level in proportion to the size of the building, leading to a lively mix of foyers, arcades and atria in New York's office buildings.

Such regulation could improve the use of land and public space, but better-quality architecture will come about only if there is a change of attitude, on the part not just of clients, whether public or private, but of the key participants, the general public and architects themselves. The initiatives discussed in the previous chapter – greater consultation with, and involvement of, the community, wider dissemination of information about planning and architecture by means of architecture centres, a higher profile for architecture and related matters in schools education – all have a part to play, as does more and better coverage of architecture and planning in the media. All these measures should seek to bring architects and the public closer, so that the one can serve the other better.

There is no doubt that, at present, the gulf between the two is wide and that architects should bear considerable responsibility for this. As Plutarch observed more than 2,000 years ago, 'Those who love to build are their own undoers and need no other enemies.' Few members of the public seem to believe that many architects embody the ideals set out by Vitruvius: 'The architect should be a man of letters, a skilful draughtsman, a mathematician, familiar with music, not ignorant of medicine, learned in the response of jurisconsults, familiar with astronomy and astronomical calculations ... but perhaps it will be wonderful to inexperienced persons that human nature can master and hold in recollection so large a number of subjects.' Perhaps indeed!

Many of the criticisms of contemporary architecture and buildings are valid and are rooted not just in the durability of materials or the levels of maintenance and repair but in the designs themselves. We have built too many blocks of flats and estates like Broadwater Farm, which are little short of misery to live in. There are shopping centres, like many of the Arndales or the Tricorn in Portsmouth, that are bleak and make shopping an endurance test. In almost every town and city we continue to tolerate multi-storey car parks that are concrete labyrinths, unsafe and frightening at night, a constant invitation to theft and graffiti. The architectural profession could and should make more effort to listen to, and work with, communities and particularly the elderly and those with disabilities. In spite of some improvements in both thinking and practice, the needs of people with disabilities continue to be ignored. Architect Andrew Lisicki writes, 'The argument that people with disabilities have the same rights as those who temporarily have none is irrefutable. So why is it proving so difficult for us to assert those rights? We have won the argument but we still can't go to the cinema or the shops. We can't use the public transport. We can't choose our education. We can't even choose where we live.'[18]

Architects can help, but 'The first real change must be in the minds of the legislators ... those who make this environment in physical terms should be controlled by those who make the law.'[19] Changes to the Building Regulations, to the Codes of Practice issued by the British Standards Institution and to disability legislation generally would be a constructive start,[20] all of them only recommendations that can be, and are, ignored by planning authorities and the Department of the Environment itself. Legislation changes that are needed include the 1970 Chronically Sick and Disabled Persons Act (amended 1976), whose Section 3 places duties on housing authorities, and the 1981 Disabled Persons Act. Both these pieces of legislation contain large and well-used loopholes in phrases such as 'in so far as it is in the circumstances both practicable and reasonable' and 'appropriate provision'. A further weakness is the number of bodies and properties that can, and do, claim exemption from the above, including 'Crown properties, government buildings, British Rail properties, most educational establishments, military establishments, agricultural buildings, temporary buildings, virtually all existing buildings, open spaces and all housing. Should any of these escape the net, English Heritage can be relied upon to keep disabled people at bay in the interests of preserving historical purity.'[21]

But we should beware too great a beating of breasts. Shoddy and thoughtless building has occurred in every generation and, since we are fallible beings, will no doubt continue. But it should also be accepted that architects are not solely responsible for such disasters. Planners and developers provide the briefs for buildings; politicians determine construction budgets and maintenance costs. Those who frame the political and financial parameters should share the responsibility. However, to recognize that is to carry the argument into the centre of the political arena. Since many of those who criticize contemporary architecture are reluctant to address this political reality, they back off and limit their criticism to appearance and style, often with particular reference to the past.

Of course, style is important, but there is room in this, as in any generation, for a wide variety of styles and of ways of expressing the needs and concerns of our generation in the form of buildings. We would do well to leaven the debate over the merits of different styles with the generous open-mindedness of David Mackay, when he accepted that, in commissioning all the past winners of Barcelona's Building of the Year Award to contribute to the Olympic Village, there would inevitably be a wide variety of style and even of quality.

'But isn't that part of a city?' he asked. 'Surely we can accommodate that human variety?'

In Britain, if you look at buildings of the early nineteenth century, you see John Nash's remodelling of Buckingham Palace (1820s), Decimus Burton's neo-classical screen at Hyde Park Corner (from 1825), Charles Barry's Gothic extravaganza in the Houses of Parliament (1839–52), William Butterfield's highly decorated Arts and Crafts All Saints, Margaret Street (1849–59), the high technology of Paxton's Crystal Palace (1851) and Brunel's Paddington Station (1850–55), all built within a period of thirty years. If the Victorians could enjoy such a profusion of styles, why can't we?

Contemporary architects, whether described as Modernist, Neo-Modernist, Post-Modernist, High-tech or Community, will go on fighting their own corner, many arguing that architecture should reflect, and grow out of, not just the social and individual needs of people but also society's capabilities, including, in particular, technological advances. Throughout the ages architects have been prepared to make use of those advances, whether they be bricks, tiles, or sheets of glass or the ability to construct an arch or a dome. In doing so they have celebrated the skill of humans to explore problems, to innovate and to discover new solutions. Just as the double-span flying buttresses of Notre Dame in the twelfth century (1163–1250), and the steel joints in the Eiffel Tower in the nineteenth century (1889) made those buildings possible, so too did the structural rose connections and the 8.2-metre-long brackets made of 10-ton steel casting open up possibilities for the construction of the Pompidou Centre. Already, since 1971, technology has moved on. The computer, the microchip and bio-technology offer new opportunities, replacing industrial mechanical systems and allowing buildings to interact with changes in temperature and climate to reduce energy costs, for instance.

These advances, and the changes they bring about in how people live and work, are happening with increasing speed. Lloyd's has outgrown three buildings this century, so it is no wonder that its brief required 'flexibility to meet changing needs well into the next century',[22] which led to a solution involving not only adaptable interior spaces but also a structure that would allow parts and services to be added or removed without destroying the overall integrity of the design. At INMOS (1982), Britain's first microchip factory, three quarters of the budget and most of the space are devoted to mechanical services that are continually changing. In buildings such as these we are moving away from the Classical, platonic principle of a stable world, expressed by the Parthenon in balance, proportion, volume and line, from which nothing can be removed or added, and are seeking a more fluid approach to functions, uses and materials.

We cannot be certain about the ways in which architecture should respond to these changes or to the balance of our needs for buildings that have to reflect change, such as those places of work where technological advance is crucial, and others, such as churches or monuments, where we rightly seek stability and continuity. What is certain is that we have to respond to change and thus must innovate and build, and it is here that the public confronts the other criticism of much contemporary architecture, that it is not familiar, not the same as the past. Should we innovate or repeat? It is a question that is often misrepresented as a choice between innovating and conserving.

There is no doubt that there is public demand for buildings that are friendly, reassuring and comfortable, particularly in the field of domestic housing. But achieving that does not necessarily mean that designs should ape the past. Buildings that have stood the test of time have done so precisely because they expressed the best of their age and responded to contemporary needs. Pastiche is mere mimicry and seeks, with decoration, to distract attention from its failure to create designs that grow out of the functions of a building or a space. In doing so it pays no homage to the great architecture of the past but rather distorts it, with columns that support nothing and detail slapped on at random as a cosmetic.

As for the debate between innovation and conservation, it is often conducted with more emotion than sense, focusing on subjective aesthetics. William Morris hated the new. When asked, on a visit to Paris, why he loved the recently constructed Eiffel Tower so much that he spent all his time sitting in it, he replied that it was the only place in the city where he could avoid looking at the damned thing. By contrast, Ruskin was a determined supporter of innovation, maintaining that 'Great Art, whether expressing itself in words, colours or stones, does not say the same thing over and over again ... the merit of architecture as of every other Art consists in saying new and different things.'

Most people would take a median position, believing that we should conserve the best of the past while building for the future. As Martha Graham, the choreographer, once said, 'The absolute thing is now ... but there could be no present without the past. I don't believe in throwing away the past but in using it.'[23] As has been discussed in Chapter Three, Paris and Barcelona demonstrate that a respect for, and celebration of, past architectural glories need be no constraint on innovative building and can be a positive inspiration. 'Identity' and 'modernity', as David Mackay defines them, can be complementary.[24]

Indeed, we have much past to 'use' in Britain and have, on the whole, conserved it well. London in particular has an architectural heritage of glorious variety and quality. We must do everything we can to conserve and maintain in good condition the work of Inigo Jones, Christopher Wren, Nicholas Hawksmoor, James Gibbs, John Nash, John Soane, Charles Barry, George Dance, Thomas Cubitt, Francis Fowke, Norman Shaw, Edwin Lutyens, Berthold Lubetkin, Charles Holden and Leslie Martin. Their buildings are what make London such a beautiful city, but their conservation should ensure that London is not an architectural museum but a suitable setting for the contemporary work of their successors.

Planning legislation, with the help of organizations like the Campaign for the Protection of Rural England, has meant that the British countryside is relatively unscarred by urban sprawl or by the advertising hoarding found in many fields and on hillsides in Europe. If we have been slightly less successful in stopping the outbreak of a rash of signs, shopfronts and extraneous wires in towns, we have still achieved a reasonable balance in their environments, and some places, like Bath and Carlisle, are models of how to retain the spirit of an urban centre while restraining the car and retail commerce.

Almost all our great buildings, though not our archaeological sites, are intact, even if we have failed to invest in their fabric to such an extent that Lord Palumbo, the Chairman of the Arts Council, has estimated that over £1 billion is needed to restore them.

Indeed, in some respects we have conserved our heritage too well. Our concern has tended to be general rather than particular; our listing system[25] itemizes 35,000 structures in grades that are so broad that they can offer little guide to quality. When in 1990 the Japanese company Daiwa purchased a disused telephone exchange (1929) in the City of London, it was taken aback to discover later that planning permission for a new building on the site was to be refused because the exchange had become a Grade II listed building in 1991. As a building it had undoubted curiosity value but no outstanding architectural merit. Since there were other, similar, exchanges in the City, it was not even a rarity. Nevertheless the case had to be taken to the Secretary of State before it could be resolved. The exchange was delisted four months later.

The buildings behind Mappin and Webb, at No. 1 Poultry, are also listed, though they too were late additions, having been added in 1984. They have period charm but little intrinsic architectural merit. Their one distinction is that they are built on a medieval street pattern, though this has little obvious relevance to their Victorian façades or their historic use. Yet it was to preserve these and John Belcher's Mappin and Webb building – or, more pertinently, to prevent the construction first of a Mies van der Rohe building and then one by James Stirling – that the conservation lobby pursued a battle for over a decade.

The system is also inflexible, as organizations like English Heritage tend to be distracted by minutiae from their main objectives. Sir Horace Jones's Billingsgate (1875) is a fine Victorian building, well proportioned, in a magnificent site beside the Thames. It was built as a fish market, now redundant. A more enlightened age might have seen this as an opportunity to convert it to a grand public use, following the example of the French Government, which, in a comparable location on the left bank of the Seine, converted the Gare d'Orsay into the magnificent Musée d'Orsay. Instead in Billingsgate commercial considerations were put first, and it was redesigned as rentable office accommodation. In supervising this scheme English Heritage was rightly concerned to retain the proportions and the detail, both exterior and interior, and was well satisfied with the results. However, when asked to approve some additional lighting to the lower storey by means of inserting glass in the holes in the floor through which fish had been shovelled in times past, it objected.

In spite of such imperfections the conservation of our heritage, whether in our city centres or in our countryside, is generally applauded, but our punctiliousness has been in marked contrast to our lack of concern about conserving communities in the poorer areas of our cities. During the same decades in which English Heritage has been saving our monuments, local authorities have been demolishing rows of terraced houses under slum-clearance schemes.

Again the policy has been a blanket one, and little time has been devoted to considering the individual merits of properties, to assessing the social impact of demolition, the views of people who lived there, the relative costs of refurbishment compared with those of new buildings and the likely life span of the existing buildings or to distinguishing between the general condition of the structures in a street as distinct from the absence of modern amenities in otherwise sound houses. Action areas were declared, red lines drawn on maps and improvement grants and mortgages refused. No doubt many of the streets couldn't, and shouldn't, have been renovated, but it has been demonstrated convincingly by, among others, Rod Hackney at Black Road, Macclesfield, and at Hawes Road, Stoke-on-Trent, and by Hunt Thompson's conversion of Lea View in Hackney, that communities could be kept intact and regenerated by the refurbishment of old buildings. Such refurbishment can be economically viable and is undoubtedly popular.

If we had put as much ingenuity and energy into saving our communities as we have into saving our heritage, London and certain other cities would look very different today, and there would be fewer Hoxtons. Perhaps the reason why we didn't is political. Our monuments are mainly in high-profile sites. Black Road, Hawes Road and the rest are in the poorest areas of our cities (though it has

seldom proved difficult to restore and modernize equally old properties in affluent areas such as Bloomsbury or Chelsea). What is vital is
that our passion for the past should not be used as a weapon by the
heritage lobby to prevent us from creating a future by means of new
and innovative building. Unless we look to that future we are lost, as
was recognized by Lord Chesterfield when he wrote to his son,
'Speak of the Moderns without contempt, and of the Ancients without idolatry.'[26]

But the excitement of the new has as many opponents as advocates. Some object to new buildings on aesthetic grounds. It was
ever thus. Nash's Regent's Park terraces were criticized at the time
(1844) as 'violent transgressions of true taste'; Horace Walpole
declared Blenheim Palace (1760) 'execrable within, without and
almost all around'; and Disraeli believed that Charles Barry 'should
be hanged, in public' for his design of the Houses of Parliament.
Some opponents reject new buildings because they do not 'fit' into
their context, whether in style, scale, mass or materials. By this non-
sensical criterion Christopher Wren's churches in the City of
London would never have been built, his soaring piles of white
stone being totally out of scale and sympathy with the surrounding
remains of seventeenth-century London, whose houses were constructed mainly with timber and had pitched, tiled roofs. At Trinity
College, Cambridge, his classically proportioned Renaissance library,
banged across the end of the Jacobean courtyard, would have been
unacceptable. When at Hampton Court, with its soft plum-red
brick, he proposed to add to the old fabric of the Palace his extension in white stone and orange brick he would have been con-
demned as a vandal rather than praised for designing a building of
dazzling beauty and flair. Consider James Gibbs's Fellows' Building
(1723–9) beside the great Gothic chapel of King's College, Cambridge (1446–1515), the Royal Pavilion next door to Brighton's
Georgian squares, the bulk of the Foreign and Commonwealth
Office looking over the domestic neatness of Downing Street. The
list of incongruities is endless, and all would breach the criteria that
many in today's conservation lobby employ.[27] Other opponents
object to the 'inappropriate' use of new materials and techniques,

refusing to accept that beauty, or the lack of it, is not intrinsic but lies in the use of those materials. A building can as easily be a failure in Portland stone as in steel.

All these views are subjective, and many buildings defy definitive assessment. Who can say whether Nash's Regent's Park is 'better designed' than Norman Shaw's Bedford Park? The comparison is not a proper one. The best we can do is to trust our judgement and be prepared to take risks. As Charles Correa, the 1984 RIBA Royal Gold Medallist, said, 'Only a decadent architecture looks obsessively backwards ... At its most vital, architecture is an agent for change. To invent tomorrow, that is its finest function.' 'Great nations write their autobiographies in three manuscripts – the book of their Deeds, the book of their Words and the book of their Art,' wrote John Ruskin. The Parthenon, Angkor Wat, the Pyramids, St Peter's demonstrate that, of all the arts, architecture is the most enduring and the one that has perhaps the greatest impact on our individual lives. For that reason the acid test is whether a building adds to the enjoyment or the quality of our lives, be it St Paul's, the house in which we live or children's schools, like Stoke Park Infant School at Bishopstoke in Hampshire. But one thing is certain. If we are to invent an architectural future of quality, we must follow policies that give us the maximum chance of creating more Stoke Parks.

There are clear limits to what can be achieved by policy initiatives. Governments cannot determine the quality of architecture, but they can create a framework within which good architecture has a chance of being made. They can set a good example by their own actions in commissioning new public buildings. They can ensure that architectural education and training is of the highest standards and they can promote interest in, and understanding of, architecture and urban design among as wide a public as possible. Learning from the example of the French Government's Loi sur l'Architecture, the Dutch Government's White Paper on architecture[28] and the good practice of local authorities such as Hampshire, the Government should use its power of procurement to give a lead to other public bodies and to prime developers. That power of procurement is substantial, since, as we have noted, central government spending amounted to £3 billion on new building and renovation in 1990.[29]

Improving the quality of the largest new public buildings must be a priority. The Government should end its use of Design and Build contracts and employ named architects. Design quality should be a central feature of briefs and contracts. The design of buildings with budgets of over £3 million should be determined by competition. Competitions are far from being a cure-all, and we have, earlier in this chapter, seen that they can create almost as many problems as they solve, particularly when they are adopted on a one-off basis. However, as part of a wider policy, with the adoption of a consistent line on the size and formation of juries, attention to the writing of briefs and commitment, whenever possible, to building the winning design, competitions could help to promote both a new vigour and a new interest in British architecture, just as in France over the past fifteen years they have been invaluable in raising standards.

The French experience shows that, to be successful, any competition policy needs to be flexible, the size of the building determining the nature of the competition. This would encourage less elaborate and formal competitions for smaller projects, such as court houses or regional offices, to be decided by interview or from among entries restricted by the age, experience or geographical location of the architects. Used in this way, competitions could offer the prospect of a career structure for the best of our young architects, but that should be part of a wider policy to foster talent. We should organize an annual competition for young architects, modelled on the French PAN, to design a nominated subject (a library, a leisure centre, a public housing scheme) with the guarantee that the winning design would be built. In conjunction with that, Britain ought to rejoin the EUROPAN competition and so give international experience and opportunity to our young architects.

The French Loi sur l'Architecture, arising out of a centralized legal and political system, makes architectural competitions mandatory for local authorities. Britain's less centralized traditions would make compulsory competitions undesirable, and the scale of new building and renovation by local government would turn such a policy into a nightmare. Indeed, the sheer volume of work entailed by their competitions is causing the French to consider the simplification of their system. However, prompted by ministerial guidelines and circulars, there are initiatives that local authorities could take here. They should be encouraged to use their procurement and consumer power to set a good example to local developers and builders, in imitation of central government, not least by commissioning named architects. They should favour the employment of local architects who have a knowledge and understanding of local circumstances, particularly where housing is concerned. They should, wherever possible, forge links with local schools of architecture or architecture departments in higher-education institutions in order to offer work placements and work experience for students. They should use their position to promote interest in, and understanding of, urban design and planning by means of public exhibitions, publications, debates and forums, either in local architecture centres, in the largest cities, or in public libraries, community centres or other appropriate places.

Influencing the private sector will be more difficult. In France, in spite of the success of its public policies, there has been little or no visible impact on commercial developers except, possibly, at the most expensive end of the market. In Britain, on the other hand, there are encouraging signs that some private developers are very conscious of the potential of good architecture and urban design to improve the quality of their buildings, to add value to them, to make them easier to sell or let and to reduce running and maintenance costs. Such developers have demonstrated that innovative architecture need not be an additional expense in real terms.

However, there is a long way to go before such attitudes are the norm. Perhaps the most effective way in which government could help would be to disseminate up-to-date information. We should publish an annual *Album of Architecture* illustrating the work of the best young architects graduating from colleges and architecture schools and distribute this, free, to local authorities, public companies and bodies and all government departments. Private developers and voluntary organizations could buy copies.

Further promotion of good practice and talent should be provided by national exhibitions held biannually. The French Government organizes such exhibitions for all government departments and publicly funded organizations in order to display the best of their work, whether new building or renovation. For architects the prospect of exhibiting their best should be stimulating – or salutary. A similar exhibition for the private sector might encourage developers to move away from Design and Build and would give a boost to design students, as would prizes for the Building of the Year.

Finally, it would be impossible to implement a programme of competitions, or to introduce any of the other initiatives proposed above, unless someone were appointed to assume responsibility for them. We need a national Director of Architecture, not to impose on the country his or her taste or uniformity of style but to coordinate the Government's architectural programme.

These initiatives would not transform the quality of public architecture in Britain overnight or guarantee a new generation of good architects or fine buildings. They would not necessarily even influence directly the quality of architecture commissioned by local authorities or the private sector, but they would set an example and provide a national framework. They would also demonstrate the commitment to quality and design that the Government must make if we are to leave a legacy of architectural achievement to our children.

The 1990s are certain to be an important decade for British architecture. We enter it at a low point in both public and private sectors. The recession has led to a freeze on many of the office and retail developments that were in the planning pipeline, while local authorities have been forcibly prevented by central government from building the homes and schools for which there is such strong local demand. Depressingly, but not surprisingly, it is estimated that half of the country's architects have lost their jobs in the past two years as both local authorities and private practices have shed staff. Yet our failure in the public sector to build schools, libraries and, especially, homes has created a pent-up demand for public buildings that is likely to turn the rest of the 1990s into a period of construction. In responding to that demand it is vital that we put quality of design and function before cheapness. If we do not, we will store up maintenance problems for the future and blight Britain with a decade of cheap and drab buildings.

The choice is ours. The 1990s offer an opportunity to build and innovate. We have the talent and the skills to produce a generation of great buildings and urban landscapes and to create a framework that encourages and promotes quality architecture. With a policy for architecture such as is proposed in this chapter we could at least give ourselves a chance of, in Charles Correa's phrase, inventing a future of which our children can be proud.

CHAPTER TEN

A New London

London has to change. The evidence of its decline is clear. The complexity of its problems is challenging. The case for new policies and new investment is overwhelming. Fortunately, its qualities and strengths provide a foundation on which to build, but before all else change must start with London's attitude to the whole idea of city culture, to Europe and to itself.

What is lacking is self-confidence. Since the Second World War London has experienced a steady decline in population and in international importance. Inevitably this has affected the spirit of the city, and of Britain generally. With characteristic resourcefulness we have coped with this, in the main, by choosing not to see. Since traditionally our attitude to Europe has been parochial, it has not been hard to avoid confronting the gap that has widened, and is continuing to widen, between the quality of education, training, housing and public transport in London and that available in other European cities.

People have also perfected the habit of averting their eyes from what is all around us in London. For many who live in the south-west or the north-west of the city there is no call to visit Hackney or Peckham or Walthamstow. For all that the problems of these areas impinge on the life of the rest of London, they might as well be on the other side of the globe, not merely the other side of the city. The only aspects of London life that intrude on everyone are the state of the roads, litter, public transport and, recently, people sleeping rough on the streets and begging in the entrances to Underground stations in the centre of London. Most people have developed personal strategies to deal with these unfortunate reminders of the realities that lurk just out of sight, and meanwhile there are enough new shops, cleaned buildings and good programmes on the television (sometimes) to offer a semblance of novelty and progress. So, with a mixture of resilience, ignorance and endurance in equal parts, we have learned to cope with London's failings. Consequently, far from being galvanized into action by recognition of its relative decline, London life lacks a sense of urgency or adventure.

The two exceptions to this are, perhaps not surprisingly, London's two greatest strengths, the City and the arts, in both of which we continue to innovate and to excel. We need to infect the other areas of the city's life with their virus of curiosity and continual renewal and to start by asking questions about what is happening in other cities, both in Britain and on the Continent.

London must learn to see itself not just as the British capital but as a European city. Unless it does so it will become marginalized on the north-western edge of a European community whose centre of gravity is inexorably moving east. The new Europeanism can be symbolized by better communications with the rest of Europe: first, through the development of Heathrow's Terminal 5 and faster links between the centre of London and the main airports and, second, through government support for the completion of the Channel Tunnel rail link well in advance of the date presently envisaged, 2005. Following Maastricht, the ability to translate its European perspective into reality will depend on a future British Government's enthusiasm for co-operation with our EC partners. If Britain has to be coaxed or cajoled unwillingly into monetary union, who will consider London to be the appropriate place for the new European Central Bank which will symbolize that union? A decision to locate the Bank in Frankfurt or Paris would greatly prejudice London's commercial, as well as financial, future.

Adopting a European perspective does not mean slavish imitation. The examples of Paris, Barcelona, Rotterdam and other cities abroad should be viewed with interest rather than awe. The nature of London's development must grow out of its own circumstances and strengths, must be rooted in its own culture and multi-cultural identity. But at the same time it must and will become increasingly open to what is happening elsewhere in Europe. If we lag behind the pace of European change, London's future will be circumscribed.

Our first initiative should be the re-establishment of a strategic authority and the adoption of a city-wide policy. We need a democratically elected London authority, which should have limited responsibilities, a small staff and a small number of members, full-time and paid.[1] Boroughs should retain their responsibilities for existing services such as housing, education and social services, leaving the new city-wide council to concentrate on strategy and co-ordination. Its leader would be able to speak for London, to promote the city as a world-class financial and cultural centre and to negotiate with central government for investment.

The strategy adopted by this new London authority should, for instance, embrace the European concept of urbanism and concern for the quality of the public domain. We have seen how, in Rotterdam, urbanist policies can, in practice, be implemented in a variety of ways. London needs to be led by a determination to attract people back to live in the centre of the city, with consequently higher densities of population in some areas. At the same time the city should move towards 'decentralized concentration', becoming polycentric with a number of nodes or villages dispersed around that stronger inner-city area. Taken together, these changes would facilitate the process of rebalancing jobs, services and amenities in London, particularly towards the east of the city.

They are also changes that would alleviate London's transport problems by contributing to some reduction in commuting and in cross-city journeys, but they themselves would be dependent on the city's taking control of its transport networks. Unless we promote a major shift from private to public transport, and do so fast, almost all other initiatives will fail. To achieve that shift we will have to have new buses and new Underground lines, orbital rail routes and an RER-type regional service. We will need pilot schemes on road pricing and on park-and-ride. We must introduce more traffic-calming measures and keep lorries out of the city's centre at peak times. We should give more streets back to pedestrians at weekends. This would be a strategy made up of equal measures of encouragement and deterrent and one that would demand the integration of the different transport systems. With such a policy London could once again become, as it was in the 1930s, a city admired for its public transport. Without it life for Londoners will be increasingly unattractive, and, as CBI research demonstrates, the economy of the city will suffer. There are useful initiatives – for instance, affordable rent schemes – that could be taken, particularly by the boroughs, to encourage the expansion of small new businesses in London, but it is transport that will determine the rate of expansion of London's economy as a whole.

It will also have a major effect on our efforts to make London's environment greener and cleaner. There is no shortage of projects that we could emulate: early-morning street cleaning, for instance, to the standard set by Jacques Chirac with his 'weeping streets' at 6 a.m., when millions of gallons of water sluice down Paris's gutters, followed by an army of 4,000 cleaners equipped with motorized vehicles that vacuum and sweep; better-quality litter bins and more of them; incentives to cut down the use of leaded petrol; tighter controls over the discharge of effluent into the Thames. We need more parks, the linkage of existing parks by means of green walkways through the city and the creation of smaller green spaces, adapting the ideas, in landscaping and public art, of Oriol Bohigas in Barcelona and of Bob McGilvray in Blackness, Dundee.

As for the built environment, the initiatives that will have the most dramatic impact are those that will open up the Thames. To develop its derelict spaces, such as the Greenwich Peninsula, to find exciting new uses for major empty buildings like County Hall, Bankside and Battersea power stations, to create a park at Barn Elms, simply to give people unimpeded access to the river along its length and on both banks – those actions would send out a message, loud and clear: London is changing.

The same is true of progress on some of the key developments in the city. King's Cross, Spitalfields and Paddington Basin have hung fire for too long. It is not too late for sanity to prevail over the East London River Crossing, for a better settlement to be reached with environmentalist groups over Oxleas Wood and for the Santiago Calatrava bridge design to be adopted. If Riek Bakker could push through the Ben van Berkel bridge in Rotterdam, surely we can do better than the Department of Transport's tawdry effort? If Barcelona can use architects and artists to transform places, both large and small, throughout the city, why can't London? If Birmingham can make Centenary Square, why can't we remake Trafalgar Square?

What is needed is a sense of urgency, a desire for a quality environment and a presumption that agreements can be reached that will satisfy communities as well as planners and politicians. With these attitudes a priority for the new strategic authority will be to put behind us the do-nothing sluggishness of the 1980s and grasp the opportunities that exist all over the city. If we created a museums quarter running from the Albert Memorial to the Natural History Museum, it would be the envy of Europe. Vauxhall Cross, where a huge coach park and a mess of billboard hoardings make a mockery of what should be a fine public space beside the river, could be transformed. The marvellous opportunity to give coherence to the South Bank, and to make the river walkway between there and London Bridge one of the delights of the city, is one that we must grasp.

Sites such as these should be the highlights of a wider strategy stemming from a sense of urban design that would improve all areas of London. The strategy should incorporate a city-wide policy relating to signs; the greening of public spaces, with the target of planting 100,000 new trees a year; improved access to all public buildings and public places in order to make London a city that respects the needs of those with disabilities; and, perhaps most effective and immediate of all, a policy for improving the lighting of London's main public buildings, public spaces and, especially, the Thames. As part of that policy improvements are urgently needed to the lighting of the city's streets, which are so under-lit that they give women and the elderly no sense of safety after dark.

All these are projects that could proceed quickly. What is more, they would build on the city's existing strengths and would command widespread support. The same would doubtless be true of changes that are needed in the city's cultural life. The evidence of central-government neglect in recent years is all around us – in the disrepair of our museums, in the memory of the closure of the RSC at the Barbican in 1990. It would seem a relatively uncontentious matter, at least for anyone who is not a blinkered Conservative Government apologist, to agree on a programme of revival. A start could be made on repairing the 945 historic London buildings reported to be at risk in a recent English Heritage report,[2] as it could on the maintenance work that is necessary at the Tate, the Royal National Theatre, the National Gallery and the Victoria and Albert Museum. There is even likely to be a consensus on the need to finance this revival from the public purse, with some assistance on capital from a national lottery, particularly now that it is generally accepted that the arts, and the cultural industries that depend on them, contribute substantially to London's economy.

It is possible that the consensus would hold further and assert, if only for pragmatic economic reasons, that the arts in London ought to be expanding. The Lyceum Theatre in Covent Garden should be renovated. Where better to locate the architecture centre that London needs than in Bankside Power Station, on the river opposite St Paul's, in the heart of the City? A world city like London ought to have an annual arts festival, linked perhaps with the Thames, in addition to its excellent specialist festivals such as the biannual London International Festival of Theatre, the London Film Festival and Dance Umbrella. If there were any appetite to learn from the French, we might be daring enough to ask the Inland Revenue to vacate Somerset House, just as Mitterrand moved his Ministry of Finance from the Louvre. To tuck the Courtauld Gallery into the Aldwych side of Somerset House is to ignore the potential of the rest of the building, the splendid courtyard and one of the finest terraces in London, overlooking the Embankment.

It is possible to imagine at least some of these projects being achieved in the 1990s, but there are other cultural needs in London that might attract less widespread support but are vitally necessary. Theatre in Education, disability arts, public libraries, Black and Asian arts, local museums, the non-professional arts, women's theatre groups – all these have borne the brunt of cuts in recent years for no other reason than that they are funded by local authorities, and local-government expenditure has been seen by the Government as self-evidently bad. To revive these parts of London's cultural life, which are so important to the widening of audiences and the nurturing of new talent, will require a new attitude to local government. As all political parties except the Conservatives agree, the arts ought to be a statutory responsibility of local authorities, thus making them eligible for Revenue Support Grant funding from central government. Without such a move the grass roots of London's cultural life will continue to wither, regardless of what happens to the glamorous and commanding heights.

If such political differences stand in the way of agreement on how to proceed with respect to cultural policy, they are even more in evidence when considering housing or education. Since neither could conceivably be considered one of London's strengths, so both offer little on which to build. Consensus evaporates, to be replaced by conventional party-political disagreement. What most people agree on is that education needs additional money if class sizes are to be reduced and books and other resources provided. Even the Government implicitly accepts this, since the schools that opt out of local-authority control find their budgets magically augmented, even if the increases do not match the £4,000 spent per pupil per year in independent schools. Most people would also agree that money alone is not the answer to the problems of education, but there is precious little agreement on issues such as teaching methods and the structure of education. Meanwhile London's education system is drifting further and further behind that of most other world cities and continues to be a major cause for concern. An under-educated and under-trained London will not prosper. One act that would send out a signal that London values education would be to make the empty County Hall into a new university. It would be the first to be created from scratch since Stirling University in 1967. To establish a new seat of learning in the heart of the capital, opposite the Houses of Parliament, would be a powerful symbol of intent.

Similarly in housing there is little political agreement beyond an acknowledgement, first, of the effectiveness of involving tenants in decisions and, second, of the fact that the scale of housing need is so great that it will require all the resources of both public and private sectors to tackle it. But discussion of any form of government investment, or of the role of local authorities in such a programme, reveals a policy gap as wide as the gap in recent years between the minute number of public-sector homes built in London (302 in 1990) and the large number of families who need housing (there are currently 239,000 families on council waiting lists).[3]

Although the issues of housing, education investment and local democracy generate real political differences, many people share a vision of the environment they want to see in London. They want a cleaner and greener city, in which the traffic flows. They want a better-designed public domain, centred on the Thames. They want a city that is more accessible and friendlier to its people, especially those with disabilities, the elderly, women and children. The realization of their vision is going to involve considerable cost, running into billions of pounds, over the next ten years.

Can we afford it? The answer is that we *must* afford it if we wish London to thrive. As in the cases of Barcelona, Paris and Rotterdam, the public share of that money will have to be provided by both national and local government, and all of it will have to come ultimately from individual and corporate taxation. Unlike those other cities, London has the unique advantage of access to North Sea oil revenue; even allowing for this boon, however, every one of us will have to contribute, and the success of every initiative discussed in this book will depend on whether the people of London, and of Britain, want a modern capital badly enough to pay for it. It is clear that the cheap option, doing nothing, will mean the competitive death of London, almost certainly within a generation.

London has to change. History shows that it has done so before with great success. The rebuilding after the Great Fire of 1666, which bequeathed to the city its fine heritage of churches by Wren,

Hawksmoor and Gibbs; the continuation of that church-building tradition in the early nineteenth century, after Parliament had voted, in 1818, to allocate £1 million to build 600 churches throughout Britain (often called the Waterloo Churches), which gave us master-pieces in London by Barry, Soane, Nash, Smirke, Cundy and Basevi;[4] the creation of late-Victorian London made possible by the huge investment of the Metropolitan Water Board and the London County Council; the carving out of modern London as Shaftesbury Avenue and Charing Cross Road and, later, Kingsway were driven through the slums of Soho and Holborn; the forging of the London Underground system in the 1920s and 1930s; the rebuilding of the city after the bomb damage of the Second World War; the Festival of Britain in 1951: all show that London can change if it so wills.

Its revitalization will be contingent on a fresh attitude towards urban design and architecture and towards the regeneration of com-munities. We will have to begin to discuss the issues relating to our built environment. For that a major cultural change will be needed: we must recognize that art and architecture are not simply decora-tive but are part of the essential fabric of a city's identity. Attitudes must also change towards the words 'public' and 'civic', putting aside the presumption of recent years that the concept of 'public' is bad and that we can run cities without local government, with as few public services as possible and with the minimum of regulation. The condition of London today is proof enough that we cannot.

So London has to change. All who love this city can feel that its pulse is uncertain. If that pulse is to quicken and strengthen, now is the time, in the last years before a new millennium, to act. The London we create will be the London in which our children and grandchildren will live. It is right therefore that we should provide opportunities for young people in particular to contribute their tal-ents to the city's regeneration. For it will be with their energy and commitment that we will begin to make a new London.

Notes and References

London: a Call for Action

1. 'London into Europe', LWT, 9 November 1990.
2. *Green Paper on the Urban Environment*, Commission of the European Community, Brussels, 1990, p. 10.
3. Richard Sennett, *The Fall of Public Man*, New York, Random House, 1977.
4. Jane Jacobs, *The Death and Life of Great American Cities*, Harmondsworth, Penguin, 1985.
5. M. Hamer and S. Potter, *Vital Travel Statistics*, London, Transport 2000, 1990.
6. Harley Sherlock, *Cities are Good for Us*, London, Paladin, 1991, p. 154.
7. Stephen Cook, 'Ministers shun advice on tackling housing crisis', *Guardian*, 8 June 1991.
8. Philip Gumuchdjian, Project for South Kensington Museums Site, 1986 (see p. 120 in this volume).

I A Sense of Urgency

1. Aristotle, *Poetics*, Harmondsworth, Penguin, 1981.
2. The Rev. Andrew Mearns, 'The Bitter Cry of Outcast London', London, 1883.
3. Cumulative loss since 1978/79 in 1991/92. Prices from Department of the Environment papers and GDP deflator.
4. Department of the Environment, UK housing and construction statistics, 1972–90. A further 2,000 Housing Association homes were started in 1990, giving a total of 2,302 public-sector homes. This is far short of the 1979 total of 10,944 public-sector homes started. Private-sector starts, which are subject to economic trends, fluctuate enormously, so rarely make up the difference lost by cuts in pub-

lic-sector house building, which only fifteen years ago were running at 24,000 per annum.

5. Department of the Environment Information Bulletin No. 527, 10 September 1991, quarterly press release on homelessness in England. The number of those accepted as homeless is subject to ever tightening criteria. The number who were acknowledged to be homeless in 1990/91 was 89,000 (Department of the Environment, quarterly homeless bulletin, 10 December 1991); the number of those who are registered on council waiting lists is 240,000 (1990/91 Housing Investment Programme returns). This indicates the real situation.

6. Frank Duffy and Alex Henney, *The Changing City*, London, Bulstrode Press, 1989.

7. Patrick Abercrombie, *Greater London Plan: 1944*, London, HMSO, 1945, together with his *London County Plan*, with J. Forshaw, London, HMSO, 1943.

8. *London: World City Moving into the 21st Century*, London, HMSO, 1991, p. 141.

9. *Our Common Future: The World Commission on Environment and Development*, Oxford, Oxford University Press, 1987.

10. D. Pearce, A. Markandya and E. Barber, *Blueprint for a Green Economy*, London, Earthscan, 1989.

2 The Rights and Wrongs of London

1. London Underground Entry Census, Spring 1991.

2. London Regional Transport Statistics, quoted in Harley Sherlock, *Cities are Good for Us*, London, Paladin, 1991 (the number was 101,000 in 1988).

3. British Rail, Network South East, annual survey of commuters, 1990.

4. CBI report, 'Trade Routes to the Future: Meeting the Transport Infrastructure for the 1990s', November 1989.

5. Department of Education and Science, *London: World City Moving into the 21st Century*, London, HMSO, 1991, p. 127.

6. Colin Clark, 'Transport: Maker and Breaker of Cities', *Town Planning Review*, 28, 1957, pp. 237–50.

7. Quoted consistently by Wilfred Newton, Chairman of London Underground, and endorsed by the Monopolies and Mergers Commission's report 'A Report on Passenger and Other Services Supplied by the Company', July 1991.

8. Project Manager, Liverpool Street Station, British Rail, December 1991.

9. Patrick Abercrombie, *Greater London Plan: 1944*, London, HMSO, 1945.

10. *Traffic in Towns: A Study of the Long Term Problems of Traffic in Urban Areas*, London, HMSO, 1963.

11. Advisory Committee on Trunk Road Assessment, 1971.

12. Peter Hall, *London 2001*, London, Unwin Hyman, 1984, pp. 129–32.

13. ibid., p. 129.

14. Personnel Department, Metropolitan Police: number in November 1991 and recruitment aims for 1995.

15. Dr Tim Elkin and Duncan McLaren, with Mayer Hillman, *Reviving the City*, London, Friends of the Earth, 1991, p. 72.

16. *Environmental Policies for Cities in the 1990s*, Organization for Economic Cooperation and Development, 1990, pp. 74–5.

17. ibid., p. 78.

18. SERPLAN, 'Regional Trends in the South East', *South East Regional Monitor*, 1984–5, RPC 369.

19. *London in Prospect*, Institute of Metropolitan Studies, London, 1991.

20. *The United Kingdom Balance of Payments*, Central Statistical Office Pink Book, London, HMSO, 1987.

21. Frank Duffy and Alex Henney, *The Changing City*, London, Bulstrode Press, 1989, p. 27.

22. ibid., p. 24.

23. *London 2000*, Henley Centre, for the Association of London Authorities, March 1991.

24. *Local Futures: The Geography of British Prosperity 1990–95*, Henley Centre, July 1990, p. 112.

25. Hall, *London 2001*, p. 54.

26. Nomis De Database, CACI Market Research, October 1991.

27. 'Unemployment Rates by Ethnic Origin and Region: Average 1987–1990', *Unemployment Gazette*, February 1991.

28. See J. D. Kasarda and J. Friedrichs in *The Future of the Metropolis: Economic Aspects*, Berlin, de Gruyter, 1986, pp. 221–49; Hall, *London 2001*, pp. 59–64.

29. *London: World City*, p. 158. DES statistics show full-time participation rates in 1986 as 33 per cent in the UK, 47 per cent in Germany, 66 per cent in France, 77 per cent in Japan and 79 per cent in the USA.

30. Hall, *London 2001*, p. 64; N. Buck and I. Gordon, 'The Beneficiaries of Employment Growth', *In Hasner*, volume II, 1987, pp. 77–115.

31. Ebenezer Howard, *Tomorrow: A Peaceful Path to Real Reform* (1898), reissued under the title *Garden Cities of Tomorrow*, London, Swan, Sonnenschein and Co., 1902.

32. Buck and Gordon, 'The Beneficiaries of Employment Growth', p. 24.

33. *Annual Census of Employment*, London, HMSO, 1989.

34. *Green Paper on the Urban Environment*, Commission of the European Community, Brussels, 1990, p. 53.

35. Buck and Gordon, 'The Beneficiaries of Employment Growth', p. 99.

36. Demographical and statistical studies, London Research Centre, 1990.

37. *Royal Parks Review*, chaired by Dame Jennifer Jenkins, July 1991.

38. *London: World City*, p. 45.

39. Labour Party survey, May 1991.

40. ALA survey, 'Taking Stock: Resources Needed for London's Education Service', May 1991.

41. DES letter, 2 December 1991. Approved for closure under Section 12 of the Education Act 1980.

42. LACFAB survey, 1991: 23.5 per cent primary and 20.5 per cent secondary.

43. Department of the Environment, local housing statistics, England and Wales, 1980 and 1990.

44. UK housing and construction statistics, 1972–90.

45. Metropolitan Police, Commissioner's Annual Reports, 1980 and 1990.

46. Parliamentary Answer, HC Debates, 4 May 1990, Hansard, col. 676W.

47. Department of the Environment Deposited Paper 6036.

48. Office of Population Censuses and Surveys, 1984, 1987. Exact figures: 1961–71, -460,944; 1971–81, -53,957; 1981–6, -38,500.

49. Hall, *London 2001*, p. 79.

50. ILEA was coterminous with LCC except that it included Greenwich and excluded Newham and Haringey.

51. Buck and Gordon, 'The Beneficiaries of Employment Growth'.

52. *London in Prospect*, Institute of Metropolitan Studies, 1991.

53. See note 31.

54. Department of the Environment Deposited Paper 6036.

55. LPAC, *Strategic Planning Advice for London*, Romford, 1988.

56. Abercrombie, *Greater London Plan: 1944*.

57. *Streamlining the Cities: Government Proposals for Reorganizing Local Government in London and the Metropolitan Counties*, Command 9063, London, HMSO, 1983.

58. ibid., p. 3.

3 The European Example

1. In *Civics as Applied Sociology*, 1905.

2. *The Urban Spaces of Barcelona: 1981–1987*, Harvard University Graduate School of Design, Boston, MA, 1990, pp. 40–45, gives a complete inventory of the projects.

3. Henry N. Cobb, 'The Public Realm as a Theatre of Inquiry', in ibid., p.11.

4. At 1984 prices this figure covered the period 1981–9; a further £1,370 million (1990 prices) is projected for the period 1989–95.

5. Richard Rogers (UK) and Renzo Piano (Italy) for the Pompidou Centre; Gae Aulenti (Italy) for the Musée d'Orsay; I. M. Pei (USA) for the Louvre; Bernard Tschumi (Switzerland) for the Parc de la Villette; Carlos Ott (Canada) for the Opéra de la Bastille; and Johann Otto von Spreckelson (Denmark) for L'Arche de la Défense.

6. *Le Livre Blanc de l'Ile-de-France: Document préalable à la révision du Schéma Directeur d'Aménagement et de l'Urbanisme de la Région Ile-de-France*, 1990.

7. National Commission for Districts' Social Development, Annual Report, 1991.

8. Paul Webster, 'La Grande Illusion', *Guardian*, 3 May 1991.

9. Lewis Mumford, *The City in History*, London, Secker & Warburg, 1961.

10. For a fuller discussion of urban development and design in Rotterdam, see Maarten Hajer's 'Designing the Public Domain', in Franco Bianchini and Michael Parkinson, eds., *Cultural Policy and Urban Regeneration: The West European Experience*, Manchester, Manchester University Press, forthcoming (1992).

11. Richard Sennett, *The Conscience of the Eye: The Design and Social Life of Cities*, London, Faber & Faber, 1991.

12. ibid.; see also Robert Park, 'The City: Suggestions for the Investigation of Behavior', in *The Urban Environment* (1916), reprinted in Richard Sennett, ed., *Classic Essays on the Culture of Cities*, New York, Prentice-Hall, 1969, p. 126.

4 Turning to the Thames

1. *Wise Children*, London, Chatto & Windus, 1991, p. 1.

2. Judy Hillman, *A New Look for London*, London, RFAC, 1988.

3. *Miscellaneous Sonnets*, part II, xxxvi.

4. River Thames Unit, Museum of London.

5. *Thames-Side Guidelines: An Environmental Design Handbook for London's River*, Department of Transportation and Development, GLC, 1986, p. 8.

6. *Port Greenwich*, LBA Greenwich, Planning Application for Greenwich Peninsula, September 1990.

7. Josep Martorell, Oriol Bohigas, David Mackay, Albert Puigdomènech, *Transformation of a Seafront: Barcelona – the Olympic Village 1992*, translated by Clare Nelson and Graham Thompson, Barcelona, Editorial Gustavo Gili, 1988.

8. Until local government reorganization the Borough of Woolwich also covered both sides of the river.

9. Interview with Jonathan Glancey, *Independent*, 24 October 1990.

10. Port of London Authority, Statistics Department.

11. See note 8.

12. LDDC, Annual Report, 1991.

13. Rémi Loth, in a speech presented to the London Rivers Association Conference, 'The Working Thames: Industry, Planning and the Environment', Royal Festival Hall, London, 9 July 1991.

14. John Stow, *A Survey of London*, published in London by John Wolfe, 1598.

15. Pepys's *Diary*, Everyman's Library edn (3 vols.), nos. 53–5, London, 1953.

16. Nigel Spearing, MP, 'A Plan for a Thames Passenger Service', 1973.

17. Sir Alan Herbert, *The Water Gypsies*, Harmondsworth, Penguin 1960.

18. A. P. Herbert, *The Thames*, Weidenfeld & Nicolson, London, 1966.

19. Ministry of Transport, *Public Enquiry into the Desirability and Practicability of*

the Provision of a Regular Transport Service on the River Thames, London, HMSO, November 1934.

20. Department of the Environment *Strategic Guidance for London*, July 1989, paragraph 48.

21. P. Merlin, 'Energy Savings in Transport', *Transport and Planning Technology*, vol. 8, 1938, pp. 39–52.

22. *No Boats on the River*, London, Methuen, 1932.

23. *Tideless Thames in a Future London*, London, Frederick Muller, 1944.

24. Hansard, vol. 345, col. 2055, 29 March 1939.

25. Port of London Authority, Statistics Department.

26. Unpublished speech, entitled 'Recent Achievements, Popular Misconceptions and Future Prospects', presented to the London Rivers Association Conference, 'The Working Thames: Industry, Planning and the Environment', at the Royal Festival Hall, London, 9 July 1991.

27. *Building Design*, 10 May 1991.

28. Herbert, *The Thames*.

29. Professor Sir H. Bondi, for the Ministry of Housing and Local Government, *A London Flood Barrier*, February 1968.

30. Hansard, HL, 21 December 1985.

31. Westminster (1750), Blackfriars (1769), Battersea (wooden, 1772), Richmond (1774) and Kew (modern, 1789).

32. Vauxhall, the first iron bridge (1816), Waterloo (1817), Southwark (1819), Hungerford, the first suspension bridge (1845), Grosvenor (or Victoria), the first railway bridge (1860), Chelsea (1858), Lambeth (1862), Hammersmith (1887) and Tower Bridge (1894).

33. Putney (1886), Westminster (1862), Blackfriars (1869) and Battersea (1890).

34. Chiswick, Twickenham and Hampton Court (all 1933).

35. Kew (1903), Vauxhall (1904), Southwark (1921), Lambeth (1929), Chelsea (1937), Richmond (1939), Waterloo (1942) and London Bridge (1972).

36. Department of Transport press release, 27 September 1991.

37. Hansard, HC, 12 July 1990. Robert Atkins, MP, in reply to a question from Mark Fisher, MP.

38. Jane Bowden, Thames Coordinator, Countryside Commission, in a speech entitled 'Riverside Industry and the Thames Path: Conflict or Opportunity?', presented to the London Rivers Association Conference at the Royal Festival Hall, London, 9 July 1991.

39. Jonathan Raban, 'On the Water Margin', in *For Love and Money,* London, Picador, 1988, p. 297.

40. The Western Riverside Waste Authority.

41. Foster, Rogers, Stirling, *London as it Could Be*, Royal Academy, autumn 1986.

42. *Building Design*, 10 May 1991.

43. Held at the Royal Festival Hall, London, 9 July 1991.

44. *Building Design*, 10 May 1991.

45. Bondi, *A London Flood Barrier*.

46. Spearing, 'A Plan for a Thames Passenger Service'.

47. Mr and Mrs Hall, *The Book of the Thames*, London, Charlotte James, 1975, p. 407.

48. Interview with Jonathan Glancey, *Independent*, 24 October 1990.

49. Carter, *Wise Children*, p. 194.

5 Designing Public Space

1. Charles Dickens, *Bleak House*, Harmondsworth, Penguin, 1971, p. 49.

2. Lewis Mumford, *Art and Technics*, Oxford, Oxford University Press, 1952, p. 112.

3. Martial, *De spectaculis*, II, 12.

4. Jacob Larwood, *The Story of the London Parks*, London, 1886.

5. October 1986 to October 1990.

6. Steen Eiler Rasmussen, *London: The Unique City*, Cambridge, MA, MIT Press, 1982, pp. 165–202.

7. *Surveys of the Use of Open Space*, London, GLC, 1969.

8. The admission price was reduced to one shilling after the opening weeks, and 6 million people attended.

9. Richard Cork, 'Art in the City', in Mark Fisher and Ursula Owen, eds., *Whose Cities?*, Harmondsworth, Penguin, 1991, p. 134.

6 Regenerating Communities

1. Anne Power, *Running to Stand Still*, London, Priority Estates Project, 1991, pp. 31–2.

2. Professor David Donnison, submission to the Commission on Urban Priority Areas, in *Faith in the City: Report on the Archbishop of Canterbury's Commission on Urban Priority Areas*, London, Church House, 1985, p. 247.

3. Oscar Newman, *Architectural Journal*, 8 April 1987, p. 39.

4. Alice Coleman, *Utopia on Trial*, London, Hilary Shipman, 1985.

5. Anne Power, 'Housing, Community and Crime', in David Downes, ed., *Crime and the City*, London, Macmillan, 1989.

6. Lord Scarman, *The Scarman Report: The Brixton Disorders 10–12 April*, Harmondsworth, Penguin, 1982. Also J. Parker and K. Dugmore, *Colour and the Allocation of GLC Housing: The Report of the GLC Lettings Survey, 1974–75*, Research Report 21, London, GLC, 1976.

7. Housing Investment Programme, April 1990. (NB: A new definition of 'unfit' was introduced in the Local Government and Housing Act 1989.)

8. 'Unemployment Rates by Ethnic Origin and Region: Average 1987–1990', *Unemployment Gazette*, February 1991.

9. Letter from David Riggs to Mildred Gordon, MP, in reply to HC Deb., 24 July 1991, col. 6471W.

10. M. Hough and P. Mayhew, *The British Crime Survey*, Home Office Research Study 76, London, HMSO, 1983.

11. Department of the Environment, City Estate Action Programme, London Region, as of December 1991. A small number remain outstanding.

12. Bernard Shaw, *Pygmalion*, London, Constable, 1916, Act II, p. 138.

13. Power, *Running to Stand Still*.

14. Interviews conducted by Mark Fisher, MP, with Hoxton residents, summer 1991.

15. *The Feasibility Report*, Volume 3.1, *The Arden Estate*, London, Borough of Hackney, 1988.

16. Jane Jacobs, *The Death and Life of Great American Cities*, Harmondsworth, Penguin, 1985.

17. Rod Hackney, *The Good, the Bad and the Ugly*, London, Frederick Muller, 1990, pp. 118–20.

18. ibid, p. 119.

19. M. Burbridge, for the Department of the Environment, *An Investigation of Difficult to Let Housing*, Vol. 2 *Case Studies of Post-War Estates*, London, HMSO, 1980, p. 31.

20. Nomis De Database, CACI Market Research, October 1991.

21. Survey by the BWFYA Co-op, 'Lordship Project – House-to-House Survey', July 1987.

22. 'Cultivating the Farm', booklet published by the BWFYA Co-op, June 1988, p. 10.

23. 'Lordship Project – House-to-House Survey', p. 8.

24. *Faith in the City: Report of the Archbishop of Canterbury's Commission on Urban Priority Areas*, London, Church House, 1985, p. 230.

25. Power, *Running to Stand Still*.

26. 'Lordship Project – House-to-House Survey', p. 29.

27. ibid., p. 31.

28. ibid., p. 27.

29. Audit Commission Survey, *Managing the Crisis in Council Housing*, March 1986, p. 41.

30. Burbridge, *An Investigation of Difficult to Let Housing*, Vol. 1 *General Findings*, Vol. 2 *Case Studies of Post-War Estates*, Vol. 3 *Case Studies of Pre-War Estates*.

31. 'Lordship Project – House-to-House Survey', p. 55.

32. Trevor Bell, *Joining Forces: Estate Management Boards – A Practical Guide for Residents and Councils*, London, Priority Estates Project, 1991.

33. Anne Power, *Local Housing Management*, Department of the Environment, 1984. Also Anne Power, *Property Before People*, London, Unwin Hyman, 1987.

34. Department of the Environment, *Survey of Housing Investment Programmes*, London, HMSO, 1991.

7 Planning Changes

1. Foster Associates, 'Masterplan for the King's Cross Railway Lands', February 1988.

2. LRC plc, Planning Application, July 1990.

3. John Delafons, *Aesthetic Control: A Report on the Methods Used in the USA to Control the Design of Buildings*, Berkeley, CA, University of California at Berkeley, 1990, p. 1.

4. Unpublished lecture delivered on 13 February 1991 as part of a series, 'Art and Architecture', organized by the Arts Council of Great Britain and sponsored by Blue Circle Cement and Olympia and York.

5. Published in London by Weidenfeld & Nicolson, 1983.

6. *Green Paper on the Urban Environment*, Brussels, Commission of the European Community, 1990.

7. Patrick Abercrombie, *Greater London Plan: 1944*, London, HMSO, 1945.

8. Peter Hall, *Cities of Tomorrow*, Oxford, Blackwell, 1988, p. 151.

9. Lewis Mumford, 'The Fourth Migration', in *Survey*, New York, Regional Planning Association of America, 1925.

10. ibid.

11. *Tomorrow: A Peaceful Path to Real Reform* (1898), reissued under the title *Garden Cities of Tomorrow*, London, Swan, Sonnenschein and Co., 1902.

12. Mumford, 'The Fourth Migration'.

13. Jane Jacobs, *The Death and Life of Great American Cities*, Harmondsworth, Penguin, 1985.

14. Greater London census, 1981, and Housing Investment Programme returns (number of dwellings), April 1991.

15. Dr Tim Elkin and Duncan McLaren, with Mayer Hillman, *Reviving the City*, London, Friends of the Earth, 1991, p. 17.

16. E. Milner-Holland, *Report of the Committee on Housing in Greater London*, Command 2605, London, HMSO, 1965.

17. Patrick Geddes, *Cities in Evolution*, London, Norgate & Williams, 1915.

18. Ian Miles, 'Telecommunications: Space and Reinforcing Distance?', in John Brotchie, Michael Batty, Peter Hall and John Newton, eds., *Cities of the 21st Century: New Technologies and Spatial Systems*, London, Longman, 1991, p. 88.

19. Office of Population Censuses and Surveys, census, 1981, *Greater London County Report*, Part 2, Table 44.

20. H. W. E. Davies, 'The Preparation of Development Plans', in *Planning Control in Western Europe*, London, HMSO, 1989, pp. 58–9.

21. M. Bruton and D. Nicholson, *Local Planning in Practice*, London, Hutchinson, 1987.

22. *The Future of Development Plans*, Department of the Environment, 1986.

23. Nan Fairbrother, *New Lives, New Landscapes*, Harmondsworth, Penguin, 1972.

24. Robin Thompson, 'An Achievable Alternative for Planning', in Andy Thorney and John Montgomery, eds., *Radical Planning Initiatives*, London, Gower, 1990, pp. 300–311.

25. See Adrian Salt and Henry Brown, *Planning Applications: The RMJM Guide*, London, BSP Professional Books, 1987.

26. Both the Urban Development Corporation and Enterprise Zones were established in 1981.

27. LDDC, *Corporate Plan*, 1991, p. 9.

28. Rod Hackney, *The Good, the Bad and the Ugly*, London, Frederick Muller, 1990, p. 170.

29. Town and Country Planning Act 1990, Section 55 (2) (a) (ii).

30. ibid., Section 75 (3).

31. Department of the Environment, Circular 142/1973, 'Streamlining the Planning Machine'; Circular 22/1980, 'Development Control: Policy and Practice'.

32. Delafons, *Aesthetic Control*, p. 2.

33. Research by the Centre for Environmental Research at Sheffield, 1981.

34. See John Punter, *The Control of the External Appearance of Development in England and Wales*, 3 vols., Reading, Department of Land Management and Development at University of Reading, 1984.

35. Ian Nairn, *Outrage* (1955) and *Counter Attack Against Suburbia* (1957).

36. Department of the Environment, Circular 22/1980, 'Development Control: Policy and Practice'.

37. Department of the Environment, Circular 113/1975, 'Review of the Development Control System'.

38. Circular 22/1980.

39. See note 4.

40. *Draft Planning Policy Guidance: General Policy and Principles*, Department of the Environment, 1 October 1991.

41. Reyner Banham, Peter Hall, Paul Barker and Cedric Price, 'Non-planning: an Experiment in Freedom', *New Society*, 29 March 1969.

42. Davies, 'The Preparation of Development Plans', in *Planning Control in Western Europe*, p. 439. The study surveys England, Denmark, France, the Federal Republic of Germany and the Netherlands.

43. J. Punter, 'France', in Davies, *Planning Control in Western Europe*, p. 152, quoting J. F. Tribillon, *Le Vocabulaire critique du droit de l'urbanisme*, Paris, Les Editions de la Villette, 1985.

44. For Housing, Physical Planning and the Environment.

45. The Rijksplanologische Dienst (the National Physical Planning Agency); the Rijksplanologische Commissie (the National Physical Planning Committee); and the Raad van Advies voor de Ruimtelijke Ordening (the Advisory Physical Planning Council).

46. See John Ellis, 'US Planning Codes and Controls', *Architectural Review*, November 1988.

47. The Downtown Plan Ordinance, containing zoning regulations; the Downtown Plan, containing objectives and policies in the form of design guidelines; and the Downtown Area Plan, a condensed version of the Plan.

48. Delafons, *Aesthetic Control*, p.48.

49. See note 47.

50. *Mission Bay Plan: Proposal for Adoption*, Department of City Planning, City and County of San Francisco, January 1990.

51. Judy Hillman, *Planning for Beauty: The Case for Design*, London, Royal Fine Art Commission, 1990.

52. Thompson, 'An Achievable Alternative for Planning'.

53. Planning and Compensation Act 1991, Sections 70 (2) and 54A.

54. *Chief Planning Inspector's Report, April 1990–March 1991*, London, HMSO, 1991, p. 9.

8 Involving People

1. 1988.

2. Quoted in 'Architecture Centres', in *Architects' Journal*, No. 16. Vol. 193, 17 April 1991.

3. The Architecture Foundation, *A New Centre for London*, Preliminary Report, 29 May 1991, Summary 1.6 and 1.7.

4. The Architecture Foundation, *Scope and Aims*, 28 June 1991.

5. The Architecture Foundation, *Mission Statement*, 3 April 1990.

6. Jean-Louis Cohen, Co-Director, Permanent Exhibition, Pavillon de l'Arsenal, and V. Magnago-Lampugnani, the Director of the Deutsches Architekturmuseum, Frankfurt. Other members of the Council include Phyllis Lambert, the founder and Director of the Canadian Centre for Architecture, and Manuel Solà-Morales, Professor of Urban Design at the University of Barcelona. The Foundation has fourteen trustees, including architects David Chipperfield, Sir Norman Foster and James Stirling; historian Mark Girouard; Lord Palumbo, Chairman of the Arts Council of Great Britain; Nicholas Serota, Director of the Tate; and Stuart Lipton of Stanhope Properties.

7. HRH The Prince of Wales, *Vision of Britain: A Personal View of Architecture*, London, Doubleday, 1989.

8. Ian Record and Nigel Frost, *Design Technology and Built Environment*, London, Building Experiences Trust, 1991.

9. Marcy Abhau et al., eds., *Architecture in Education: A Resource of Imaginative Ideas and Tested Activities*, Foundation for Architecture, Philadelphia, 1987.

10. Patrick Abercrombie, *Greater London Plan: 1944*, London, HMSO, 1945.

11. *Old Houses to New Homes*, White Paper, Ministry of Housing and Local Government, April 1968.

12. 1982: Fitzrovia, Hammersmith, Southall, South Bank, South Hackney and Spitalfields; 1984: Finsbury and West Docklands; 1985: Battersea, Fulham, King's Cross/Somers Town, Lambeth Walk, Notting Hill, Paddington, Pimlico and Soho.

13. For further details of grants and expenditure, and for a wider discussion of these issues, see *Community Areas Policy: A Record of Achievement*, London, GLC, 1985, pp. 24–6.

14. Richard Weston, *Schools of Thought*, Hampshire County Council, 1991, p. 55.

9 Inventing Tomorrow

1. Hansard, 5 and 10 December 1990.

2. Letter of 25 July 1990 from Private Secretary to Minister for Roads and Transport to Ben Evans.

3. Written reply, 25 April 1991.

4. Incomplete figures: only ten departments were able to provide statistics. The real total is likely to be much higher.

5. Letter to Mark Fisher, MP, 10 September 1990.

6. Richard Weston, *Schools of Thought*, Hampshire County Council, 1991, p. 55.

7. Letter to Mark Fisher, MP, from Patrick Nicholls, MP, 5 September 1989.

8. ibid.

9. House of Commons Debate, 1 March 1984, and House of Commons Debate, 13 December 1991, Hansard, col. 555–6W.

10. Weston, *Schools of Thought*, p. 6.

11. ibid., p. 6.

12. Colin Stansfield Smith, unpublished lecture, Winchester, 1991.

13. Weston, *Schools of Thought*, p. 21.

14. Hansard, 8 January 1990, col. 566, answer to a written question asked by Tam Dalyell, MP.

15. Michael Wigginton, 'Compulsory Competitive Tendering: What Difference Will It Make to Design?', paper from Joint RSA/RIBA Seminar on Compulsory Competitive Tendering, October 1991.

16. The Essex Design Guide was introduced in 1973 by Essex County Council to deal with new developments in the county and was given a prominent position at the 1974 RIBA conference, which acted as an endorsement. The idea was to get away from road standards designed to keep traffic moving with gentle curves and wider lanes. The Design Guide encouraged a villagesque layout, cul-de-sacs, twisting roads, even a neo-vernacular aesthetic to encourage a relationship between the house and the road. It became a pattern-book standard for developers, who often imposed this totally inappropriate village environment in conurbations. The approach is still widespread today.

17. Steen Eiler Rasmussen, *London: The Unique City*, Cambridge, MA, MIT Press, 1982.

18. Andrew Lisicki, 'Access Law: the Case for Change', unpublished paper, November 1991, p. 4.

19. ibid., p. 6.

20. Specifically Parts M (1987) and T (1985) of the Building Regulations, which apply only to new buildings. The BSI Codes of Practice, BS 5619 (design of housing for the convenience of disabled people), BS 5810 (access of the disabled to buildings), BS 5655 (lifts and service lifts) and BS 5588 (means of escape for disabled people).

21. Lisicki, 'Access Law: the Case for Change', p. 3.

22. Brief to Richard Rogers Partnership from Lloyd's for the new buildings.

23. Obituary of Martha Graham, *Independent*, 3 April 1990.

24. David Mackay, *Modern Architecture in Barcelona, 1854–1939*, London, BSP Professional Books, 1989.

25. 'The Green Book', annual listings for each London Borough by the Department of the Environment.

26. *Letters Written to His Son ... Philip Stanhope*, 1774.

27. Michael Manser, 'Conservation's gone too far', *Financial Times*, 11 January 1991.

28. *Dutch Government Policy on Architecture*, Ministry of Welfare, Health and Cultural Affairs and Ministry of Housing, Physical Planning and the Environment, Amsterdam, 1991.

29. See note 1.

10 A New London

1. That number could be either twenty – two for each of London's ten European Parliamentary constituencies – or thirty-three, one from each borough and from the City of London. In either case London could set the pace for electoral reform by being the first local authority to have its members elected by proportional representation.

2. 'Buildings at Risk in Greater London', London Division, English Heritage, April 1991.

3. UK Housing and Conservation statistics, 1990, and letter to Mildred Gordon, MP, from Benefits Agency, 24 July 1991.

4. M. H. Port, *600 New Churches*, London, SPCK, 1961. Examples include Nash's All Soul's, Langham Place (1822); Smirke's St Anne's, Wandsworth (1820); Barry's Holy Trinity, Choudsley Square, Islington (1826); Grundy's St Paul's, Knightsbridge (1845); Basevi's St Saviour's, Chelsea (1839); Soane's Holy Trinity, Marylebone Road (1826).

Index